CAMBRIDGE LIBRARY COLLECTION

Books of enduring scholarly value

Philosophy

This series contains both philosophical texts and critical essays about
philosophy, concentrating especially on works originally published in the
eighteenth and nineteenth centuries. It covers a broad range of topics including
ethics, logic, metaphysics, aesthetics, utilitarianism, positivism, scientific
method and political thought. It also includes biographies and accounts of
the history of philosophy, as well as collections of papers by leading figures.
In addition to this series, primary texts by ancient philosophers, and works
with particular relevance to philosophy of science, politics or theology, may be
found elsewhere in the Cambridge Library Collection.

The Data of Ethics

Herbert Spencer (1820–1903), Victorian philosopher, biologist, sociologist
and political theorist, author of the famous phrase 'survival of the fittest'
and one of the founders of Social Darwinism, was nominated for the
Nobel Prize for Literature in 1902, losing out to Theodor Mommsen.
Spencer left his post at *The Economist* in 1857 to focus on writing his ten-
volume *System of Synthetic Philosophy*, a work that offers an ethics-based
guide to human conduct to replace that provided by conventional religious
belief. Published in 1879, this volume seeks to demonstrate that social
evolution tends towards greater individualism, altruism and co-operation.
Spencer argues that it is possible to establish rules of right conduct on a
scientific basis, and declares that this work is the culmination of his life's study.
He was anxious to publish it outside the planned order of the *System*, because
he feared (wrongly) that his death would prevent its completion.

Cambridge University Press has long been a pioneer in the reissuing of out-of-print titles from its own backlist, producing digital reprints of books that are still sought after by scholars and students but could not be reprinted economically using traditional technology. The Cambridge Library Collection extends this activity to a wider range of books which are still of importance to researchers and professionals, either for the source material they contain, or as landmarks in the history of their academic discipline.

Drawing from the world-renowned collections in the Cambridge University Library and other partner libraries, and guided by the advice of experts in each subject area, Cambridge University Press is using state-of-the-art scanning machines in its own Printing House to capture the content of each book selected for inclusion. The files are processed to give a consistently clear, crisp image, and the books finished to the high quality standard for which the Press is recognised around the world. The latest print-on-demand technology ensures that the books will remain available indefinitely, and that orders for single or multiple copies can quickly be supplied.

The Cambridge Library Collection brings back to life books of enduring scholarly value (including out-of-copyright works originally issued by other publishers) across a wide range of disciplines in the humanities and social sciences and in science and technology.

The Data of Ethics

HERBERT SPENCER

CAMBRIDGE
UNIVERSITY PRESS

CAMBRIDGE UNIVERSITY PRESS

Cambridge, New York, Melbourne, Madrid, Cape Town,
Singapore, São Paolo, Delhi, Mexico City

Published in the United States of America by Cambridge University Press, New York

www.cambridge.org
Information on this title: www.cambridge.org/9781108040853

© in this compilation Cambridge University Press 2012

This edition first published 1879
This digitally printed version 2012

ISBN 978-1-108-04085-3 Paperback

THE DATA OF ETHICS.

THE DATA

OF

E T H I C S.

BY

HERBERT SPENCER.

WILLIAMS AND NORGATE,

14, HENRIETTA STREET, COVENT GARDEN, LONDON;
AND 20, SOUTH FREDERICK STREET, EDINBURGH.

1879.

PREFACE.

A REFERENCE to the programme of the "System of Synthetic Philosophy," will show that the chapters herewith issued, constitute the first division of the work on the *Principles of Morality*, with which the System ends. As the second and third volumes of the *Principles of Sociology* are as yet unpublished, this instalment of the succeeding work appears out of its place.

I have been led thus to deviate from the order originally set down, by the fear that persistence in conforming to it might result in leaving the final work of the series unexecuted. Hints, repeated of late years with increasing frequency and distinctness, have shown me that health may permanently fail, even if life does not end, before I reach the last part of the task I have marked out for myself. This last part of the task it is, to which I regard all the preceding parts as subsidiary. Written as far back as 1842, my first essay, consisting of letters on *The Proper Sphere of Government*, vaguely indicated what I conceived to be certain general principles of right and wrong in political conduct; and from that time onwards my ultimate purpose, lying behind all proximate purposes, has been that of finding for the principles of right and wrong in conduct at large, a scientific basis. To leave this purpose unfulfilled after making so extensive a preparation for fulfilling it, would be a failure the probability of which I do not like to contemplate; and I am anxious to preclude it, if not wholly, still partially. Hence the step I now take. Though this first division of the work terminating the Synthetic Philosophy, cannot, of course, contain the specific conclusions to be set forth in the entire work; yet it implies them in such wise that, definitely to formulate them requires nothing beyond logical deduction.

I am the more anxious to indicate in outline, if I cannot complete, this final work, because the establishment of rules of right conduct on a scientific basis is a pressing need. Now that moral injunctions are losing the authority given by their supposed sacred origin, the secularization of morals is becoming imperative. Few things can happen more disastrous than the decay and death of a regulative system no longer fit, before another and fitter regulative system has grown up to replace it. Most of those who reject the current creed, appear to assume that the controlling agency furnished by it may safely be thrown aside, and the vacancy left unfilled by any other controlling agency. Meanwhile, those who defend the current creed allege that in the absence of the guidance it yields, no guidance can exist: divine commandments they think the only possible guides. Thus between these extreme opponents there is a certain community. The one holds that the gap left by disappearance of the code of supernatural ethics, need not be filled by a code of natural ethics; and the other holds that it cannot be so filled. Both contemplate a vacuum, which the one wishes and the other fears. As the change which promises or threatens to bring about this state, desired or dreaded, is rapidly progressing, those who believe that the vacuum can be filled, and that it must be filled, are called on to do something in pursuance of their belief.

To this more special reason I may add a more general reason. Great mischief has been done by the repellent aspect habitually given to moral rule by its expositors; and immense benefits are to be anticipated from presenting moral rule under that attractive aspect which it has when undistorted by superstition and asceticism. If a father, sternly enforcing numerous commands, some needful and some needless, adds to his severe control a behaviour wholly unsympathetic—if his children have to take their pleasures by stealth, or, when timidly looking up from their play, ever meet a cold glance or more frequently a frown; his government will inevitably be disliked, if not hated; and the aim will be to evade it as much as possible. Contrariwise, a father who, equally firm in maintaining restraints needful for the well-being of his children or the well-being of other persons, not only avoids needless restraints, but, giving his sanction to all legitimate gratifications and providing the means for them, looks on at their gambols with an approving smile, can scarcely fail to gain an influence which, no less efficient for the time being, will also be permanently efficient. The controls of such two fathers symbolize the controls of Morality as it is and Morality as it should be.

Nor does mischief result only from this undue severity of the ethical doctrine bequeathed us by the harsh past. Further mischief results from the impracticability of its ideal. In violent reaction against the utter selfishness of life as carried on in barbarous societies, it has insisted on a life utterly unselfish. But just as the rampant egoism of a brutal militancy, was not to be remedied by attempts at the absolute subjection of the ego in convents and monasteries; so neither is the misconduct of ordinary humanity as now existing, to be remedied by upholding a standard of abnegation beyond human achievement. Rather the effect is to produce a despairing abandonment of all attempts at a higher life. And not only does an effort to achieve the impossible, end in this way, but it simultaneously discredits the possible. By association with rules that cannot be obeyed, rules that can be obeyed lose their authority.

Much adverse comment will, I doubt not, be passed on the theory of right conduct which the following pages shadow forth. Critics of a certain class, far from rejoicing that ethical principles otherwise derived by them, coincide with ethical principles scientifically derived, are offended by the coincidence. Instead of recognizing essential likeness they enlarge on superficial difference. Since the days of persecution, a curious change has taken place in the behaviour of so-called orthodoxy towards so-called heterodoxy. The time was when a heretic, forced by torture to recant, satisfied authority by external conformity : apparent agreement sufficed, however profound continued to be the real disagreement. But now that the heretic can no longer be coerced into professing the ordinary belief, his belief is made to appear as much opposed to the ordinary as possible. Does he diverge from established theological dogma? Then he shall be an atheist; however inadmissible he considers the term. Does he think spiritualistic interpretations of phenomena not valid? Then he shall be classed as a materialist; indignantly though he repudiates the name. And in like manner, what differences exist between natural morality and supernatural morality, it has become the policy to exaggerate into fundamental antagonisms. In pursuance of this policy, there will probably be singled out for reprobation from this volume, doctrines which, taken by themselves, may readily be made to seem utterly wrong. With a view to clearness, I have treated separately some correlative aspects of conduct, drawing conclusions either of which becomes untrue if divorced from the other; and have thus given abundant opportunity for misrepresentation.

The relations of this work to works preceding it in the series, are such as to involve frequent reference. Containing, as it does, the outcome of principles set forth in each of them, I have found it impracticable to dispense with re-statements of those principles. Further, the presentation of them in their relations to different ethical theories, has made it needful, in every case, briefly to remind the reader what they are, and how they are derived. Hence an amount of repetition which to some will probably appear tedious. I do not, however, much regret this almost unavoidable result; for only by varied iteration can alien conceptions be forced on reluctant minds.

June, 1879.

CONTENTS.

CHAPTER I.

CONDUCT IN GENERAL.

§ 1. The doctrine that correlatives imply one another —that a father cannot be thought of without thinking of a child, and that there can be no consciousness of superior without a consciousness of inferior—has for one of its common examples the necessary connexion between the conceptions of whole and part. Beyond the primary truth that no idea of a whole can be framed without a nascent idea of parts constituting it, and that no idea of a part can be framed without a nascent idea of some whole to which it belongs, there is the secondary truth that there can be no correct idea of a part without a correct idea of the correlative whole. There are several ways in which inadequate knowledge of the one involves inadequate knowledge of the other.

If the part is conceived without any reference to the whole, it becomes itself a whole—an independent entity; and its relations to existence in general are misapprehended. Further, the size of the part as compared with the size of the whole, must be misapprehended unless the whole is not only recognized as including it, but is figured in its total extent. And again, the position which the part occupies in relation to other parts, cannot be rightly conceived unless there is some conception of the whole in its distribution as well as in its amount.

1 *

Still more when part and whole, instead of being statically related only, are dynamically related, must there be a general understanding of the whole before the part can be understood. By a savage who has never seen a vehicle, no idea can be formed of the use and action of a wheel. To the unsymmetrically-pierced disk of an eccentric, no place or purpose can be ascribed by a rustic unacquainted with machinery. Even a mechanician, if he has never looked into a piano, will, if shown a damper, be unable to conceive its function or relative value.

Most of all, however, where the whole is organic, does complete comprehension of a part imply extensive comprehension of the whole. Suppose a being ignorant of the human body to find a detached arm. If not misconceived by him as a supposed whole, instead of being conceived as a part, still its relations to other parts, and its structure, would be wholly inexplicable. Admitting that the co-operation of its bones and muscles might be divined, yet no thought could be framed of the share taken by the arm in the actions of the unknown whole it belonged to ; nor could any interpretation be put upon the nerves and vessels ramifying through it, which severally refer to certain central organs. A theory of the structure of the arm implies a theory of the structure of the body at large.

And this truth holds not of material aggregates only, but of immaterial aggregates—aggregated motions, deeds, thoughts, words. The Moon's movements cannot be fully interpreted without taking into account the movements of the Solar System at large. The process of loading a gun is meaningless until the subsequent actions performed with the gun are known. A fragment of a sentence, if not unintelligible, is wrongly interpreted in the absence of the remainder. Cut off its beginning and end, and the rest of a demonstration proves nothing. Evidence given by a plaintiff often misleads until the evidence which the defendant produces is joined with it.

§ 2. Conduct is a whole; and, in a sense, it is an organic whole—an aggregate of inter-dependent actions performed by an organism. That division or aspect of conduct with which Ethics deals, is a part of this organic whole—a part having its components inextricably bound up with the rest. As currently conceived, stirring the fire, or reading a newspaper, or eating a meal, are acts with which Morality has no concern. Opening the window to air the room, putting on an overcoat when the weather is cold, are thought of as having no ethical significance. These, however, are all portions of conduct. The behaviour we call good and the behaviour we call bad, are included, along with the behaviour we call indifferent, under the conception of behaviour at large. The whole of which Ethics forms a part, is the whole constituted by the theory of conduct in general; and this whole must be understood before the part can be understood. Let us consider this proposition more closely.

And first, how shall we define conduct? It is not co-extensive with the aggregate of actions, though it is nearly so. Such actions as those of an epileptic in a fit, are not included in our conception of conduct: the conception excludes purposeless actions. And in recognizing this exclusion, we simultaneously recognize all that is included. The definition of conduct which emerges is either—acts adjusted to ends, or else—the adjustment of acts to ends; according as we contemplate the formed body of acts, or think of the form alone. And conduct in its full acceptation must be taken as comprehending all adjustments of acts to ends, from the simplest to the most complex, whatever their special natures and whether considered separately or in their totality.

Conduct in general being thus distinguished from the somewhat larger whole constituted by actions in general, let us next ask what distinction is habitually made between the conduct on which ethical judgments are passed and the remainder of conduct. As already said, a large part of

ordinary conduct is indifferent. Shall I walk to the waterfall to-day ? or shall I ramble along the sea-shore ? Here
the ends are ethically indifferent. If I go to the waterfall,
shall I go over the moor or take the path through the
wood? Here the means are ethically indifferent. And
from hour to hour most of the things we do are not to
be judged as either good or bad in respect of either ends or
means.   No less clear is it that the transition
from indifferent acts to acts which are good or bad is
gradual. If a friend who is with me has explored the sea-
shore but has not seen the waterfall, the choice of one or
other end is no longer ethically indifferent. And if, the
waterfall being fixed on as our goal, the way over the moor
is too long for his strength, while the shorter way through
the wood is not, the choice of means is no longer ethically
indifferent. Again, if a probable result of making the
one excursion rather than the other, is that I shall not be
back in time to keep an appointment, or if taking the longer
route entails this risk while taking the shorter does not, the
decision in favour of one or other end or means acquires in
another way an ethical character; and if the appointment
is one of some importance, or one of great importance, or
one of life-and-death importance, to self or others, the
ethical character becomes pronounced. These instances will
sufficiently suggest the truth that conduct with which
Morality is not concerned, passes into conduct which is moral
or immoral, by small degrees and in countless ways.

But the conduct that has to be conceived scientifically
before we can scientifically conceive those modes of conduct
which are the objects of ethical judgments, is a conduct
immensely wider in range than that just indicated. Complete comprehension of conduct is not to be obtained by
contemplating the conduct of human beings only : we have
to regard this as a part of universal conduct—conduct as
exhibited by all living creatures. For evidently this comes
within our definition—acts adjusted to ends. The con-

duct of the higher animals as compared with that of man, and the conduct of the lower animals as compared with that of the higher, mainly differ in this, that the adjustments of acts to ends are relatively simple and relatively incomplete. And as in other cases, so in this case, we must interpret the more developed by the less developed. Just as, fully to understand the part of conduct which Ethics deals with, we must study human conduct as a whole; so, fully to understand human conduct as a whole, we must study it as a part of that larger whole constituted by the conduct of animate beings in general.

Nor is even this whole conceived with the needful fulness, so long as we think only of the conduct at present displayed around us. We have to include in our conception the less-developed conduct out of which this has arisen in course of time. We have to regard the conduct now shown us by creatures of all orders, as an outcome of the conduct which has brought life of every kind to its present height. And this is tantamount to saying that our preparatory step must be to study the evolution of conduct.

CHAPTER II.

THE EVOLUTION OF CONDUCT.

§ 3. We have become quite familiar with the idea of an evolution of structures throughout the ascending types of animals. To a considerable degree we have become familiar with the thought that an evolution of functions has gone on *pari passu* with the evolution of structures. Now advancing a step, we have to frame a conception of the evolution of conduct, as correlated with this evolution of structures and functions.

These three subjects are to be definitely distinguished. Obviously the facts comparative morphology sets forth, form a whole which, though it cannot be treated in general or in detail without taking into account facts belonging to comparative physiology, is essentially independent. No less clear is it that we may devote our attention exclusively to that progressive differentiation of functions, and combination of functions, which accompanies the development of structures—may say no more about the characters and connexions of organs than is implied in describing their separate and joint actions. And the subject of conduct lies outside the subject of functions, if not as far as this lies outside the subject of structures, still, far enough to make it substantially separate. For those functions which are already variously compounded to achieve what we regard as single bodily acts, are endlessly re-compounded to achieve that co-ordination of bodily acts which is known as conduct.

We are concerned with functions in the true sense, while we think of them as processes carried on within the body; and, without exceeding the limits of physiology, we may treat of their adjusted combinations, so long as these are regarded as parts of the vital *consensus*. If we observe how the lungs aërate the blood which the heart sends to them; how heart and lungs together supply aërated blood to the stomach, and so enable it to do its work; how these co-operate with sundry secreting and excreting glands to further digestion and to remove waste matter; and how all of them join to keep the brain in a fit condition for carrying on those actions which indirectly conduce to maintenance of the life at large; we are dealing with functions. Even when considering how parts that act directly on the environment—legs, arms, wings—perform their duties, we are still concerned with functions in that aspect of them constituting physiology, so long as we restrict our attention to internal processes, and to internal combinations of them. But we enter on the subject of conduct when we begin to study such combinations among the actions of sensory and motor organs as are externally manifested. Suppose that instead of observing those contractions of muscles by which the optic axes are converged and the foci of the eyes adjusted (which is a portion of physiology), and that instead of observing the co-operation of other nerves, muscles, and bones, by which a hand is moved to a particular place and the fingers closed (which is also a portion of physiology), we observe a weapon being seized by a hand under guidance of the eyes. We now pass from the thought of combined internal functions to the thought of combined external motions. Doubtless if we could trace the cerebral processes which accompany these, we should find an inner physiological co-ordination corresponding with the outer co-ordination of actions. But this admission is consistent with the assertion, that when we ignore the internal combination and attend only to the external combination, we pass from a portion of physiology to a portion of conduct. For though it may be objected that the external combination instanced, is too simple to be rightly included under the name conduct, yet a moment's thought shows that it is joined with what we call conduct by insensible gradations. Suppose the weapon seized is used to ward off a blow. Suppose a counter-blow is given. Suppose the aggressor runs and is chased. Suppose there comes a struggle and a handing him over to the police. Suppose there follow the many and varied acts constituting a prosecution. Obviously the initial adjustment of an act to an end, inseparable from the rest, must be included with them under the same general head; and obviously from this initial simple adjustment, having intrinsically no moral character, we pass by degrees to the most complex adjustments and to those on which moral judgments are passed.

Hence, excluding all internal co-ordinations, our subject here is the aggregate of all external co-ordinations; and this aggregate includes not only the simplest as well as the most complex performed by human beings, but also those performed by all inferior beings considered as less or more evolved.

§ 4. Already the question—What constitutes advance in the evolution of conduct, as we trace it up from the lowest types of living creatures to the highest? has been answered by implication. A few examples will now bring the answer into conspicuous relief.

We saw that conduct is distinguished from the totality of actions by excluding purposeless actions; but during evolution this distinction arises by degrees. In the very lowest creatures most of the movements from moment to moment made, have not more recognizable aims than have the struggles of an epileptic. An infusorium swims randomly about, determined in its course not by a perceived object to be pursued or escaped, but, apparently, by varying stimuli in its medium; and its acts, unadjusted in any appreciable way to ends, lead it now into contact with some nutritive substance which it absorbs, and now into the neighbourhood of some creature by which it is swallowed and digested. Lacking those developed senses and motor powers which higher animals possess, ninety-nine in the hundred of these minute animals, severally living for but a few hours, disappear either by innutrition or by destruction. The conduct is constituted of actions so little adjusted to ends, that life continues only as long as the accidents of the environment are favourable. But when, among aquatic creatures, we observe one which, though still low in type, is much higher than the infusorium—say a rotifer—we see how, along with larger size, more developed structures, and greater power of combining functions, there goes an advance in conduct. We see how by its whirling cilia it sucks in as food these small animals moving around; how by its prehensile tail it fixes itself to some fit object; how by withdrawing its outer organs and contracting its body, it preserves itself from this or that injury from time to time threatened; and how thus, by better adjusting its own actions, it becomes less dependent on the actions going on around, and so preserves itself for a longer period.

A superior sub-kingdom, as the Mollusca, still better exemplifies this contrast. When we compare a low mollusc, such as a floating ascidian, with a high mollusc, such as a cephalopod, we are again shown that greater organic evolution is accompanied by more evolved conduct. At the mercy of every marine creature large enough to swallow it, and drifted about by currents which may chance to keep it at sea or may chance to leave it fatally stranded, the ascidian displays but little adjustment of acts to ends in comparison with the cephalopod; which, now crawling over the beach, now exploring the rocky crevices, now swimming

through the open water, now darting after a fish, now hiding
itself from some larger animal in a cloud of ink, and using
its suckered arms at one time for anchoring itself and at
another for holding fast its prey; selects, and combines, and
proportions, its movements from minute to minute, so as
to evade dangers which threaten, while utilizing chances of
food which offer: so showing us varied activities which, in
achieving special ends, achieve the general end of securing
continuance of the activities.

Among vertebrate animals we similarly trace up, along
with advance in structures and functions, this advance in
conduct. A fish roaming about at hazard in search of
something to eat, able to detect it by smell or sight only
within short distances, and now and again rushing away in
alarm on the approach of a bigger fish, makes adjustments of
acts to ends that are relatively few and simple in their kinds;
and shows us, as a consequence, how small is the average
duration of life. So few survive to maturity that, to
make up for destruction of unhatched young and small
fry and half-grown individuals, a million ova have to be
spawned by a cod-fish that two may reach the spawning age.
Conversely, by a highly-evolved mammal, such as an ele-
phant, those general actions performed in common with the
fish are far better adjusted to their ends. By sight as well,
probably, as by odour, it detects food at relatively great
distances; and when, at intervals, there arises a need for
escape, relatively-great speed is attained. But the chief
difference arises from the addition of new sets of adjustments. We have combined actions which facilitate nutrition
—the breaking off of succulent and fruit-bearing branches, the
selecting of edible growths throughout a comparatively wide
reach; and, in case of danger, safety can be achieved not by
flight only, but, if necessary, by defence or attack : bringing
into combined use tusks, trunk, and ponderous feet. Further, we see various subsidiary acts adjusted to subsidiary
ends—now the going into a river for coolness, and using the

trunk as a means of projecting water over the body; now the employment of a bough for sweeping away flies from the back; now the making of signal sounds to alarm the herd, and adapting the actions to such sounds when made by others. Evidently, the effect of this more highly-evolved conduct is to secure the balance of the organic actions throughout far longer periods.

And now, on studying the doings of the highest of mammals, mankind, we not only find that the adjustments of acts to ends are both more numerous and better than among lower mammals; but we find the same thing on comparing the doings of higher races of men with those of lower races. If we take any one of the major ends achieved, we see greater completeness of achievement by civilized than by savage; and we also see an achievement of relatively numerous minor ends subserving major ends. Is it in nutrition? The food is obtained more regularly in response to appetite; it is far higher in quality; it is free from dirt; it is greater in variety; it is better prepared. Is it in warmth? The characters of the fabrics and forms of the articles used for clothing, and the adaptations of them to requirements from day to day and hour to hour, are much superior. Is it in dwellings? Between the shelter of boughs and grass which the lowest savage builds, and the mansion of the civilized man, the contrast in aspect is not more extreme than is the contrast in number and efficiency of the adjustments of acts to ends betrayed in their respective constructions. And when with the ordinary activities of the savage we compare the ordinary civilized activities—as the business of the trader, which involves multiplied and complex transactions extending over long periods, or as professional avocations, prepared for by elaborate studies and daily carried on in endlessly-varied forms, or as political discussions and agitations, directed now to the carrying of this measure and now to the defeating of that,—we see sets of adjustments of acts to ends, not only immensely exceeding

those seen among lower races of men in variety and intri-
cacy, but sets to which lower races of men present nothing
analogous. And along with this greater elaboration of life
produced by the pursuit of more numerous ends, there
goes that increased duration of life which constitutes the
supreme end.

And here is suggested the need for supplementing this
conception of evolving conduct. For besides being an
improving adjustment of acts to ends, such as furthers prolongation of life, it is such as furthers increased amount of
life. Reconsideration of the examples above given, will
show that length of life is not by itself a measure of evolution of conduct; but that quantity of life must be taken into
account. An oyster, adapted by its structure to the diffused
food contained in the water it draws in, and shielded by its
shell from nearly all dangers, may live longer than a cuttle-
fish, which has such superior powers of dealing with
numerous contingencies; but then, the sum of vital
activities during any given interval is far less in the oyster
than in the cuttle-fish. So a worm, ordinarily sheltered from
most enemies by the earth it burrows through, which also
supplies a sufficiency of its poor food, may have greater
longevity than many of its annulose relatives, the insects;
but one of these during its existence as larva and imago,
may experience a greater quantity of the changes which constitute life. Nor is it otherwise when we compare the more
evolved with the less evolved among mankind. The difference between the average lengths of the lives of savage and
civilized, is no true measure of the difference between the
totalities of their two lives, considered as aggregates of
thought, feeling, and action. Hence, estimating life by
multiplying its length into its breadth, we must say that the
augmentation of it which accompanies evolution of conduct,
results from increase of both factors. The more multiplied
and varied adjustments of acts to ends, by which the more
developed creature from hour to hour fulfils more numerous

requirements, severally add to the activities that are carried on abreast, and severally help to make greater the period through which such simultaneous activities endure. Each further evolution of conduct widens the aggregate of actions while conducing to elongation of it.

§ 5. Turn we now to a further aspect of the phenomena, separate from, but necessarily associated with, the last. Thus far we have considered only those adjustments of acts to ends which have for their final purpose complete individual life. Now we have to consider those adjustments which have for their final purpose the life of the species.

Self-preservation in each generation has all along depended on the preservation of offspring by preceding generations. And in proportion as evolution of the conduct subserving individual life is high, implying high organization, there must previously have been a highly-evolved conduct subserving nurture of the young. Throughout the ascending grades of the animal kingdom, this second kind of conduct presents stages of advance like those which we have observed in the first. Low down, where structures and functions are little developed, and the power of adjusting acts to ends but slight, there is no conduct, properly so named, furthering salvation of the species. Race-maintaining conduct, like self-maintaining conduct, arises gradually out of that which cannot be called conduct: adjusted actions are preceded by unadjusted ones.   Protozoa spontaneously divide and sub-divide, in consequence of physical changes over which they have no control; or, at other times, after a period of quiescence, break up into minute portions which severally grow into new individuals. In neither case can conduct be alleged. Higher up, the process is that of ripening, at intervals, germ-cells and sperm-cells, which, on occasion, are sent forth into the surrounding water and left to their fate: perhaps one in ten thousand surviving to maturity. Here, again, we see only development and dispersion going on apart from parental care. Types above these, as fish which choose fit places in which to deposit their ova, or as the higher crustaceans which carry masses of ova about until they are hatched, exhibit adjustments of acts to ends which we may properly call conduct; though it is of the simplest kind. Where, as among certain fish, the male keeps guard over the eggs, driving away intruders, there is an additional adjustment of acts to ends; and the applicability of the name conduct is more decided. Passing at once to creatures far superior, such as birds which, building nests and sitting on their eggs, feed their broods for considerable periods, and give them aid after they can fly; or such as mammals which, suckling their young for a time, continue afterwards to bring them food or protect them while they feed, until they reach ages at which they can provide for themselves; we are shown how this conduct which furthers race-maintenance evolves hand-in-hand with the conduct which furthers self-maintenance. That better organization which makes possible the last, makes possible the first also.   Mankind exhibit a great progress of like nature. Compared with brutes, the savage, higher in his self-maintaining conduct, is higher too in his race-maintaining conduct. A larger number of the wants of offspring are provided for; and parental care, enduring longer, extends to the disciplining of offspring in arts and habits which fit them for their conditions of existence. Conduct of this order, equally with conduct of the first order, we see becoming evolved in a still greater degree as we ascend from savage to civilized. The adjustments of acts to ends in the rearing of children become far more elaborate, alike in number of ends met, variety of means used, and efficiency of their adaptations; and the aid and oversight are continued throughout a much greater part of early life.

In tracing up the evolution of conduct, so that we may frame a true conception of conduct in general, we have thus to recognize these two kinds as mutually dependent. Speaking generally, neither can evolve without evolution of the other; and the highest evolutions of the two must be reached simultaneously.

§ 6. To conclude, however, that on reaching a perfect adjustment of acts to ends subserving individual life and the rearing of offspring, the evolution of conduct becomes complete, is to conclude erroneously. Or rather, I should say, it is an error to suppose that either of these kinds of conduct can assume its highest form, without its highest form being assumed by a third kind of conduct yet to be named.

The multitudinous creatures of all kinds which fill the Earth, cannot live wholly apart from one another, but are more or less in presence of one another—are interfered with by one another. In large measure the adjustments of acts to ends which we have been considering, are components of that "struggle for existence" carried on both between members of the same species and between members of different species; and, very generally, a successful adjustment made by one creature involves an unsuccessful adjustment made by another creature, either of the same kind or of a different kind. That the carnivore may live herbivores must die; and that its young may be reared the young of weaker creatures must be orphaned. Maintenance of the hawk and its brood involves the deaths of many small birds; and that small birds may multiply, their progeny must be fed with innumerable sacrificed worms and larvæ. Competition among members of the same species has allied, though less conspicuous, results. The stronger often carries off by force the prey which the weaker has caught. Monopolizing certain hunting grounds, the more ferocious drive others of their kind into less favourable places. With plant-eating animals, too, the like holds: the better food is secured by the more vigorous individuals, while the less vigorous and worse fed, succumb either directly from innutrition or indirectly from resulting inability to escape enemies. That is to say, among creatures whose lives are carried on antagonistically, each of the two kinds of conduct delineated above, must remain imperfectly evolved. Even in such few kinds of them as have little to fear from enemies or competitors, as lions or tigers, there is still inevitable failure in the adjustments of acts to ends towards the close of life. Death by starvation from inability to catch prey, shows a falling short of conduct from its ideal.

This imperfectly-evolved conduct introduces us by antithesis to conduct that is perfectly evolved. Contemplating these adjustments of acts to ends which miss completeness because they cannot be made by one creature without other creatures being prevented from making them, raises the thought of adjustments such that each creature may make them without preventing them from being made by other creatures. That the highest form of conduct must be so distinguished, is an inevitable implication; for while the form of conduct is such that adjustments of acts to ends by some necessitate non-adjustments by others, there remains room for modifications which bring conduct into a form avoiding this, and so making the totality of life greater.

From the abstract let us pass to the concrete. Recognizing men as the beings whose conduct is most evolved, let us ask under what conditions their conduct, in all three aspects of its evolution, reaches its limit. Clearly while the lives led are entirely predatory, as those of savages, the adjustments of acts to ends fall short of this highest form of conduct in every way. Individual life, ill carried on from hour to hour, is prematurely cut short; the fostering of offspring often fails, and is incomplete when it does not fail; and in so far as the ends of self-maintenance and race-maintenance are met, they are met by destruction of other beings, of different kind or of like kind. In social groups formed by compounding and re-compounding primitive hordes, conduct remains imperfectly evolved in proportion as there continue antagonisms between the groups and antagonisms between members of the same group—two traits necessarily associated; since the nature which prompts international aggression prompts aggression of individuals on one another. Hence the limit of evolution can be reached by conduct only in permanently peaceful societies. That perfect adjustment of acts to ends in maintaining individual life and rearing new individuals, which is effected by each without hindering others from effecting like perfect adjustments, is, in its very definition, shown to constitute a kind of conduct that can be approached only as war decreases and dies out.

A gap in this outline must now be filled up. There remains a further advance not yet even hinted. For beyond so behaving that each achieves his ends without preventing others from achieving their ends, the members of a society may give mutual help in the achievement of ends. And if, either indirectly by industrial co-operation, or directly by volunteered aid, fellow citizens can make easier for one another the adjustments of acts to ends, then their conduct assumes a still higher phase of evolution; since whatever facilitates the making of adjustments by each, increases the totality of the adjustments made, and serves to render the lives of all more complete.

§ 7. The reader who recalls certain passages in *First Principles*, in the *Principles of Biology*, and in the *Principles of Psychology*, will perceive above a re-statement, in another form, of generalizations set forth in those works. Especially will he be reminded of the proposition that Life is "the definite combination of heterogeneous changes, both simultaneous and successive, in correspondence with external coexistences and sequences;" and still more of that abridged and less specific formula, in which Life is said to be "the continuous adjustment of internal relations to external relations."

The presentation of the facts here made, differs from the

2 *

presentations before made, mainly by ignoring the inner
part of the correspondence and attending exclusively to that
outer part constituted of visible actions. But the two are in
harmony; and the reader who wishes further to prepare himself for dealing with our present topic from the evolution
point of view, may advantageously join to the foregoing
more special aspect of the phenomena, the more general
aspects before delineated.

After this passing remark, I recur to the main proposition set forth in these two chapters, which has, I think,
been fully justified. Guided by the truth that as the conduct with which Ethics deals is part of conduct at large,
conduct at large must be generally understood before this
part can be specially understood; and guided by the further
truth that to understand conduct at large we must understand the evolution of conduct; we have been led to see
that Ethics has for its subject-matter, that form which
universal conduct assumes during the last stages of its
evolution. We have also concluded that these last stages
in the evolution of conduct are those displayed by the
highest type of being, when he is forced, by increase of
numbers, to live more and more in presence of his fellows.
And there has followed the corollary that conduct gains
ethical sanction in proportion as the activities, becoming
less and less militant and more and more industrial,
are such as do not necessitate mutual injury or hindrance,
but consist with, and are furthered by, co-operation and
mutual aid.

These implications of the Evolution-Hypothesis, we shall
now see harmonize with the leading moral ideas men have
otherwise reached.

CHAPTER III.

GOOD AND BAD CONDUCT.

§ 8. By comparing its meanings in different connexions and observing what they have in common, we learn the essential meaning of a word; and the essential meaning of a word that is variously applied, may best be learnt by comparing with one another those applications of it which diverge most widely. Let us thus ascertain what good and bad mean.

In which cases do we distinguish as good, a knife, a gun, a house? And what trait leads us to speak of a bad umbrella or a bad pair of boots? The characters here predicated by the words good and bad, are not intrinsic characters; for apart from human wants, such things have neither merits nor demerits. We call these articles good or bad according as they are well or ill adapted to achieve prescribed ends. The good knife is one which will cut; the good gun is one which carries far and true; the good house is one which duly yields the shelter, comfort, and accommodation sought for. Conversely, the badness alleged of the umbrella or the pair of boots, refers to their failures in fulfilling the ends of keeping off the rain and comfortably protecting the feet, with due regard to appearances.   So is it when we pass from inanimate objects to inanimate actions. We call a day bad in which storms prevent us from satisfying certain of our desires. A

good season is the expression used when the weather
has favoured the production of valuable crops.   If
from lifeless things and actions we pass to living ones, we
similarly find that these words in their current applications
refer to efficient subservience. The goodness or badness of
a pointer or a hunter, of a sheep or an ox, ignoring all other
attributes of these creatures, refer in the one case to the
fitness of their actions for effecting the ends men use them
for, and in the other case to the qualities of their flesh as
adapting it to support human life.   And those doings of
men which, morally considered, are indifferent, we class as
good or bad according to their success or failure. A good
jump is a jump which, remoter ends ignored, well achieves
the immediate purpose of a jump; and a stroke at billiards
is called good when the movements are skilfully adjusted to
the requirements. Oppositely, the badness of a walk that
is shuffling and an utterance that is indistinct, is alleged
because of the relative non-adaptations of the acts to the
ends.

Thus recognizing the meanings of good and bad as otherwise used, we shall understand better their meanings as
used in characterizing conduct under its ethical aspects.
Here, too, observation shows that we apply them according
as the adjustments of acts to ends are, or are not, efficient.
This truth is somewhat disguised. The entanglement of
social relations is such, that men's actions often simultaneously affect the welfares of self, of offspring, and of
fellow-citizens. Hence results confusion in judging of
actions as good or bad; since actions well fitted to achieve
ends of one order, may prevent ends of the other orders from
being achieved. Nevertheless, when we disentangle the
three orders of ends, and consider each separately, it becomes clear that the conduct which achieves each kind
of end is regarded as relatively good; and is regarded as
relatively bad if it fails to achieve it.

Take first the primary set of adjustments—those sub-

serving individual life. Apart from approval or disapproval
of his ulterior aims, a man who fights is said to make a good
defence, if his defence is well adapted for self-preservation ;
and, the judgments on other aspects of his conduct remaining the same, he brings down on himself an unfavourable
verdict, in so far as his immediate acts are concerned, if
these are futile. The goodness ascribed to a man of
business, as such, is measured by the activity and ability
with which he buys and sells to advantage; and may
coexist with a hard treatment of dependents which is reprobated. Though in repeatedly lending money to a friend who
sinks one loan after another, a man is doing that which, considered in itself is held praiseworthy ; yet, if he does it to the
extent of bringing on his own ruin, he is held blameworthy
for a self-sacrifice carried too far. And thus is it with the
opinions we express from hour to hour on those acts of
people around which bear on their health and personal welfare. "You should not have done that;" is the reproof
given to one who crosses the street amid a dangerous rush
of vehicles. "You ought to have changed your clothes ;" is
said to another who has taken cold after getting wet. "You
were right to take a receipt;" "you were wrong to invest
without advice ;" are common criticisms. All such approving
and disapproving utterances make the tacit assertion that,
other things equal, conduct is right or wrong according as
its special acts, well or ill adjusted to special ends, do or
do not further the general end of self-preservation.

These ethical judgments we pass on self-regarding acts
are ordinarily little emphasized ; partly because the promptings of the self-regarding desires, generally strong enough,
do not need moral enforcement, and partly because the
promptings of the other-regarding desires, less strong, and
often over-ridden, do need moral enforcement. Hence
results a contrast. On turning to that second class of
adjustments of acts to ends which subserve the rearing of
offspring, we no longer find any obscurity in the application

of the words good and bad to them, according as they are efficient or inefficient. The expressions good nursing and bad nursing, whether they refer to the supply of food, the quality and amount of clothing, or the due ministration to infantine wants from hour to hour, tacitly recognize as special ends which ought to be fulfilled, the furthering of the vital functions, with a view to the general end of continued life and growth. A mother is called good who, ministering to all the physical needs of her children, also adjusts her behaviour in ways conducive to their mental health; and a bad father is one who either does not provide the necessaries of life for his family, or otherwise acts in a manner injurious to their bodies or minds. Similarly of the education given to them, or provided for them. Goodness or badness is affirmed of it (often with little consistency, however) according as its methods are so adapted to physical and psychical requirements, as to further the children's lives for the time being, while preparing them for carrying on complete and prolonged adult life.

Most emphatic, however, are the applications of the words good and bad to conduct throughout that third division of it comprising the deeds by which men affect one another. In maintaining their own lives and fostering their offspring, men's adjustments of acts to ends are so apt to hinder the kindred adjustments of other men, that insistance on the needful limitations has to be perpetual; and the mischiefs caused by men's interferences with one another's life-subserving actions are so great, that the interdicts have to be peremptory. Hence the fact that the words good and bad have come to be specially associated with acts which further the complete living of others and acts which obstruct their complete living. Goodness, standing by itself, suggests, above all other things, the conduct of one who aids the sick in re-acquiring normal vitality, assists the unfortunate to recover the means of maintaining themselves, defends those who are threatened with harm in person, property, or reputation, and aids whatever promises to improve the living of all his fellows. Contrariwise, badness brings to mind, as its leading correlative, the conduct of one who, in carrying on his own life, damages the lives of others by injuring their bodies, destroying their possessions, defrauding them, calumniating them.

Always, then, acts are called good or bad, according as they are well or ill adjusted to ends; and whatever inconsistency there is in our uses of the words, arises from inconsistency of the ends. Here, however, the study of conduct in general, and of the evolution of conduct, have prepared us to harmonize these interpretations. The foregoing exposition shows that the conduct to which we apply the name good, is the relatively more evolved conduct; and that bad is the name we apply to conduct which is relatively less evolved. We saw that evolution, tending ever towards self-preservation, reaches its limit when individual life is the greatest, both in length and breadth; and now we see that, leaving other ends aside, we regard as good the conduct furthering self-preservation, and as bad the conduct tending to self-destruction. It was shown that along with increasing power of maintaining individual life, which evolution brings, there goes increasing power of perpetuating the species by fostering progeny, and that in this direction evolution reaches its limit when the needful number of young, preserved to maturity, are then fit for a life that is complete in fulness and duration; and here it turns out that parental conduct is called good or bad as it approaches or falls short of this ideal result. Lastly, we inferred that establishment of an associated state, both makes possible and requires a form of conduct such that life may be completed in each and in his offspring, not only without preventing completion of it in others, but with furtherance of it in others; and we have found above, that this is the form of conduct most emphatically termed good. Moreover, just as we there saw that evolution becomes the highest possible when the conduct simultaneously achieves the greatest totality of life in self, in offspring, and in fellow men; so here we see that the conduct called good rises to the conduct conceived as best, when it fulfils all three classes of ends at the same time.

§ 9. Is there any postulate involved in these judgments on conduct? Is there any assumption made in calling good the acts conducive to life, in self or others, and bad those which directly or indirectly tend towards death, special or general? Yes; an assumption of extreme significance has been made—an assumption underlying all moral estimates.

The question to be definitely raised and answered before entering on any ethical discussion, is the question of late much agitated—Is life worth living? Shall we take the pessimist view? or shall we take the optimist view? or shall we, after weighing pessimistic and optimistic arguments, conclude that the balance is in favour of a qualified optimism?

On the answer to this question depends entirely every decision concerning the goodness or badness of conduct. By those who think life is not a benefit but a misfortune, conduct which prolongs it is to be blamed rather than praised : the ending of an undesirable existence being the thing to be wished, that which causes the ending of it must be applauded; while actions furthering its continuance, either in self or others, must be reprobated. Those who, on the other hand, take an optimistic view, or who, if not pure optimists, yet hold that in life the good exceeds the evil, are committed to opposite estimates ; and must regard as conduct to be approved that which fosters life in self and others, and as conduct to be disapproved that which injures or endangers life in self or others.

The ultimate question, therefore, is—Has evolution been a mistake; and especially that evolution which improves the adjustment of acts to ends in ascending stages of organization ? If it is held that there had better not have been any animate existence at all, and that the sooner it comes to an end the better; then one set of conclusions with respect to conduct emerges. If, contrariwise, it is held that there is a balance in favour of animate existence, and if, still further, it is held that in the future this balance may be increased; then the opposite set of conclusions emerges. Even should it be alleged that the worth of life is not to be judged by its intrinsic character, but rather by its extrinsic sequences— by certain results to be anticipated when life has passed —the ultimate issue re-appears in a new shape. For though the accompanying creed may negative a deliberate shortening of life that is miserable, it cannot justify a gratuitous lengthening of such life. Legislation conducive to increased longevity would, on the pessimistic view, remain blameable; while it would be praiseworthy on the optimistic view.

But now, have these irreconcilable opinions anything in common? Men being divisible into two schools differing on this ultimate question, the inquiry arises—Is there anything which their radically-opposed views alike take for granted? In the optimistic proposition, tacitly made when using the words good and bad after the ordinary manner; and in the pessimistic proposition overtly made, which implies that the words good and bad should be used in the reverse senses; does examination disclose any joint proposition—any proposition which, contained in both of them, may be held more certain than either—any universally-asserted proposition?

§ 10. Yes, there is one postulate in which pessimists and optimists agree. Both their arguments assume it to be self-evident that life is good or bad, according as it does, or does not, bring a surplus of agreeable feeling. The pessimist says he condemns life because it results in more pain than pleasure. The optimist defends life in the belief that it.

brings more pleasure than pain. Each makes the kind of sentiency which accompanies life the test. They agree that the
justification for life as a state of being, turns on this issue—
whether the average consciousness rises above indifference-
point into pleasurable feeling or falls below it into painful
feeling. The implication common to their antagonist views
is, that conduct should conduce to preservation of the individual, of the family, and of the society, only supposing that
life brings more happiness than misery.

Changing the venue cannot alter the verdict. If either
the pessimist, while saying that the pains of life predominate,
or the optimist, while saying that the pleasures predominate,
urges that the pains borne here are to be compensated by
pleasures received hereafter; and that so life, whether
or not justified in its immediate results, is justified in
its ultimate results; the implication remains the same.
The decision is still reached by balancing pleasures against
pains. Animate existence would be judged by both a
curse, if to a surplus of misery borne here, were added
a surplus of misery to be borne hereafter. And for either
to regard animate existence as a blessing, if here its pains
were held to exceed its pleasures, he must hold that hereafter its pleasures will exceed its pains. Thus there is no
escape from the admission that in calling good the conduct
which subserves life, and bad the conduct which hinders or
destroys it, and in so implying that life is a blessing and not
a curse, we are inevitably asserting that conduct is good or
bad according as its total effects are pleasurable or painful.

One theory only is imaginable in pursuance of which
other interpretations of good and bad can be given. This
theory is that men were created with the intention that they
should be sources of misery to themselves; and that they are
bound to continue living that their creator may have the
satisfaction of contemplating their misery. Though this is
not a theory avowedly entertained by many—though it is
not formulated by any in this distinct way; yet not a few do

accept it under a disguised form. Inferior creeds are pervaded by the belief that the sight of suffering is pleasing to the gods. Derived from bloodthirsty ancestors, such gods are naturally conceived as gratified by the infliction of pain : when living they delighted in torturing other beings; and witnessing torture is supposed still to give them delight. The implied conceptions long survive. It needs but to name Indian fakirs who hang on hooks and Eastern dervishes who gash themselves, to show that in societies considerably advanced, are still to be found many who think that submission to anguish brings divine favour. And without enlarging on fasts and penances, it will be clear that there has existed, and still exists, among Christian peoples, the belief that the Deity whom Jephthah thought to propitiate by sacrificing his daughter, may be propitiated by self-inflicted pains. Further, the conception accompanying this, that acts pleasing to self are offensive to God, has survived along with it, and still widely prevails; if not in formulated dogmas, yet in beliefs that are manifestly operative.

Doubtless, in modern days such beliefs have assumed qualified forms. The satisfactions which ferocious gods were supposed to feel in contemplating tortures, has been, in large measure, transformed into the satisfaction felt by a deity in contemplating that self-infliction of pain which is held to further eventual happiness. But clearly those who entertain this modified view, are excluded from the class whose position we are here considering. Restricting ourselves to this class—supposing that from the savage who immolates victims to a cannibal god, there are descendants among the civilized, who hold that mankind were made for suffering, and that it is their duty to continue living in misery for the delight of their maker, we can only recognize the fact that devil-worshippers are not yet extinct.

Omitting people of this class, if there are any, as beyond or beneath argument, we find that all others avowedly or tacitly hold that the final justification for maintaining life, can only be the reception from it of a surplus of pleasurable feeling over painful feeling; and that goodness or badness can be ascribed to acts which subserve life or hinder life, only on this supposition.

And here we are brought round to those primary meanings of the words good and bad, which we passed over when considering their secondary meanings. For on remembering that we call good and bad the things which immediately produce agreeable and disagreeable sensations, and also the sensations themselves—a good wine, a good appetite, a bad smell, a bad headache—we see that by referring directly to pleasures and pains, these meanings harmonize with those which indirectly refer to pleasures and pains. If we call good the enjoyable state itself, as a good laugh—if we call good the proximate cause of an enjoyable state, as good music—if we call good any agent which conduces immediately or remotely to an enjoyable state, as a good shop, a good teacher—if we call good considered intrinsically, each act so adjusted to its end as to further self-preservation and that surplus of enjoyment which makes self-preservation desirable—if we call good every kind of conduct which aids the lives of others, and do this under the belief that life brings more happiness than misery; then it becomes undeniable that, taking into account immediate and remote effects on all persons, the good is universally the pleasurable.

§ 11. Sundry influences—moral, theological, and political —conspire to make people disguise from themselves this truth. As in narrower cases so in this widest case, they become so pre-occupied with the means by which an end is achieved, as eventually to mistake it for the end. Just as money, which is a means of satisfying wants, comes to be regarded by a miser as the sole thing to be worked for, leaving the wants unsatisfied; so the conduct men have found preferable because most conducive to happiness, has come to be thought of as intrinsically preferable : not only to be made a proximate end (which it should be), but to be made an ultimate end, to the exclusion of the true ultimate end. And yet cross-examination quickly compels everyone to confess the true ultimate end. Just as the miser, asked to justify himself, is obliged to allege the power of money to purchase desirable things, as his reason for prizing it; so the moralist who thinks this conduct intrinsically good and that intrinsically bad, if pushed home, has no choice but to fall back on their pleasure-giving and pain-giving effects. To prove this it needs but to observe how impossible it would be to think of them as we do, if their effects were reversed.

Suppose that gashes and bruises caused agreeable sensations, and brought in their train increased power of doing work and receiving enjoyment; should we regard assault in the same manner as at present? Or suppose that self-mutilation, say by cutting off a hand, was both intrinsically pleasant and furthered performance of the processes by which personal welfare and the welfare of dependents is achieved; should we hold as now, that deliberate injury to one's own body is to be reprobated? Or again, suppose that picking a man's pocket excited in him joyful emotions, by brightening his prospects; would theft be counted among crimes, as in existing law-books and moral codes? In these extreme cases, no one can deny that what we call the badness of actions is ascribed to them solely for the reason that they entail pain, immediate or remote, and would not be so ascribed did they entail pleasure.

If we examine our conceptions on their obverse side, this general fact forces itself on our attention with equal distinctness. Imagine that ministering to a sick person always increased the pains of illness. Imagine that an orphan's relatives who took charge of it, thereby necessarily brought miseries upon it. Imagine that liquidating another man's pecuniary claims on you redounded to his disadvantage.

Imagine that crediting a man with noble behaviour hindered
his social welfare and consequent gratification. What should
we say to these acts which now fall into the class we call
praiseworthy ?   Should we not contrariwise class them as
blameworthy ?

Using, then, as our tests, these most pronounced forms of
good and bad conduct, we find it unquestionable that our
ideas of their goodness and badness really originate from
our consciousness of the certainty or probability that they will
produce pleasures or pains somewhere. And this truth is
brought out with equal clearness by examining the standards
of different moral schools; for analysis shows that every
one of them derives its authority from this ultimate standard.
Ethical systems are roughly distinguishable according as
they take for their cardinal ideas (1) the character of the
agent ; (2) the nature of his motive ; (3) the quality of his
deeds ; and (4) the results. Each of these may be characterized as good or bad ; and those who do not estimate a mode
of life by its effects on happiness, estimate it by the implied
goodness or badness in the agent, in his motive, or in his
deeds. We have perfection in the agent set up as a test by
which conduct is to be judged. Apart from the agent we
have his feeling considered as moral. And apart from the
feeling we have his action considered as virtuous.

Though the distinctions thus indicated have so little
definiteness that the words marking them are used inter-
changeably, yet there correspond to them doctrines partially
unlike one another ; which we may here conveniently examine
separately, with the view of showing that all their tests of
goodness are derivative.

§ 12. It is strange that a notion so abstract as that of
perfection, or a certain ideal completeness of nature, should
ever have been thought one from which a system of guidance
can be evolved ; as it was in a general way by Plato
and more distinctly by Jonathan Edwardes. Perfection is

synonymous with goodness in the highest degree; and hence to define good conduct in terms of perfection, is indirectly to define good conduct in terms of itself. Naturally, therefore, it happens that the notion of perfection like the notion of goodness can be framed only in relation to ends.

We allege imperfection of any inanimate thing, as a tool, if it lacks some part needful for effectual action, or if some part is so shaped as not to fulfil its purpose in the best manner. Perfection is alleged of a watch if it keeps exact time, however plain its case; and imperfection is alleged of it because of inaccurate time-keeping, however beautifully it is ornamented. Though we call things imperfect if we detect in them any injuries or flaws, even when these do not detract from efficiency; yet we do this because they imply that inferior workmanship, or that wear and tear, with which inefficiency is commonly joined in experience: absence of minor imperfections being habitually associated with absence of major imperfections.

As applied to living things, the word perfection has the same meaning. The idea of perfect shape in a race-horse is derived by generalization from those observed traits of race-horses which have usually gone along with attainment of the highest speed; and the idea of perfect constitution in a race-horse similarly refers to the endurance which enables him to continue that speed for the longest time. With men, physically considered, it is the same: we are able to furnish no other test of perfection, than that of complete power in all the organs to fulfil their respective functions. That our conception of perfect balance among the internal parts, and of perfect proportion among the external parts, originates thus, is made clear by observing that imperfection of any viscus, as lungs, heart, or liver, is ascribed for no other reason than inability to meet in full the demands which the activities of the organism make on it; and on observing that the conception of insufficient size, or of too great size, in a limb, is derived from accumulated experiences

3

respecting that ratio among the limbs which furthers in the highest degree the performance of all needful actions.

And of perfection in mental nature we have no other measure. If imperfection of memory, of judgment, of temper, is alleged, it is alleged because of inadequacy to the requirements of life; and to imagine a perfect balance of the intellectual powers and of the emotions, is to imagine that proportion among them which ensures an entire discharge of each and every obligation as the occasion calls for it.

So that the perfection of man considered as an agent, means the being constituted for effecting complete adjustment of acts to ends of every kind. And since, as shown above, the complete adjustment of acts to ends is that which both secures and constitutes the life that is most evolved, alike in breadth and length; while, as also shown, the justification for whatever increases life is the reception from life of more happiness than misery; it follows that conduciveness to happiness is the ultimate test of perfection in a man's nature. To be fully convinced of this it needs but to observe how the proposition looks when inverted. It needs but to suppose that every approach towards perfection involved greater misery to self, or others, or both, to show by opposition that approach to perfection really means approach to that which secures greater happiness.

§ 13. Pass we now from the view of those who make excellence of being the standard, to the view of those who make virtuousness of action the standard. I do not here refer to moralists who, having decided empirically or rationally, inductively or deductively, that acts of certain kinds have the character we call virtuous, argue that such acts are to be performed without regard to proximate consequences: these have ample justification. But I refer to moralists who suppose themselves to have conceptions of virtue as an end, underived from any other end—who think that the idea of virtue is not resolvable into simpler ideas.

This is the doctrine which appears to have been entertained by Aristotle. I say, appears to have been, because his statements are far from consistent with one another. Recognizing happiness as the supreme end of human endeavour, it would at first sight seem that he cannot be taken as typical of those who make virtue the supreme end. Yet he puts himself in this category by seeking to define happiness in terms of virtue, instead of defining virtue in terms of happiness. The imperfect separation of words from things, which characterizes Greek speculation in general, seems to have been the cause of this. In primitive thought the name and the object named, are associated in such wise that the one is regarded as a part of the other—so much so, that knowing a savage's name is considered by him as having some of his being, and a consequent power to work evil on him. This belief in a real connexion between word and thing, continuing through lower stages of progress, and long surviving in the tacit assumption that the meanings of words are intrinsic, pervades the dialogues of Plato, and is traceable even in Aristotle. For otherwise it is not easy to see why he should have so incompletely dissociated the abstract idea of happiness from particular forms of happiness. Naturally where the divorcing of words as symbols, from things as symbolized, is imperfect, there must be difficulty in giving to abstract words a sufficiently abstract meaning. If in the first stages of language the concrete name cannot be separated in thought from the concrete object it belongs to, it is inferable that in the course of forming successively higher grades of abstract names, there will have to be resisted the tendency to interpret each more abstract name in terms of some one class of the less abstract names it covers. Hence, I think, the fact that Aristotle supposes happiness to be associated with some one order of human activities, rather than with all orders of human activities. Instead of including in it the pleasurable feelings accompanying actions that constitute mere living, which actions he says man has in common with vegetables; and instead of making it include the mental states which the life of external perception yields, which he says man has in common with animals at large; he excludes these from his idea of happiness, and includes in it only the modes of consciousness accompanying rational life. Asserting that the proper work of man " consists in the active exercise of the mental capacities conformably to reason;" he concludes that " the supreme good of man will consist in performing this work with excellence or virtue: herein he will obtain happiness." And he finds confirmation for his view in its correspondence with views previously enunciated; saying—" our notion nearly agrees with theirs who place happiness in virtue; for we say that it consists in the action of virtue; that is, not merely in the possession, but in the use."

Now the implied belief that virtue can be defined other-wise than in terms of happiness (for else the proposition is that happiness is to be obtained by actions conducive to happiness) is allied to the Platonic belief that there is an ideal or absolute good, which gives to particular and relative goods their property of goodness; and an argument analogous to that which Aristotle uses against Plato's conception of good, may be used against his own conception of virtue. As with good so with virtue—it is not singular but plural: in Aristotle's own classification, virtue, when treated of at large, is transformed into virtues. Those which he calls virtues, must be so called in consequence of some common character that is either intrinsic or extrinsic. We may class things together either because they are made alike by all having in themselves some peculiarity, as we do vertebrate animals because they all have vertebral columns; or we may class them together because of some community in their outer relations, as when we group saws, knives, mallets, harrows, under the head of tools. Are the virtues classed as such because of some intrinsic community of nature? Then

there must be identifiable a common trait in all the cardinal
virtues which Aristotle specifies—"Courage, Temperance,
Liberality, Magnanimity, Magnificence, Meekness, Amiability
or Friendliness, Truthfulness, Justice." What now is the trait
possessed in common by Magnificence and Meekness? and
if any such common trait can be disentangled, is it that
which also constitutes the essential trait in Truthfulness?
The answer must be—No. The virtues, then, not being classed
as such because of an instrinsic community of character, must
be classed as such because of something extrinsic; and this
something can be nothing else than the happiness which
Aristotle says consists in the practice of them. They are
united by their common relation to this result; while they
are not united by their inner natures.

Perhaps still more clearly may the inference be drawn
thus :—If virtue is primordial and independent, no reason
can be given why there should be any correspondence
between virtuous conduct and conduct that is pleasure-
giving in its total effects on self, or others, or both; and if
there is not a necessary correspondence, it is conceivable
that the conduct classed as virtuous should be pain-giving
in its total effects. That we may see the consequence
of so conceiving it, let us take the two virtues considered as typically such in ancient times and in modern
times—courage and chastity. By the hypothesis, then,
courage, displayed alike in self-defence and in defence of
country, is to be conceived as not only entailing pains
incidentally, but as being necessarily a cause of misery to
the individual and to the State; while, by implication, the
absence of it redounds to personal and general well-being.
Similarly, by the hypothesis, we have to conceive that
irregular sexual relations are directly and indirectly beneficial—that adultery is conducive to domestic harmony and
the careful rearing of children; while marital relations in
proportion as they are persistent, generate discord between
husband and wife and entail on their offspring, suffering,

disease, and death. Unless it is asserted that courage and chastity could still be thought of as virtues though thus productive of misery, it must be admitted that the conception of virtue cannot be separated from the conception of happiness-producing conduct; and that as this holds of all the virtues, however otherwise unlike, it is from their conduciveness to happiness that they come to be classed as virtues.

§ 14. When from those ethical estimates which take perfection of nature, or virtuousness of action, as tests, we pass to those which take for test rectitude of motive, we approach the intuitional theory of morals; and we may conveniently deal with such estimates by a criticism on this theory.

By the intuitional theory I here mean, not that which recognizes as produced by the inherited effects of continued experiences, the feelings of liking and aversion we have to acts of certain kinds; but I mean the theory which regards such feelings as divinely given, and as independent of results experienced by self or ancestors. "There is therefore," says Hutcheson, "as each one by close attention and reflection may convince himself, a natural and immediate determination to approve certain affections, and actions consequent upon them;" and since, in common with others of his time, he believes in the special creation of man, and all other beings, this "natural sense of immediate excellence" he considers as a supernaturally-derived guide. Though he says that the feelings and acts thus intuitively recognized as good, "all agree in one general character, of tending to the happiness of others;" yet he is obliged to conceive this as a pre-or-dained correspondence. Nevertheless, it may be shown that conduciveness to happiness, here represented as an incidental trait of the acts which receive these innate moral approvals, is really the test by which these approvals are recognized as moral. The intuitionists place confidence in these verdicts of conscience, simply because they vaguely, if not distinctly,

perceive them to be consonant with the disclosures of that
ultimate test. Observe the proof.

By the hypothesis, the wrongness of murder is known
by a moral intuition which the human mind was originally
constituted to yield; and the hypothesis therefore negatives
the admission that this sense of its wrongness arises, immediately or remotely, from the consciousness that murder
involves deduction from happiness, directly and indirectly.
But if you ask an adherent of this doctrine to contrast his
intuition with that of the Fijian, who, considering murder an
honourable action, is restless until he has distinguished
himself by killing some one; and if you inquire of him in
what way the civilized intuition is to be justified in
opposition to the intuition of the savage; no course is open
save that of showing how conformity to the one conduces
to well-being, while conformity to the other entails suffering,
individual and general. When asked why the moral
sense which tells him that it is wrong to take another man's
goods, should be obeyed rather than the moral sense of a
Turcoman, who proves how meritorious he considers theft
to be by making pilgrimages to the tombs of noted robbers
to make offerings; the intuitionist can do nothing but
urge that, certainly under conditions like ours, if not also
under conditions like those of the Turcomans, disregard of
men's claims to their property not only inflicts immediate
misery, but involves a social state inconsistent with happiness.
Or if, again, there is required from him a justification for
his feeling of repugnance to lying, in contrast with
the feeling of an Egyptian, who prides himself on skill
in lying (even thinking it praiseworthy to deceive without
any further end than that of practising deception); he can
do no more than point to the social prosperity furthered
by entire trust between man and man, and the social dis-
organization that follows universal untruthfulness—consequences that are necessarily conducive to agreeable feelings
and disagreeable feelings respectively.

The unavoidable conclusion is, then, that the intuitionist
does not, and cannot, ignore the ultimate derivations of
right and wrong from pleasure and pain. However much
he may be guided, and rightly guided, by the decisions of
conscience respecting the characters of acts; he has come
to have confidence in these decisions because he perceives,
vaguely but positively, that conformity to them furthers
the welfare of himself and others, and that disregard of
them entails in the long run suffering on all. Require
him to name any moral-sense judgment by which he
knows as right, some kind of act that will bring a surplus
of pain, taking into account the totals in this life and in
any assumed other life, and you find him unable to name
one: a fact proving that underneath all these intuitions
respecting the goodness or badness of acts, there lies the
fundamental assumption that acts are good or bad according
as their aggregate effects increase men's happiness or
increase their misery.

§ 14. It is curious to see how the devil-worship of the
savage, surviving in various disguises among the civilized,
and leaving as one of its products that asceticism which in
many forms and degrees still prevails widely, is to be found
influencing in marked ways, men who have apparently
emancipated themselves, not only from primitive superstitions but from more developed superstitions. Views of
life and conduct which originated with those who propitiated
deified ancestors by self-tortures, enter even still into the
ethical theories of many persons who have years since cast
away the theology of the past, and suppose themselves to be
no longer influenced by it.

In the writings of one who rejects dogmatic Christianity
together with the Hebrew cult which preceded it, a career
of conquest costing tens of thousands of lives, is narrated
with a sympathy comparable to that rejoicing which the
Hebrew traditions show us over destruction of enemies in

the name of God. You may find, too, a delight in contemplating the exercise of despotic power, joined with insistance on the salutariness of a state in which the wills of slaves and citizens, are humbly subject to the wills of masters and rulers—a sentiment also reminding us of that ancient Oriental life which biblical narratives portray. Along with this worship of the strong man—along with this justification of whatever force may be needed for carrying out his ambition—along with this yearning for a form of society in which supremacy of the few is unrestrained and the virtue of the many consists in obedience to them; we not unnaturally find repudiation of the ethical theory which takes, in some shape or other, the greatest happiness as the end of conduct : we not unnaturally find this utilitarian philosophy designated by the contemptuous title of "pig-philosophy." And then, serving to show what comprehension there has been of the philosophy so nicknamed, we are told that not happiness but blessedness must be the end.

Obviously, the implication is that blessedness is not a kind of happiness; and this implication at once suggests the question—What mode of feeling is it? If it is a state of consciousness at all, it is necessarily one of three states— painful, indifferent, or pleasurable. Does it leave the possessor at the zero point of sentiency? Then it leaves him just as he would be if he had not got it. Does it not leave him at the zero point? Then it must leave him below zero or above zero.

Each of these possibilities may be conceived under two forms. That to which the term blessedness is applied, may be a particular state of consciousness—one among the many states that occur; and on this supposition we have to recognize it as a pleasurable state, an indifferent state, or a painful state. Otherwise, blessedness is a word not applicable to a particular state of consciousness, but characterizes the aggregate of its states; and in this case the average of the aggregate is to be conceived as one in which the pleasurable predominates, or one in which the painful predominates, or one in which pleasures and pains exactly cancel one another. Let us take in turn these two imaginable applications of the word.

"Blessed are the merciful;" "Blessed are the peace-makers;" "Blessed is he that considereth the poor;" are sayings which we may fairly take as conveying the accepted meaning of blessedness. What now shall we say of one who is, for the time being, blessed in performing an act of mercy? Is his mental state pleasurable? If so the hypothesis is abandoned: blessedness is a particular form of happiness. Is the state indifferent or painful? In that case the blessed man is so devoid of sympathy that relieving another from pain, or the fear of pain, leaves him either wholly unmoved, or gives him an unpleasant emotion. Again, if one who is blessed in making peace receives no gratification from the act, then seeing men injure each other does not affect him at all, or gives him a pleasure which is changed into a pain when he prevents the injury. Once more, to say that the blessedness of one who "considereth the poor" implies no agreeable feeling, is to say that his consideration for the poor leaves him without feeling or entails on him a disagreeable feeling. So that if blessedness is a particular mode of con-sciousness temporarily existing as a concomitant of each kind of beneficent action, those who deny that it is a pleasure, or constituent of happiness, confess themselves either not pleased by the welfare of others or displeased by it.

Otherwise understood, blessedness must, as we have seen, refer to the totality of feelings experienced during the life of one who occupies himself with the actions the word con-notes. This also presents the three possibilities—surplus of pleasures, surplus of pains, equality of the two. If the pleasurable states are in excess, then the blessed life can be distinguished from any other pleasurable life only by the relative amount, or the quality, of its pleasures: it is a life which makes happiness of a certain kind and degree its end;

and the assumption that blessedness is not a form of happiness, lapses.   If the blessed life is one in which the pleasures and pains received balance one another, so producing an average that is indifferent; or if it is one in which the pleasures are out-balanced by the pains; then the blessed life has the character which the pessimist alleges of life at large, and therefore regards it as cursed.   Annihilation is best, he will argue; since if an average that is indifferent is the outcome of the blessed life, annihilation at once achieves it; and if a surplus of suffering is the outcome of this highest kind of life called blessed, still more should life in general be ended.

A possible rejoinder must be named and disposed of. While it is admitted that the particular kind of consciousness accompanying conduct that is blessed, is pleasurable; it may be contended that pursuance of this conduct and receipt of the pleasure, brings by the implied self-denial, and persistent effort, and perhaps bodily injury, a suffering that exceeds it in amount.   And it may then be urged that blessedness, characterized by this excess of aggregate pains over aggregate pleasures, should nevertheless be pursued as an end, rather than the happiness constituted by excess of pleasures over pains.   But now, defensible though this conception of blessedness may be when limited to one individual, or some individuals, it becomes indefensible when extended to all individuals; as it must be if blessedness is taken for the end of conduct.   To see this we need but ask for what purpose are these pains in excess of pleasures to be borne.   Blessedness being the ideal state for all persons; and the self-sacrifices made by each person in pursuance of this ideal state, having for their end to help all other persons in achieving the like ideal state; it results that the blessed though painful state of each, is to be acquired by furthering the like blessed though painful states of others : the blessed consciousness is to be constituted by the contemplation of their consciousnesses in a condition of average suffering. Does any one accept this inference ? If not, his rejection of it involves the admission that the motive for bearing pains in performing acts called blessed, is not the obtaining for others like pains of blessedness, but the obtaining of pleasures for others ; and that thus pleasure somewhere is the tacitly-implied ultimate end.

In brief, then, blessedness has for its necessary condition of existence, increased happiness, positive or negative, in some consciousness or other ; and disappears utterly if we assume that the actions called blessed, are known to cause decrease of happiness in óthers as well as in the actor.

§ 15. To make clear the meaning of the general argument set forth in this chapter, its successive parts must be briefly summarized.

That which in the last chapter we found to be highly-evolved conduct, is that which, in this chapter, we find to be what is called good conduct; and the ideal goal to the natural evolution of conduct there recognized, we here recognize as the ideal standard of conduct ethically considered.

The acts adjusted to ends, which while constituting the outer visible life from moment to moment further the continuance of life, we saw become, as evolution progresses, better adjusted; until finally they make the life of each individual entire in length and breadth, at the same time that they efficiently subserve the rearing of young, and do both these not only without hindering other individuals from doing the like, but while giving aid to them in doing the like. And here we see that goodness is asserted of such conduct under each of these three aspects. Other things equal, well-adjusted self-conserving acts we call good ; other things equal, we call good the acts that are well adjusted for bringing up progeny capable of complete living; and other things equal, we ascribe goodness to acts which further the complete living of others.

This judging as good, conduct which conduces to life in each and all, we found to involve the assumption that animate existence is desirable. By the pessimist, conduct which subserves life cannot consistently be called good: to call it good implies some form of optimism. We saw, however, that pessimists and optimists both start with the postulate that life is a blessing or a curse, according as the average consciousness accompanying it is pleasurable or painful. And since avowed or implied pessimists, and optimists of one or other shade, taken together constitute all men, it results that this postulate is universally accepted. Whence it follows that if we call good the conduct conducive to life, we can do so only with the implication that it is conducive to a surplus of pleasures over pains.

The truth that conduct is considered by us as good or bad, according as its aggregate results, to self or others or both, are pleasurable or painful, we found on examination to be involved in all the current judgments on conduct: the proof being that reversing the applications of the words creates absurdities. And we found that every other proposed standard of conduct derives its authority from this standard. Whether perfection of nature is the assigned proper aim, or virtuousness of action, or rectitude of motive, we saw that definition of the perfection, the virtue, the rectitude, inevitably brings us down to happiness experienced in some form, at some time, by some person, as the fundamental idea. Nor could we discover any intelligible conception of blessedness, save one which implies a raising of consciousness, individual or general, to a happier state; either by mitigating pains or increasing pleasures.

Even with those who judge of conduct from the religious point of view, rather than from the ethical point of view, it is the same. Men who seek to propitiate God by inflicting pains on themselves, or refrain from pleasures to avoid offending him, do so to escape greater ultimate pains or to get greater ultimate pleasures. If by positive or negative

suffering here, they expected to achieve more suffering hereafter, they would not do as they do. That which they now
think duty they would not think duty if it promised eternal
misery instead of eternal happiness. Nay, if there be any
who believe that human beings were created to be unhappy,
and that they ought to continue living to display their
unhappiness for the satisfaction of their creator, such
believers are obliged to use this standard of judgment; for
the pleasure of their diabolical god is the end to be
achieved.

So that no school can avoid taking for the ultimate moral
aim a desirable state of feeling called by whatever name—
gratification, enjoyment, happiness. Pleasure somewhere, at
some time, to some being or beings, is an inexpugnable
element of the conception. It is as much a necessary form
of moral intuition as space is a necessary form of intellectual
intuition.

CHAPTER IV.

WAYS OF JUDGING CONDUCT.

§ 17. Intellectual progress is by no one trait so adequately characterized, as by development of the idea of
causation; since development of this idea involves development of so many other ideas. Before any way can be made,
thought and language must have advanced far enough to
render properties or attributes thinkable as such, apart from
objects; which, in low stages of human intelligence, they are
not. Again, even the simplest notion of cause, as we understand it, can be reached only after many like instances have
been grouped into a simple generalization; and through all
ascending steps, higher notions of causation imply wider
notions of generality. Further, as there must be clustered
in the mind, concrete causes of many kinds before there can
emerge the conception of cause, apart from particular causes;
it follows that progress in abstractness of thought is implied.
Concomitantly, there is implied the recognition of constant
relations among phenomena, generating ideas of uniformity
of sequence and of co-existence—the idea of natural law.
These advances can go on only as fast as perceptions and
resulting thoughts, are made definite by the use of measures;
serving to familarize the mind with exact correspondence,
truth, certainty. And only when growing science accumulates
examples of quantitative relations, foreseen and verified,
throughout a widening range of phenomena, does causation

come to be conceived as necessary and universal. So that though all these cardinal conceptions aid one another in developing, we may properly say that the conception of causation especially depends for its development on the developments of the rest; and therefore is the best measure of intellectual development at large.

How slowly, as a consequence of its dependence, the conception of causation evolves, a glance at the evidence shows. We hear with surprise of the savage who, falling down a precipice, ascribes the failure of his foothold to a malicious demon; and we smile at the kindred notion of the ancient Greek, that his death was prevented by a goddess who unfastened for him the thong of the helmet by which his enemy was dragging him. But daily, without surprise, we hear men who describe themselves as saved from ship-wreck by "divine interposition," who speak of having "providentially" missed a train which met with a fatal disaster, and who call it a "mercy" to have escaped injury from a falling chimney-pot—men who, in such cases, recognize physical causation no more than do the uncivilized or semi-civilized. The Veddah who thinks that failure to hit an animal with his arrow, resulted from inadequate invocation of an ancestral spirit, and the Christian priest who says prayers over a sick man in the expectation that the course of his disease will so be stayed, differ only in respect of the agent from whom they expect supernatural aid and the phenomena to be altered by him : the necessary relations among causes and effects are tacitly ignored by the last as much as by the first. Deficient belief in causation is, indeed, exemplified even in those whose discipline has been specially fitted to generate this belief—even in men of science. For a generation after geologists had become uniformitarians in Geology, they remained catastrophists in Biology : while recognizing none but natural agencies in the genesis of the Earth's crust, they ascribed to supernatural agency the genesis of the organisms on its surface. Nay more—among

those who are convinced that living things in genera
have been evolved by the continued inter-action of forces
everywhere operating, there are some who make an excep-
tion of man; or who, if they admit that his body has been
evolved in the same manner as the bodies of other creatures,
allege that his mind has been not evolved but specially
created. If, then, universal and necessary causation is only
now approaching full recognition, even by those whose
investigations are daily re-illustrating it, we may expect to
find it very little recognized among men at large, whose
culture has not been calculated to impress them with it;
and we may expect to find it least recognized by them in
respect of those classes of phenomena amid which, in
consequence of their complexity, causation is most difficult
to trace—the psychical, the social, the moral.

Why do I here make these reflections on what seems an
irrelevant subject ? I do it because on studying the various
ethical theories, I am struck with the fact that they are all
characterized either by entire absence of the idea of
causation, or by inadequate presence of it. Whether
theological, political, intuitional, or utilitarian, they all
display, if not in the same degree, still, each in a large
degree, the defects which result from this lack. We will
consider them in the order named.

§ 18. The school of morals properly to be considered as
the still-extant representative of the most ancient school, is
that which recognizes no other rule of conduct than the
alleged will of God. It originates with the savage whose
only restraint beyond fear of his fellow man, is fear of an
ancestral spirit; and whose notion of moral duty as distinguished from his notion of social prudence, arises from
this fear. Here the ethical doctrine and the religious
doctrine are identical—have in no degree differentiated.

This primitive form of ethical doctrine, changed only by
the gradual dying out multitudinous minor supernatural

4

agents and accompanying development of one universal supernatural agent, survives in great strength down to our own day. Religious creeds, established and dissenting, all embody the belief that right and wrong are right and wrong simply in virtue of divine enactment. And this tacit assumption has passed from systems of theology into systems of morality; or rather, let us say that moral systems in early stages of development, little differentiated from the accompanying theological systems, have participated in this assumption. We see this in the works of the Stoics, as well as in the works of certain Christian moralists. Among recent ones I may instance the *Essays on the Principles of Morality*, by Jonathan Dymond, a Quaker, which makes "the authority of the Deity the sole ground of duty, and His communicated will the only ultimate standard of right and wrong." Nor is it by writers belonging to so relatively unphilosophical a sect only, that this view is held; it is held with a difference by writers belonging to sects contrariwise distinguished. For these assert that in the absence of belief in a deity, there would be no moral guidance; and this amounts to asserting that moral truths have no other origin than the will of God, which, if not considered as revealed in sacred writings, must be considered as revealed in conscience.

This assumption when examined, proves to be suicidal. If there are no other origins for right and wrong than this enunciated or intuited divine will, then, as alleged, were there no knowledge of the divine will, the acts now known as wrong would not be known as wrong. But if men did not know such acts to be wrong because contrary to the divine will, and so, in committing them, did not offend by disobedience; and if they could not otherwise know them to be wrong; then they might commit them indifferently with the acts now classed as right: the results, practically considered, would be the same. In so far as secular matters are concerned, there would be no difference between the two; for to say that in the affairs of life, any evils would arise from continuing to do the acts called wrong and ceasing to do the acts called right, is to say that these produce in themselves certain mischievous consequences and certain beneficial consequences; which is to say there is another source for moral rules than the revealed or inferred divine will: they may be established by induction from these observed consequences.

From this implication I see no escape. It must be either admitted or denied that the acts called good and the acts called bad, naturally conduce, the one to human well-being and the other to human ill-being. Is it admitted? Then the admission amounts to an assertion that the conduciveness is shown by experience; and this involves abandonment of the doctrine that there is no origin for morals apart from divine injunctions. Is it denied, that acts classed as good and bad differ in their effects? Then it is tacitly affirmed that human affairs would go on just as well in ignorance of the distinction; and the alleged need for commandments from God disappears.

And here we see how entirely wanting is the conception of cause. This notion that such and such actions are made respectively good and bad simply by divine injunction, is tantamount to the notion that such and such actions have not in the nature of things such and such kinds of effects. If there is not an unconsciousness of causation there is an ignoring of it.

§ 19. Following Plato and Aristotle, who make State-enactments the sources of right and wrong; and following Hobbes, who holds that there can be neither justice nor injustice till a regularly-constituted coercive power exists to issue and enforce commands; not a few modern thinkers hold that there is no other origin for good and bad in conduct than law. And this implies the belief that moral obligation originates with Acts of Parliament, and can be changed this way or that way by majorities. They ridicule

4 *

the idea that men have any natural rights, and allege that rights are wholly results of convention: the necessary implication being that duties are so too. Before considering whether this theory coheres with outside truths, let us observe how far it is coherent within itself.

In pursuance of his argument that rights and duties originate with established social arrangements, Hobbes says—

"Where no covenant hath preceded, there hath no right been transferred, and every man has right to every thing; and consequently, no action can be unjust. But when a covenant is made, then to break it is *unjust*; and the definition of *INJUSTICE*, is no other than *the not performance of covenant*. And whatsoever is not unjust, is *just*. . . . Therefore before the names of just and unjust can have place, there must be some coercive power, to compel men equally to the performance of their covenants, by the terror of some punishment, greater than the benefit they expect by the breach of their covenant."*

In this paragraph the essential propositions are :—justice is fulfilment of covenant; fulfilment of covenant implies a power enforcing it : "just and unjust *can* have no place" unless men are compelled to perform their covenants. But this is to say that men *cannot* perform their covenants without compulsion. Grant that justice is performance of covenant. Now suppose it to be performed voluntarily : there is justice. In such case, however, there is justice in the absence of coercion; which is contrary to the hypothesis. The only conceivable rejoinder is an absurd one :—voluntary performance of covenant is impossible. Assert this, and the doctrine that right and wrong come into existence with the establishment of sovereignty is defensible. Decline to assert it, and the doctrine vanishes.

From inner incongruities pass now to outer ones. The justification for his doctrine of absolute civil authority as the source of rules of conduct, Hobbes seeks in the miseries entailed by the chronic war between man and man which must exist in the absence of society ; holding that under any kind of government a better life is possible than in the state of

---

* *Leviathan*, ch. xv.

nature. Now whether we accept the gratuitous and baseless
theory that men surrendered their liberties to a sovereign
power of some kind, with a view to the promised increase
of satisfactions ; or whether we accept the rational theory,
inductively based, that a state of political subordination
gradually became established through experience of the
increased satisfactions derived under it ; it equally remains
obvious that the acts of the sovereign power have no other
warrant than their subservience to the purpose for which
it came into existence. The necessities which initiate
government, themselves prescribe the actions of government. If its actions do not respond to the necessities, they
are unwarranted. The authority of law is, then, by the
hypothesis, derived ; and can never transcend the authority
of that from which it is derived. If general good, or
welfare, or utility, is the supreme end ; and if State-enactments are justified as means to this supreme end ; then,
State-enactments have such authority only as arises from
conduciveness to this supreme end. When they are right,
it is only because the original authority endorses them ;
and they are wrong if they do not bear its endorsement.
That is to say, conduct cannot be made good or bad by law ;
but its goodness or badness is to the last determined by its
effects as naturally furthering, or not furthering, the lives
of citizens.

Still more when considered in the concrete, than when
considered in the abstract, do the views of Hobbes and his
disciples prove to be inconsistent. Joining in the general
belief that without such security for life as enables men to
go fearlessly about their business, there can be neither
happiness nor prosperity, individual or general, they agree
that measures for preventing murder, manslaughter, assault,
&c., are requisite ; and they advocate this or that penal
system as furnishing the best deterrents : so arguing, both
in respect of the evils and the remedies, that such and such
causes will, by the nature of things, produce such and such

effects. They recognize as inferable à *priori*, the truth that men will not lay by property unless they can count with great probability on reaping advantages from it; that consequently where robbery is unchecked, or where a rapacious ruler appropriates whatever earnings his subjects do not effectually hide, production will scarcely exceed immediate consumption; and that necessarily there will be none of that accumulation of capital required for social development, with all its aids to welfare. In neither case, however, do they perceive that they are tacitly asserting the need for certain restraints on conduct as deducible from the necessary conditions to complete life in the social state; and are so making the authority of law derivative and not original.

If it be said by any belonging to this school, that certain moral obligations to be distinguished as cardinal, must be admitted to have a basis deeper than legislation, and that it is for legislation not to create but merely to enforce them— if, I say, admitting this, they go on to allege a legislative origin for minor claims and duties; then we have the implication that whereas some kinds of conduct do, in the nature of things, tend to work out certain kinds of results, other kinds of conduct do not, in the nature of things, tend to work out certain kinds of results. While of these acts the naturally good or bad consequences must be allowed, it may be denied of those acts that they have naturally good or bad consequences. Only after asserting this can it be consistently asserted that acts of the last class are made right or wrong by law. For if such acts have any intrinsic tendencies to produce beneficial or mischievous effects, then these intrinsic tendencies furnish the warrant for legislative requirements or interdicts; and to say that the requirements or interdicts make them right or wrong, is to say that they have no intrinsic tendencies to produce beneficial or mischievous effects.

Here, then, we have another theory betraying deficient

consciousness of causation. An adequate consciousness of causation yields the irresistible belief that from the most serious to the most trivial actions of men in society, there must flow consequences which, quite apart from legal agency, conduce to well-being or ill-being in greater or smaller degrees. If murders are socially injurious whether forbidden by law or not—if one man's appropriation of another's gains by force, brings special and general evils, whether it is or is not contrary to a ruler's edicts—if non-fulfilment of contract, if cheating, if adulteration, work mischiefs on a community in proportion as they are common, quite irrespective of prohibitions; then, is it not manifest that the like holds throughout all the details of men's behaviour? Is it not clear that when legislation insists on certain acts which have naturally beneficial effects, and forbids others that have naturally injurious effects, the acts are not made good or bad by legislation; but the legislation derives its authority from the natural effects of the acts? Non-recognition of this implies non-recognition of natural causation.

§ 20. Nor is it otherwise with the pure intuitionists, who hold that moral perceptions are innate in the original sense—thinkers whose view is that men have been divinely endowed with moral faculties; not that these have resulted from inherited modifications caused by accumulated experiences.

To affirm that we know some things to be right and other things to be wrong, by virtue of a supernaturally-given conscience; and thus tacitly to affirm that we do not otherwise know right from wrong; is tacitly to deny any natural relations between acts and results. For if there exist any such relations, then we may ascertain by induction, or deduction, or both, what these are. And if it be admitted that because of such natural relations, happiness is produced by this kind of conduct, which is therefore to be approved, while misery is produced by that kind of conduct, which is therefore to be condemned; then it is admitted that the rightness or wrongness of actions are determinable, and must finally be determined, by the goodness or badness of the effects that flow from them; which is contrary to the hypothesis.

It may, indeed, be rejoined that effects are deliberately ignored by this school; which teaches that courses recognized by moral intuition as right, must be pursued without regard to consequences. But on inquiry it turns out that the consequences to be disregarded are particular consequences, and not general consequences. When, for example, it is said that property lost by another ought to be restored irrespective of evil to the finder, who possibly may, by restoring it, lose that which would have preserved him from starvation; it is meant that in pursuance of the principle, the immediate and special consequences must be disregarded, not the diffused and remote consequences. By which we are shown that though the theory forbids overt recognition of causation, there is an unavowed recognition of it.

And this implies the trait to which I am drawing attention. The conception of natural causation is so imperfectly developed, that there is only an indistinct consciousness that throughout the whole of human conduct, necessary relations of causes and effects prevail; and that from them are ultimately derived all moral rules, however much these may be proximately derived from moral intuitions.

§ 21. Strange to say, even the utilitarian school, which, at first sight, appears to be distinguished from the rest by recognizing natural causation, is, if not so far from complete recognition of it, yet very far.

Conduct, according to its theory, is to be estimated by observation of results. When, in sufficiently numerous cases, it has been found that behaviour of this kind works evil while behaviour of that kind works good, these kinds of behaviour are to be judged as wrong and right respectively.

Now though it seems that the origin of moral rules in natural causes, is thus asserted by implication, it is but partially asserted. The implication is simply that we are to ascertain by induction that such and such mischiefs or benefits *do* go along with such and such acts ; and are then to infer that the like relations will hold in future. But acceptance of these generalizations and the inferences from them, does not amount to recognition of causation in the full sense of the word. So long as only *some* relation between cause and effect in conduct is recognized, and not *the* relation, a completely-scientific form of knowledge has not been reached. At present, utilitarians pay no attention to this distinction. Even when it is pointed out, they disregard the fact that empirical utilitarianism is but a transitional form to be passed through on the way to rational utilitarianism.

In a letter to Mr. Mill, written some sixteen years ago, repudiating the title anti-utilitarian which he had applied to me (a letter subsequently published in Mr. Bain's work on *Mental and Moral Science*), I endeavoured to make clear the difference above indicated ; and I must here quote certain passages from that letter.

The view for which I contend is, that Morality properly so-called—the science of right conduct—has for its object to determine *how* and *why* certain modes of conduct are detrimental, and certain others modes beneficial. These good and bad results cannot be accidental, but must be necessary consequences of the constitution of things ; and I conceive it to be the business of Moral Science to deduce, from the laws of life and the conditions of existence, what kinds of action necessarily tend to produce happiness, and what kinds to produce unhappiness. Having done this, its deductions are to be recognized as laws of conduct ; and are to be conformed to irrespective of a direct estimation of happiness or misery.

Perhaps an analogy will most clearly show my meaning. During its early stages, planetary Astronomy consisted of nothing more than accumulated observations respecting the positions and motions of the sun and planets ; from which accumulated observations it came by and by to be empirically predicted, with an approach to truth, that certain of the heavenly bodies would have certain positions at certain times. But the modern science of planetary Astronomy consists of deductions from the law of gravitation—deductions showing why the celestial bodies *necessarily* occupy certain places at certain times. Now, the kind of relation which thus exists between ancient and modern Astronomy, is analogous to the kind of relation which, I conceive, exists between the Expendiency-Morality and Moral Science properly so called. And the objection which I have to the current Utilitarianism is, that it recognizes no more developed form of Morality—does not see that it has reached but the initial stage of Moral Science.

Doubtless if utilitarians are asked whether it can be by mere chance that this kind of action works evil and that works good, they will answer—No : they will admit that such sequences are parts of a necessary order among phenomena. But though this truth is beyond question ; and though if there are causal relations between acts and their results, rules of conduct can become scientific only when they are deduced from these causal relations ; there continues to be entire satisfaction with that form of utilitarianism in which these causal relations are practically ignored. It is supposed that in future, as now, utility is to be determined only by observation of results ; and that there is no possibility of knowing by deduction from fundamental principles, what conduct *must* be detrimental and what conduct *must* be beneficial.

§ 22. To make more specific that conception of ethical science here indicated, let me present it under a concrete aspect; beginning with a simple illustration and complicating this illustration by successive steps.

If, by tying its main artery, we stop most of the blood going to a limb, then, for as long as the limb performs its function, those parts which are called into play must be wasted faster than they are repaired : whence eventual disablement. The relation between due receipt of nutritive matters through its arteries, and due discharge of its duties by the limb, is a part of the physical order. If, instead of cutting off the supply to a particular limb, we bleed the patient largely, so drafting away the materials needed for repairing not one limb but all limbs, and not limbs only but viscera, there results both a muscular debility and an enfeeblement of the vital functions. Here, again, cause and effect are necessarily related. The mischief that results from great depletion, results apart from any divine command, or political enactment, or moral intuition. Now advance a step. Suppose the man to be prevented from taking in enough of the solid and liquid food containing those substances continually abstracted from his blood in repairing his tissues: suppose he has cancer of the œsophagus and cannot swallow —what happens? By this indirect depletion, as by direct depletion, he is inevitably made incapable of performing the actions of one in health. In this case, as in the other cases, the connexion between cause and effect is one that cannot be established, or altered, by any authority external to the phenomena themselves. Again, let us say that instead of being stopped after passing his mouth, that which he would swallow is stopped before reaching his mouth; so that day after day the man is required to waste his tissues in getting food, and day after day the food he has got to meet this waste, he is forcibly prevented from eating. As before, the progress towards death by starvation is inevitable—the connexion between acts and effects is independent of any alleged theological or political authority. And similarly if, being forced by the whip to labour, no adequate return in food is supplied to him, there are equally certain evils, equally independent of sacred or secular enactment. Pass now to those actions more commonly thought of as the occasions for rules of conduct. Let us assume the man to be continually robbed of that which was given him in exchange for his labour, and by which he was to make up for nervo-muscular expenditure and renew his powers. No less than before is the connexion between conduct and consequence rooted in the constitution of things; unchangeable by State-made law, and not needing establishment by empirical generalization. If the action by which the man is affected is a stage further away from the results, or produces results of a less decisive kind, still we see the same basis for morality in the physical order. Imagine that payment for

his services is made partly in bad coin ; or that it is delayed
beyond the date agreed upon; or that what he buys to eat
is adulterated with innutritive matter. Manifestly, by any
of these deeds which we condemn as unjust, and which are
punished by law, there is, as before, an interference with
the normal adjustment of physiological repair to physiological waste. Nor is it otherwise when we pass to kinds of
conduct still more remotely operative. If he is hindered
from enforcing his claim—if class-predominance prevents
him from proceeding, or if a bribed judge gives a verdict
contrary to evidence, or if a witness swears falsely ; have not
these deeds, though they affect him more indirectly, the
same original cause for their wrongness ?   Even
with actions which work diffused and indefinite mischiefs
it is the same. Suppose that the man, instead of being
dealt with fraudulently, is calumniated.   There is, as
before, a hindrance to the carrying on of life-sustaining
activities; for the loss of character detrimentally affects his
business. Nor is this all. The mental depression caused
partially incapacitates him for energetic activity, and perhaps
brings on ill-health. So that maliciously or carelessly pro-
pagating false statements, tends both to diminish his life
and to diminish his ability to maintain life. Hence its
flagitiousness.   Moreover, if we trace to their ultimate
ramifications the effects wrought by any of these acts
which morality called intuitive reprobates—if we ask what
results not to the individual himself only, but also to his
belongings—if we observe how impoverishment hinders the
rearing of his children, by entailing under-feeding or inadequate clothing, resulting perhaps in the death of some and
the constitutional injury of others ; we see that by the necessary connexions of things these acts, besides tending primarily
to lower the life of the individual aggressed upon, tend,
secondarily, to lower the lives of all his family, and, thirdly
to lower the life of society at large; which is damaged by
whatever damages its units.

A more distinct meaning will now be seen in the statement that the utilitarianism which recognizes only the principles of conduct reached by induction, is but preparatory to the utilitarianism which deduces these principles from the processes of life as carried on under established conditions of existence.

§ 22. Thus, then, is justified the allegation made at the outset, that, irrespective of their distinctive characters and their special tendencies, all the current methods of ethics have one general defect—they neglect ultimate causal connexions. Of course I do not mean that they wholly ignore the natural consequences of actions; but I mean that they recognize them only incidentally. They do not erect into a method the ascertaining of necessary relations between causes and effects, and deducing rules of conduct from formulated statements of them.

Every science begins by accumulating observations, and presently generalizes these empirically; but only when it reaches the stage at which its empirical generalizations are included in a rational generalization, does it become developed science. Astronomy has already passed through its successive stages: first collections of facts; then inductions from them; and lastly deductive interpretations of these, as corollaries from a universal principle of action among masses in space. Accounts of structures and tabulations of strata, grouped and compared, have led gradually to the assigning of various classes of geological changes to igneous and aqueous actions; and it is now tacitly admitted that Geology becomes a science proper, only as fast as such changes are explained in terms of those natural processes which have arisen in the cooling and solidifying Earth, exposed to the Sun's heat and the action of the Moon upon its ocean. The science of life has been, and is still, exhibiting a like series of steps: the evolution of organic forms at large, is being affiliated on physical actions in operation from the beginning; and the vital phenomena each organism presents, are coming to be understood as connected sets of changes, in parts formed of matters that are affected by certain forces and disengage other forces. So is it with mind. Early ideas concerning thought and feeling ignored everything like cause, save in recognizing those effects of habit which were forced on men's attention and expressed in proverbs; but there are growing up interpretations of thought and feeling as correlates of the actions and re-actions of a nervous structure, that is influenced by outer changes and works in the body adapted changes: the implication being that Psychology becomes a science, as fast as these relations of phenomena are explained as consequences of ultimate principles. Sociology, too, represented down to recent times only by stray ideas about social organization, scattered through the masses of worthless gossip furnished us by historians, is coming to be recognized by some as also a science; and such adumbrations of it as have from time to time appeared in the shape of empirical generalizations, are now beginning to assume the character of generalizations made coherent by derivation from causes lying in human nature placed under given conditions. Clearly then, Ethics, which is a science dealing with the conduct of associated human beings, regarded under one of its aspects, has to undergo a like transformation; and, at present undeveloped, can be considered a developed science only when it has undergone this transformation.

A preparation in the simpler sciences is pre-supposed. Ethics has a physical aspect; since it treats of human activities which, in common with all expenditures of energy, conform to the law of the persistence of energy: moral principles must conform to physical necessities. It has a biological aspect; since it concerns certain effects. inner and outer, individual and social, of the vital changes going on in the highest type of animal. It has a psychological aspect; for its subject-matter is an aggregate of actions

that are prompted by feelings and guided by intelligence.
And it has a sociological aspect; for these actions, some of
them directly and all of them indirectly, affect associated
beings.

What is the implication? Belonging under one aspect to
each of these sciences—physical, biological, psychological,
sociological,—it can find its ultimate interpretations only
in those fundamental truths which are common to all of them.
Already we have concluded in a general way that conduct at
large, including the conduct Ethics deals with, is to be fully
understood only as an aspect of evolving life; and now we
are brought to this conclusion in a more special way.

§ 23. Here, then, we have to enter on the consideration
of moral phenomena as phenomena of evolution; being
forced to do this by finding that they form a part of the
aggregate of phenomena which evolution has wrought out.
If the entire visible universe has been evolved—if the solar
system as a whole, the earth as a part of it, the life in
general which the earth bears, as well as that of each
individual organism—if the mental phenomena displayed
by all creatures, up to the highest, in common with the
phenomena presented by aggregates of these highest—if one
and all conform to the laws of evolution; then the necessary
implication is that those phenomena of conduct in these
highest creatures with which Morality is concerned, also
conform.

The preceding volumes have prepared the way for dealing
with morals as thus conceived. Utilizing the conclusions
they contain, let us now observe what data are furnished
by these. We will take in succession—the physical view,
the biological view, the psychological view, and the sociological view.

CHAPTER V.

THE PHYSICAL VIEW.

§ 24. Every moment we pass instantly from men's perceived actions to the motives implied by them; and so are led to formulate these actions in mental terms rather than in bodily terms. Thoughts and feelings are referred to when we speak of any one's deeds with praise or blame; not those outer manifestations which reveal the thoughts and feelings. Hence we become oblivious of the truth that conduct as actually experienced, consists of changes recognized by touch, sight and hearing.

This habit of contemplating only the psychical face of conduct, is so confirmed that an effort is required to contemplate only the physical face. Undeniable as it is that another's behaviour to us is made up of movements of his body and limbs, of his facial muscles, and of his vocal apparatus; it yet seems paradoxical to say that these are the only elements of conduct really known by us, while the elements of conduct which we exclusively think of as constituting it, are not known but inferred.

Here, however, ignoring for the time being the inferred elements in conduct, we have to deal with the perceived elements—we have to observe its traits considered as a set of combined motions. Taking the evolution point of view, and remembering that while an aggregate evolves, not only the matter composing it, but also the motion of that

matter, passes from an indefinite incoherent homogeneity
to a definite coherent heterogeneity, we have now to ask
whether conduct as it rises to its higher forms, displays in
increasing degrees these characters ; and whether it does not
display them in the greatest degree when it reaches that
highest form which we call moral.

§ 25. It will be convenient to deal first with the trait of
increasing coherence. The conduct of lowly-organized
creatures is broadly contrasted with the conduct of highly-
organized creatures, in having its successive portions feebly
connected. The random movements which an animalcule
makes, have severally no reference to movements made a
moment before; nor do they affect in specific ways the
movements made immediately after. To-day's wanderings
of a fish in search of food, though perhaps showing by
their adjustments to catching different kinds of prey at
different hours, a slightly-determined order, are unrelated to
the wanderings of yesterday and to-morrow. But such more
developed creatures as birds, show us in the building of
nests, the sitting on eggs, the rearing of chicks, and the
aiding of them after they fly, sets of motions which form a
dependent series, extending over a considerable period.
And on observing the complexity of the acts performed
in fetching and fixing the fibres of the nest or in catching
and bringing to the young each portion of food, we discover in the combined motions, lateral cohesion as well as
longitudinal cohesion.

Man, even in his lowest state, displays in his conduct far
more coherent combinations of motions. By the elaborate
manipulations gone through in making weapons that are to
serve for the chase next year, or in building canoes and
wigwams for permanent uses—by acts of aggression and
defence which are connected with injuries long since
received or committed, the savage exhibits an aggregate
of motions which, in some of its parts, holds together

5

over great periods. Moreover, if we consider the many movements implied by the transactions of each day, in the wood, on the water, in the camp, in the family; we see that this coherent aggregate of movements is composed of many minor aggregates, that are severally coherent within themselves and with one another.   In civilized man this trait of developed conduct becomes more conspicuous still. Be his business what it may, its processes involve relatively-numerous dependent motions; and day by day it is so carried on as to show connexions between present motions and motions long gone by, as well as motions anticipated in the distant future. Besides the many doings, related to one another, which the farmer goes through in looking after his cattle, directing his labourers, keeping an eye on his dairy, buying his simplements, selling his produce, &c.; the business of getting his lease involves numerous combined movements on which the movements of subsequent years depend; and in manuring his fields with a view to larger returns, or putting down drains with the like motive, he is performing acts which are parts of a coherent combination relatively extensive. That the like holds of the shopkeeper, manufacturer, banker, is manifest; and this increased coherence of conduct among the civilized, will strike us even more when we remember how its parts are often continued in a connected arrangement through life, for the purpose of making a fortune, founding a family, gaining a seat in Parliament.

Now mark that a greater coherence among its component motions, broadly distinguishes the conduct we call moral from the conduct we call immoral. The application of the word dissolute to the last, and of the word self-restrained to the first, implies this—implies that conduct of the lower kind, constituted of disorderly acts, has its parts relatively loose in their relations with one another; while conduct of the higher kind, habitually following a fixed order, so gains a characteristic unity and coherence. In proportion as the conduct is what we call moral, it exhibits comparatively settled connexions between antecedents and consequents; for the doing right implies that under given conditions the combined motions constituting conduct will follow in a way that can be specified. Contrariwise, in the conduct of one whose principles are not high, the sequences of motions are doubtful. He may pay the money or he may not; he may keep his appointment or he may fail; he may tell the truth or he may lie. The words trustworthiness and untrustworthiness, as used to characterize the two respectively, sufficiently imply that the actions of the one can be foreknown while those of the other can not; and this implies that the successive movements composing the one bear more constant relations to one another than do those composing the other—are more coherent.

§ 26. Indefiniteness accompanies incoherence in conduct that is little evolved; and throughout the ascending stages of evolving conduct, there is an increasingly-definite co-ordination of the motions constituting it.

Such changes of form as the rudest protozoa show us, are utterly vague—admit of no precise description; and though in higher kinds the movements of the parts are more definable, yet the movement of the whole in respect of direction is indeterminate: there is no adjustment of it to this or the other point in space. In such cœlenterate animals as polypes, we see the parts moving in ways which lack precision; and in one of the locomotive forms, as a medusa, the course taken, otherwise at random, can be described only as one which carries it towards the light, where degrees of light and darkness are present. Among annulose creatures the contrast between the track of a worm, turning this way or that at hazard, and the definite course taken by a bee in its flight from flower to flower or back to the hive, shows us the same thing: the bee's acts in building cells and feeding larvæ further exhibiting pre-

5 *

cision in the simultaneous movements as well as in the successive movements. Though the motions made by a fish in pursuing its prey have considerable definiteness, yet they are of a simple kind, and are in this respect contrasted with the many definite motions of body, head, and limbs gone through by a carnivorous mammal in the course of waylaying, running down, and seizing a herbivore; and further, the fish shows us none of those definitely-adjusted sets of motions which in the mammal subserve the rearing of young.

Much greater definiteness, if not in the combined movements forming single acts, still in the adjustments of many combined acts to various purposes, characterizes human conduct, even in its lowest stages. In making and using weapons and in the manœuvrings of savage warfare, numerous movements all precise in their adaptations to proximate ends, are arranged for the achievement of remote ends, with a precision not paralleled among lower creatures. The lives of civilized men exhibit this trait far more conspicuously. Each industrial art exemplifies the effects of movements which are severally definite; and which are definitely arranged in simultaneous and successive order. Business transactions of every kind are characterized by exact relations between the sets of motions constituting acts, and the purposes fulfilled, in time, place, and quantity. Further, the daily routine of each person shows us in its periods and amounts of activity, of rest, of relaxation, a measured arrangement which is not shown us by the doings of the wandering savage; who has no fixed times for hunting, sleeping, feeding, or any one kind of action.

Moral conduct differs from immoral conduct in the same manner and in a like degree. The conscientious man is exact in all his transactions. He supplies a precise weight for a specified sum; he gives a definite quality in fulfilment of understanding; he pays the full amount he bargained to do. In times as well as in quantities, his acts answer completely to anticipations. If he has made a business contract he is to the day; if an appointment he is to the minute. Similarly in respect of truth: his statements correspond accurately with the facts. It is thus too in his family life. He maintains marital relations that are definite in contrast with the relations that result from breach of the marriage contract; and as a father, fitting his behaviour with care to the nature of each child and to the occasion, he avoids the too much and the too little of praise or blame, reward or penalty. Nor is it otherwise in his miscellaneous acts. To say that he deals equitably with those he employs, whether they behave well or ill, is to say that he adjusts his acts to their deserts; and to say that he is judicious in his charities, is to say that he portions out his aid with discrimination instead of distributing it indiscriminately to good and bad, as do those who have no adequate sense of their social responsibilities.

That progress towards rectitude of conduct is progress towards duly-proportioned conduct, and that duly-proportioned conduct is relatively definite, we may see from another point of view. One of the traits of conduct we call immoral, is excess; while moderation habitually characterizes moral conduct. Now excesses imply extreme divergences of actions from some medium, while maintenance of the medium is implied by moderation ; whence it follows that actions of the last kind can be defined more nearly than those of the first. Clearly conduct which, being unrestrained, runs into great and incalculable oscillations, therein differs from restrained conduct of which, by implication, the oscillations fall within narrower limits. And falling within narrower limits necessitates relative definiteness of movements.

§ 27. That throughout the ascending forms of life, along with increasing heterogeneity of structure and function, there goes increasing heterogeneity of conduct—increasing diversity in the sets of external motions and combined sets of such motions—needs not be shown in detail. Nor need it be shown that becoming relatively great in the motions constituting the conduct of the uncivilized man, this heterogeneity has become still greater in those which the civilized man goes through. We may pass at once to that further degree of the like contrast which we see on ascending from the conduct of the immoral to that of the moral.

Instead of recognizing this contrast, most readers will be inclined to identify a moral life with a life little varied in its activities. But here we come upon a defect in the current conception of morality. This comparative uniformity in the aggregate of motions, which goes along with morality as commonly conceived, is not only not moral but is the reverse of moral. The better a man fulfils every requirement of life, alike as regards his own body and mind, as regards the bodies and minds of those dependent on him, and as regards the bodies and minds of his fellow-citizens, the more varied do his activities become. The more fully he does all these things, the more heterogeneous must be his movements.

One who satisfies personal needs only, goes through, other things equal, less multiform processes than one who also administers to the needs of wife and children. Supposing there are no other differences, the addition of family relations necessarily renders the actions of the man who fulfils the duties of husband and parent, more heterogeneous than those of the man who has no such duties to fulfil, or, having them, does not fulfil them ; and to say that his actions are more heterogeneous is to say that there is a greater heterogeneity in the combined motions he goes through. The like holds of social obligations. These, in proportion as a citizen duly performs them, complicate his movements considerably. If he is helpful to inferiors dependent on

him, if he takes a part in political agitation, if he aids in
diffusing knowledge, he, in each of these ways, adds to his
kinds of activity—makes his sets of movements more
multiform; so differing from the man who is the slave
of one desire or group of desires.

Though it is unusual to consider as having a moral aspect,
those activities which culture involves, yet to the few who
hold that due exercise of all the higher faculties, intellectual
and æsthetic, must be included in the conception of complete life, here identified with the ideally moral life, it will
be manifest that a further heterogeneity is implied by
them. For each of such activities, constituted by that play
of these faculties which is eventually added to their life-
subserving uses, adds to the multiformity of the aggregated
motions.

Briefly, then, if the conduct is the best possible on every
occasion, it follows that as the occasions are endlessly
varied the acts will be endlessly varied to suit—the heterogeneity in the combinations of motions will be extreme.

§ 28. Evolution in conduct considered under its moral
aspect, is, like all other evolution, towards equilibrium. I
do not mean that it is towards the equilibrium reached at
death, though this is, of course, the final state which the
evolution of the highest man has in common with all lower
evolution; but I mean that it is towards a moving equilibrium.

We have seen that maintaining life, expressed in physical
terms, is maintaining a balanced combination of internal
actions in face of external forces tending to overthrow it;
and we have seen that advance towards a higher life, has
been an acquirement of ability to maintain the balance for
a longer period, by the successive additions of organic
appliances which by their actions counteract, more and
more fully, the disturbing forces. Here, then, we are led
to the conclusion that the life called moral is one in which

this maintenance of the moving equilibrium reaches completeness, or approaches most nearly to completeness.

This truth is clearly disclosed on observing how those
physiological rhythms which vaguely show themselves
when organization begins, become more regular as well as
more various in their kinds, as organization advances.
Periodicity is but feebly marked in the actions, inner and
outer, of the rudest types.   Where life is low there is
passive dependence on the accidents of the environment;
and this entails great irregularities in the vital processes.
The taking in of food by a polype is at intervals now short
now very long, as circumstances determine; and the
utilization of it is by a slow dispersion of the absorbed
part through the tissues, aided only by the irregular movements of the creature's body; while such aeration as is
effected is similarly without a trace of rhythm. Much higher
up we still find very imperfect periodicities ; as in the inferior molluscs which, though possessed of vascular systems,
have no proper circulation, but merely a slow movement of
the crude blood, now in one direction through the vessels
and then, after a pause, in the opposite direction.   Only
with well-developed structures do there come a rhythmical
pulse and a rhythm of the respiratory actions.   And then
in birds and mammals, along with great rapidity and regularity in these essential rhythms, and along with a consequently great vital activity and therefore great expenditure,
comparative regularity in the rhythm of the alimentary
actions is established, as well as in the rhythm of activity
and rest; since the rapid waste to which rapid pulsation and
respiration are instrumental, necessitates tolerably regular
supplies of nutriment, as well as recurring intervals of sleep
during which repair may overtake waste.   And from
these stages the moving equilibrium characterized by such
inter-dependent rhythms, is continually made better by the
counteracting of more and more of those actions which
tend to perturb it.   So is it as we ascend

from savage to civilized and from the lowest among the civilized to the highest. The rhythm of external actions required to maintain the rhythm of internal actions, becomes at once more complicated and more complete; making them into a better moving equilibrium. The irregularities which their conditions of existence entail on primitive men, continually cause wide deviations from the mean state of the moving equilibrium—wide oscillations; which imply imperfection of it for the time being, and bring about its premature overthrow. In such civilized men as we call ill-conducted, frequent perturbations of the moving equilibrium are caused by those excesses characterizing a career in which the periodicities are much broken; and a common result is that the rhythm of the internal actions being often deranged, the moving equilibrium, rendered by so much imperfect, is generally shortened in duration. While one in whom the internal rhythms are best maintained is one by whom the external actions required to fulfil all needs and duties, severally performed on the recurring occasions, conduce to a moving equilibrium that is at once involved and prolonged.

Of course the implication is that the man who thus reaches the limit of evolution, exists in a society congruous with his nature—is a man among men similarly constituted, who are severally in harmony with that social environment which they have formed. This is, indeed, the only possibility. For the production of the highest type of man, can go on only *pari passu* with the production of the highest type of society. The implied conditions are those before described as accompanying the most evolved conduct—conditions under which each can fulfil all his needs and rear the due number of progeny, not only without hindering others from doing the like, but while aiding them in doing the like. And evidently, considered under its physical aspect, the conduct of the individual so constituted, and associated with like individuals, is one in which all the actions, that is the combined motions of all kinds, have become such as duly to meet every daily process, every ordinary occurrence, and every contingency in his environment. Complete life in a complete society is but another name for complete equilibrium between the co-ordinated activities of each social unit and those of the aggregate of units.

§ 29. Even to readers of preceding volumes, and still more to other readers, there will seem a strangeness, or even an absurdity, in this presentation of moral conduct in physical terms. It has been needful to make it however. If that re-distribution of matter and motion constituting evolution goes on in all aggregates, its laws must be fulfilled in the most developed being as in every other thing; and his actions, when decomposed into motions, must exemplify its laws. This we find that they do. There is an entire correspondence between moral evolution and evolution as physically defined.

Conduct as actually known to us in perception and not as interpreted into the accompanying feelings and ideas, consists of combined motions. On ascending through the various grades of animate creatures, we find these combined motions characterized by increasing coherence, increasing definiteness considered singly and in their co-ordinated groups, and increasing heterogeneity; and in advancing from lower to higher types of man, as well as in advancing from the less moral to the more moral type of man, these traits of evolving conduct become more marked still. Further, we see that the increasing coherence, definiteness, and heterogeneity, of the combined motions, are instrumental to the better maintenance of a moving equilibrium. Where the evolution is small this is very imperfect and soon cut short; with advancing evolution, bringing greater power and intelligence, it becomes more steady and longer continued in face of adverse actions; in the human race at large it is comparatively regular and enduring; and its regularity and enduringness are greatest in the highest.

CHAPTER VI.

THE BIOLOGICAL VIEW.

§ 30. The truth that the ideally moral man is one in whom the moving equilibrium is perfect, or approaches nearest to perfection, becomes, when translated into physiological language, the truth that he is one in whom the functions of all kinds are duly fulfilled. Each function has some relation, direct or indirect, to the needs of life : the fact of its existence as a result of evolution, being itself a proof that it has been entailed, immediately or remotely, by the adjustment of inner actions to outer actions. Consequently, non-fulfilment of it in normal proportion is non-fulfilment of a requisite to complete life. If there is defective discharge of the function, the organism experiences some detrimental result caused by the inadequacy. If the discharge is in excess, there is entailed a reaction upon the other functions, which in some way diminishes their efficiencies.

It is true that during full vigour, while the momentum of the organic actions is great, the disorder caused by moderate excess or defect of any one function, soon disappears—the balance is re-established. But it is none the less true that always some disorder results from excess or defect, that it influences every function bodily and mental, and that it constitutes a lowering of the life for the time being.

Beyond the temporary falling short of complete life

implied by undue or inadequate discharge of a function, there is entailed, as an ultimate result, decreased length of life. If some function is habitually performed in excess of the requirement, or in defect of the requirement; and if, as a consequence, there is an often-repeated perturbation of the functions at large; there results some chronic derangement in the balance of the functions. Necessarily reacting on the structures, and registering in them its accumulated effects, this derangement works a general deterioration; and when the vital energies begin to decline, the moving equilibrium, further from perfection than it would else have been, is sooner overthrown: death is more or less premature.

Hence the moral man is one whose functions—many and varied in their kinds as we have seen—are all discharged in degrees duly adjusted to the conditions of existence.

§ 31. Strange as the conclusion looks, it is nevertheless a conclusion to be here drawn, that the performance of every function is, in a sense, a moral obligation.

It is usually thought that morality requires us only to restrain such vital activities as, in our present state, are often pushed to excess, or such as conflict with average welfare, special or general; but it also requires us to carry on these vital activities up to their normal limits. All the animal functions, in common with all the higher functions, have, as thus understood, their imperativeness. While recognizing the fact that in our state of transition, characterized by very imperfect adaptation of constitution to conditions, moral obligations of supreme kinds often necessitate conduct which is physically injurious; we must also recognize the fact that, considered apart from other effects, it is immoral so to treat the body as in any way to diminish the fulness or vigour of its vitality.

Hence results one test of actions. There may in every case be put the questions—Does the action tend to main-

tenance of complete life for the time being? and does it tend
to prolongation of life to its full extent? To answer yes or
no to either of these questions, is implicitly to class the
action as right or wrong in respect of its immediate bearings,
whatever it may be in respect of its remote bearings.

The seeming paradoxicalness of this statement results
from the tendency, so difficult of avoidance, to judge a
conclusion which pre-supposes an ideal humanity, by its
applicability to humanity as now existing. The foregoing
conclusion refers to that highest conduct in which, as we
have seen, the evolution of conduct terminates—that conduct in which the making of all adjustments of acts to ends
subserving complete individual life, together with all those
subserving maintenance of offspring and preparation of
them for maturity, not only consist with the making of like
adjustments by others, but furthers it. And this conception of conduct in its ultimate form, implies the
conception of a nature having such conduct for its spontaneous outcome—the product of its normal activities.
So understanding the matter, it becomes manifest that
under such conditions, any falling short of function, as
well as any excess of function, implies deviation from the
best conduct or from perfectly moral conduct.

§ 32. Thus far in treating of conduct from the biological
point of view, we have considered its constituent actions
under their physiological aspects only; leaving out of
sight their psychological aspects. We have recognized the
bodily changes and have ignored the accompanying mental
changes. And at first sight it seems needful for us here to
do this; since taking account of states of consciousness,
apparently implies an inclusion of the psychological view in
the biological view.

This is not so however. As was pointed out in the
Principles of Psychology (§§ 52, 53) we enter upon psychology proper, only when we begin to treat of mental

states and their relations, considered as referring to external agents and their relations. While we concern ourselves exclusively with modes of mind as correlatives of nervous changes, we are treating of what was there distinguished as æstho-physiology. We pass to psychology only when we consider the correspondence between the connexions among subjective states and the connexions among objective actions. Here, then, without transgressing the limits of our immediate topic, we may deal with feelings and functions in their mutual dependencies.

We cannot omit doing this; because the psychical changes which accompany many of the physical changes in the organism, are biological factors in two ways. Those feelings, classed as sensations, which, directly initiated in the bodily framework, go along with certain states of the vital organs and more conspicuously with certain states of the external organs, now serve mainly as guides to the performance of functions but partly as stimuli, and now serve mainly as stimuli but in a smaller degree as guides. Visual sensations which, as co-ordinated, enable us to direct our movements, also, if vivid, raise the rate of respiration; while sensations of cold and heat, greatly depressing or raising the vital actions, serve also for purposes of discrimination. So, too, the feelings classed as emotions, which are not localizable in the bodily framework, act in more general ways, alike as guides and stimuli—having influences over the performance of functions more potent even than have most sensations. Fear, at the same time that it urges flight and evolves the forces spent in it, also affects the heart and the alimentary canal; while joy, prompting persistence in the actions bringing it, simultaneously exalts the visceral processes.

Hence in treating of conduct under its biological aspect, we are compelled to consider that inter-action of feelings and functions, which is essential to animal life in all its more developed forms.

§ 33. In the *Principles of Psychology,* § 124, it was shown that necessarily, throughout the animate world at large, "pains are the correlatives of actions injurious to the organism, while pleasures are the correlatives of actions conducive to its welfare;" since "it is an inevitable deduction from the hypothesis of Evolution, that races of sentient creatures could have come into existence under no other conditions." The argument was as follows :—

If we substitute for the word Pleasure the equivalent phrase—a feeling which we seek to bring into consciousness and retain there, and if we substitute for the word Pain the equivalent phrase—a feeling which we seek to get out of consciousness and to keep out ; we see at once that, if the states of consciousness which a creature endeavours to maintain are the correlatives of injurious actions, and if the states of consciousness which it endeavours to expel are the correlatives of beneficial actions, it must quickly disappear through persistence in the injurious and avoidance of the beneficial. In other words, those races of beings only can have survived in which, on the average, agreeable or desired feelings went along with activities conducive to the maintenance of life, while disagreeable and habitually-avoided feelings went along with activities directly or indirectly destructive of life ; and there must ever have been, other things equal, the most numerous and long-continued survivals among races in which these adjustments of feelings to actions were the best, tending ever to bring about perfect adjustment.

Fit connexions between acts and results must establish themselves in living things, even before consciousness arises ; and after the rise of consciousness these connexions can change in no other way than to become better established. At the very outset, life is maintained by persistence in acts which conduce to it, and desistance from acts which impede it ; and whenever sentiency make its appearance as an accompaniment, its forms must be such that in the one case the produced feeling is of a kind that will be sought— pleasure, and in the other case is of a kind that will be shunned—pain. Observe the necessity of these relations as exhibited in the concrete.

A plant which envelops a buried bone with a plexus of rootlets, or a potato which directs its blanched shoots towards a grating through which light comes into the cellar, shows us that the changes which outer agents themselves

set up in its tissues are changes which aid the utilization
of these agents. If we ask what would happen if a
plant's roots grew not towards the place where there was
moisture but away from it, or if its leaves, enabled by light
to assimilate, nevertheless bent themselves towards the darkness ; we see that death would result in the absence of the
existing adjustments. This general relation is still better
shown in an insectivorous plant, such as the *Dionœa
muscipula*, which keeps its trap closed round animal matter
but not round other matter. Here it is manifest that the
stimulus arising from the first part of the absorbed substance,
itself sets up those actions by which the mass of the substance is utilized for the plant's benefit.   When
we pass from vegetal organisms to unconscious animal
organisms, we see a like connexion between proclivity
and advantage. On observing how the tentacles of a
polype attach themselves to, and begin to close round, a
living creature, or some animal substance, while they are
indifferent to the touch of other substance; we are similarly
shown that diffusion of some of the nutritive juices
into the tentacles, which is an incipient assimilation,
causes the motions effecting prehension. And it is obvious
that life would cease were these relations reversed.   Nor
is it otherwise with this fundamental connexion between
contact with food and taking in of food, among conscious creatures, up to the very highest. Tasting a
substance implies the passage of its molecules through
the mucous membrane of the tongue and palate; and
this absorption, when it occurs with a substance serving
for food, is but a commencement of the absorption carried
on throughout the alimentary canal. Moreover, the sensation
accompanying this absorption, when it is of the kind produced by food, initiates at the place where it is strongest,
in front of the pharynx, an automatic act of swallowing,
in a manner rudely analogous to that in which the stimulus
of absorption in a polype's tentacles initiates prehension.

If from these processes and relations that imply contact between a creature's surface and the substance it takes in, we turn to those set up by diffused particles of the substance, constituting to conscious creatures its odour, we meet a kindred general truth. Just as, after contact, some molecules of a mass of food are absorbed by the part touched, and excite the act of prehension ; so are absorbed such of its molecules as, spreading through the water, reach the organism ; and, being absorbed by it, excite those actions by which contact with the mass is effected. If the physical stimulation caused by the dispersed particles is not accompanied by consciousness, still the motor changes set up must conduce to survival of the organism if they are such as end in contact; and there must be relative innutrition and mortality of organisms in which the produced contractions do not bring about this result. Nor can it be questioned that whenever and wherever the physical stimulation has a concomitant sentiency, this must be such as consists with, and conduces to, movement towards the nutritive matter : it must be not a repulsive but an attractive sentiency. And this which holds with the lowest consciousness, must hold throughout; as we see it do in all such superior creatures as are drawn to their food by odour.

Besides those movements which cause locomotion, those which effect seizure must no less certainly become thus adjusted The molecular changes caused by absorption of nutritive matter from organic substance in contact, or from adjacent organic substance, initiate motions which are indefinite where the organization is low, and which become more definite with the advance of organization. At the outset, while the undifferentiated protoplasm is everywhere absorbent and everywhere contractile, the changes of form initiated by the physical stimulation of adjacent nutritive matter are vague, and ineffectually adapted to utilization of it; but gradually, along with the specialization into parts that are contractile and parts that

6

are absorbent, these motions become better adapted; for
necessarily individuals in which they are least adapted disappear faster than those in which they are most adapted.
Recognizing this necessity we have here especially to
recognize a further necessity. The relation between these
stimulations and adjusted contractions must be such that
increase of the one causes increase of the other; since the
directions of the discharges being once established, greater
stimulation causes greater contraction, and the greater
contraction causing closer contact with the stimulating
agent, causes increase of stimulus and is thereby itself
further increased. And now we reach the corollary which
more particularly concerns us. Clearly as fast as an accompanying sentiency arises, this cannot be one that is
disagreeable, prompting desistance, but must be one that is
agreeable, prompting persistence. The pleasurable sensation
must be itself the stimulus to the contraction by which the
pleasurable sensation is maintained and increased; or must
be so bound up with the stimulus that the two increase
together. And this relation which we see is directly
established in the case of a fundamental function, must be
indirectly established with all other functions; since non-
establishment of it in any particular case implies, in so far,
unfitness to the conditions of existence.

In two ways then, it is demonstrable that there exists a
primordial connexion between pleasure-giving acts and
continuance or increase of life, and, by implication, between
pain-giving acts and decrease or loss of life. On the one
hand, setting out with the lowest living things, we see
that the beneficial act and the act which there is a tendency to perform, are originally two sides of the same;
and cannot be disconnected without fatal results. On the
other hand, if we contemplate developed creatures as now
existing, we see that each individual and species is from day
to day kept alive by pursuit of the agreeable and avoidance of the disagreeable.

Thus approaching the facts from a different side, analysis brings us down to another face of that ultimate truth disclosed by analysis in a preceding chapter. We found it was no more possible to frame ethical conceptions from which the consciousness of pleasure, of some kind, at some time, to some being, is absent, than it is possible to frame the conception of an object from which the consciousness of space is absent. And now we see that this necessity of thought originates in the very nature of sentient existence. Sentient existence can evolve only on condition that pleasure-giving acts are life-sustaining acts.

§ 34. Notwithstanding explanations already made, the naked enunciation of this as an ultimate truth, underlying all estimations of right and wrong, will in many, if not in most, cause astonishment. Having in view certain beneficial results that are preceded by disagreeable states of consciousness, such as those commonly accompanying labour; and having in view the injurious results that follow the receipt of certain gratifications, such as those which excess in drinking produces; the majority tacitly or avowedly believe that the bearing of pains is on the whole beneficial, and that the receipt of pleasures is on the whole detrimental. The exceptions so fill their minds as to exclude the rule.

When asked, they are obliged to admit that the pains accompanying wounds, bruises, sprains, are the concomitants of evils, alike to the sufferer and to those around him; and that the anticipations of such pains serve as deterrents from careless or dangerous acts. They cannot deny that the tortures of burning or scalding, and the miseries which intense cold, starvation, and thirst produce, are indissolubly connected with permanent or temporary mischiefs, tending to incapacitate one who bears them for doing things that should be done, either for his own welfare or the welfare of others. The agony of incipient suffocation they are compelled to recognize as a safeguard to life, and must allow

6 *

that avoidance of it is conducive to all that life can bring or achieve. Nor will they refuse to own that one who is chained in a cold, damp, dungeon, in darkness and silence, is injured in health and efficiency; alike by the positive pains thus inflicted on him and by the accompanying negative pains due to absence of light, of freedom, of companionship.   Conversely, they do not doubt that notwithstanding occasional excesses the pleasure which accompanies the taking of food, goes along with physical benefit; and that the benefit is the greater the keener the satisfaction of appetite. They have no choice but to acknowledge that the instincts and sentiments which so overpoweringly prompt marriage, and those which find their gratification in the fostering of offspring, work out an immense surplus of benefit after deducting all evils. Nor dare they question that the pleasure taken in accumulating property, leaves a large balance of advantage, private and public, after making all drawbacks. Yet many and conspicuous as are the cases in which pleasures and pains, sensational and emotional, serve as incentives to proper acts and deterrents from improper acts, these pass unnoticed; and notice is taken only of those cases in which men are directly or indirectly misled by them. The well-working in essential matters is ignored; and the ill-working in unessential matters is alone recognized.

Is it replied that the more intense pains and pleasures, which have immediate reference to bodily needs, guide us rightly; while the weaker pains and pleasures, not immediately connected with the maintenance of life, guide us wrongly? Then the implication is that the system of guidance by pleasures and pains, which has answered with all types of creatures below the human, fails with the human. Or rather, the admission being that with mankind it succeeds in so far as fulfilment of certain imperative wants goes, it fails in respect of wants that are not imperative. Those who think this are required, in the first place, to show us how the line is to be drawn between the two; and then to show us why the system which succeeds in the lower will not succeed in the higher.

§ 35. Doubtless, however, after all that has been said, there will be raised afresh the same difficulty—there will be instanced the mischievous pleasures and the beneficent pains. The drunkard, the gambler, the thief, who severally pursue gratifications, will be named in proof that the pursuit of gratifications misleads; while the self-sacrificing relative, the worker who perseveres through weariness, the honest man who stints himself to pay his way, will be named in proof that disagreeable modes of consciousness accompany acts that are really beneficial. But after recalling the fact pointed out in § 20, that this objection does not tell against guidance by pleasures and pains at large, since it merely implies that special and proximate pleasures and pains must be disregarded out of consideration for remote and diffused pleasures and pains; and after admitting that in mankind as at present constituted, guidance by proximate pleasures and pains fails throughout a wide range of cases; I go on to set forth the interpretation Biology gives of these anomalies, as being not necessary and permanent but incidental and temporary.

Already while showing that among inferior creatures, pleasures and pains have all along guided the conduct by which life has been evolved and maintained, I have pointed out that since the conditions of existence for each species have been occasionally changing, there have been occasionally arising partial mis-adjustments of the feelings to the requirements, necessitating re-adjustments. This general cause of derangement operating on all sentient beings, has been operating on human beings in a manner unusually decided, persistent, and involved. It needs but to contrast the mode of life followed by primitive men, wandering in the forests and living on wild food, with

the mode of life followed by rustics, artisans, traders, and
professional men in a civilized community; to see that the
constitution, bodily and mental, well-adjusted to the one is ill-
adjusted to the other. It needs but to observe the emotions
kept awake in each savage tribe, chronically hostile to
neighbouring tribes, and then to observe the emotions
which peaceful production and exchange bring into play,
to see that the two are not only unlike but opposed. And it
needs but to note how, during social evolution, the ideas
and sentiments appropriate to the militant activities
carried on by coercive co-operation, have been at variance
with the ideas and sentiments appropriate to the industrial activities, carried on by voluntary co-operation;
to see that there has ever been within each society, and
still continues, a conflict between the two moral natures
adjusted to these two unlike modes of life. Manifestly, then,
this re-adjustment of constitution to conditions, involving
re-adjustment of pleasures and pains for guidance, which
all creatures from time to time undergo, has been in the
human race during civilization, especially difficult; not only
because of the greatness of the change from small nomadic
groups to vast settled societies, and from predatory habits
to peaceful habits; but also because the old life of enmity
between societies has been maintained along with the new
life of amity within each society. While there co-exist
two ways of life so radically opposed as the militant
and the industrial, human nature cannot become properly
adapted to either.

That hence results such failure of guidance by pleasures
and pains as is daily exhibited, we discover on observing
in what parts of conduct the failure is most conspicuous.
As above shown, the pleasurable and painful sensations are
fairly well adjusted to the peremptory physical requirements:
the benefits of conforming to the sensations which prompt
us in respect of nutrition, respiration, maintenance of temperature, &c., immensely exceed the incidental evils; and

such mis-adjustments as occur may be ascribed to the change from the out-door life of the primitive man to the in-door life which the civilized man is often compelled to lead. It is the emotional pleasures and pains which are in so considerable a degree out of adjustment to the needs of life as carried on in society; and it is of these that the re-adjustment is made, in the way above shown, so tardy because so difficult.

From the biological point of view then, we see that the connexions between pleasure and beneficial action and between pain and detrimental action, which arose when sentient existence began, and have continued among animate creatures up to man, are generally displayed in him also throughout the lower and more completely-organized part of his nature; and must be more and more fully displayed throughout the higher part of his nature, as fast as his adaptation to the conditions of social life increases.

§ 36. Biology has a further judgment to pass on the relations of pleasures and pains to welfare. Beyond the connexions between acts beneficial to the organism and the pleasures accompanying performance of them, and between acts detrimental to the organism and the pains causing desistance from them, there are connexions between pleasure in general and physiological exaltation, and between pain in general and physiological depression. Every pleasure increases vitality; every pain decreases vitality. Every pleasure raises the tide of life; every pain lowers the tide of life. Let us consider, first, the pains.

By the general mischiefs that result from submission to pains, I do not mean those arising from the diffused effects of local organic lesions, such as follow an aneurism caused by intense effort spite of protesting sensations, or such as follow the varicose veins brought on by continued disregard of fatigue in the legs, or such as follow the atrophy set up in muscles that are persistently exerted when

extremely weary; but I mean the general mischiefs caused
by that constitutional disturbance which pain forthwith sets
up. These are conspicuous when the pains are acute,
whether they be sensational or emotional.   Bodily
agony long borne, produces death by exhaustion. More
frequently, arresting the action of the heart for a time, it
causes that temporary death we call fainting. On other
occasions vomiting is a consequence. And where such
manifest derangements do not result, we still, in the pallor
and trembling, trace the general prostration. Beyond the
actual loss of life caused by subjection to intense cold, there
are depressions of vitality less marked caused by cold less
extreme—temporary enfeeblement following too long an
immersion in icy water; enervation and pining away consequent on inadequate clothing. Similarly is it with
submission to great heat: we have lassitude reaching
occasionally to exhaustion; we have, in weak persons,
fainting, succeeded by temporary debilitation; and in
steaming tropical jungles, Europeans contract fevers which
when not fatal often entail life-long incapacities. Consider,
again, the evils that follow violent exertion continued in
spite of painful feelings—now a fatigue which destroys
appetite or arrests digestion if food is taken, implying
failure of the reparative processes when they are most
needed; and now a prostration of the heart, here lasting for
a time and there, where the transgression has been repeated
day after day, made permanent: reducing the rest of life to
a lower level.   No less conspicuous are the depressing
effects of emotional pains. There are occasional cases of
death from grief; and in other cases the mental suffering
which a calamity causes, like bodily suffering, shows its effects
by syncope. Often a piece of bad news is succeeded by sick-
ness; and continued anxiety will produce loss of appetite, perpetual indigestion, and diminished strength. Excessive fear,
whether aroused by physical or moral danger, will, in like
manner, arrest for a time the processes of nutrition; and,

not unfrequently, in pregnant women brings on mis-
carriage; while, in less extreme cases, the cold perspiration
and unsteady hands indicate a general lowering of the vital
activities, entailing partial incapacity of body or mind or
both. How greatly emotional pain deranges the visceral
actions is shown us by the fact that incessant worry
is not unfrequently followed by jaundice. And here,
indeed, the relation between cause and effect happens to
have been proved by direct experiment. Making such
arrangements that the bile-duct of a dog delivered its
product outside the body, Claude Bernard observed that so
long as he petted the dog and kept him in good spirits,
secretion went on at its normal rate; but on speaking
angrily, and for a time so treating him as to produce depression, the flow of bile was arrested.   Should it be said
that evil results of such kinds are proved to occur only
when the pains, bodily or mental, are great; the reply is
that in healthy persons the injurious perturbations caused by
small pains, though not easily traced, are still produced;
and that in those whose vital powers are much reduced
by illness, slight physical irritations and trifling moral
annoyances, often cause relapses.

Quite opposite are the constitutional effects of pleasure.
It sometimes, though rarely, happens that in feeble persons
intense pleasure—pleasure that is almost pain—gives a
nervous shock that is mischievous; but it does not do
this in those who are undebilitated by voluntary or enforced
submission to actions injurious to the organism. In the
normal order, pleasures, great and small, are stimulants to
the processes by which life is maintained.   Among
the sensations may be instanced those produced by bright
light. Sunshine is enlivening in comparison with gloom
—even a gleam excites a wave of pleasure; and experiments
have shown that sunshine raises the rate of respiration:
raised respiration being an index of raised vital activities in
general. A warmth that is agreeable in degree favours the

heart's action, and furthers the various functions to which this is instrumental. Though those who are in full vigour and fitly clothed, can maintain their temperature in winter, and can digest additional food to make up for the loss of heat, it is otherwise with the feeble ; and, as vigour declines, the beneficence of warmth becomes conspicuous. That benefits accompany the agreeable sensations produced by fresh air, and the agreeable sensations that accompany muscular action after due rest, and the agreeable sensations caused by rest after exertion, cannot be questioned. Receipt of these pleasures conduces to the maintenance of the body in fit condition for all the purposes of life. More manifest still are the physiological benefits of emotional pleasures. Every power, bodily and mental, is increased by "good spirits;" which is our name for a general emotional satisfaction. The truth that the fundamental vital actions—those of nutrition—are furthered by laughter-moving conversation, or rather by the pleasurable feeling causing laughter, is one of old standing ; and every dyspeptic knows that in exhilarating company, a large and varied dinner including not very digestible things, may be eaten with impunity, and indeed with benefit, while a small, carefully-chosen dinner of simple things, eaten in solitude, will be followed by indigestion. This striking effect on the alimentary system is accompanied by effects, equally certain though less manifest, on the circulation and the respiration. Again, one who, released from daily labours and anxieties, receives delights from fine scenery or is enlivened by the novelties he sees abroad, comes back showing by toned-up face and vivacious manner, the greater energy with which he is prepared to pursue his avocation. Invalids especially, on whose narrowed margin of vitality the influence of conditions is most visible, habitually show the benefits derived from agreeable states of feeling. A lively social circle, the call of an old friend, or even removal to a brighter room, will, by the induced cheerfulness, much improve the physical state. In brief, as every medical man knows, there is no such tonic as happiness.

These diffused physiological effects of pleasures and pains, which are joined with the local or special physiological effects, are, indeed, obviously inevitable. We have seen (*Principles of Psychology*, §§ 123—125) that while craving, or negative pain, accompanies the under-activity of an organ, and while positive pain accompanies its over-activity, pleasure accompanies its normal activity. We have seen that by evolution no other relations could be established; since, through all inferior types of creatures, if defect or excess of function produced no disagreeable sentiency, and medium function no agreeable sentiency, there would be nothing to ensure a proportioned performance of function. And as it is one of the laws of nervous action that each stimulus, beyond a direct discharge to the particular organ acted on, indirectly causes a general discharge throughout the nervous system (*Prin. of Psy.* §§ 21, 39), it results that the rest of the organs, all influenced as they are by the nervous system, participate in the stimulation. So that beyond the aid, more slowly shown, which the organs yield to one another through the physiological division of labour, there is the aid, more quickly shown, which mutual excitation gives. While there is a benefit to be presently felt by the whole organism from the due performance of each function, there is an immediate benefit from the exaltation of its functions at large caused by the accompanying pleasure; and from pains, whether of excess or defect, there also come these double effects, immediate and remote.

§ 37. Non-recognition of these general truths vitiates moral speculation at large. From the estimates of right and wrong habitually framed, these physiological effects wrought on the actor by his feelings are entirely omitted It is tacitly assumed that pleasures and pains have no reactions on the body of the recipient, affecting his fitness for the duties of life. The only reactions recognized are those on character; respecting which the current supposition is, that acceptance of pleasures is detrimental and submission to pains beneficial. The notion, remotely descended from the ghost-theory of the savage, that mind and body are independent, has, among its various implications, this belief that states of consciousness are in no wise related to bodily states. "You have had your gratification—it is past; and you are as you were before," says the moralist to one. And to another he says, "You have borne the suffering—it is over; and there the matter ends." Both statements are false. Leaving out of view indirect results, the direct results are that the one has moved a step away from death and the other has moved a step towards death.

Leaving out of view, I say, the indirect results. It is these indirect results, here for the moment left out of view, which the moralist has exclusively in view: being so occupied by them that he ignores the direct results. The gratification, perhaps purchased at undue cost, perhaps enjoyed when work should have been done, perhaps snatched from the rightful claimant, is considered only in relation to remote injurious effects, and no set-off is made for immediate beneficial effects. Conversely, from positive and negative pains, borne now in the pursuit of some future advantage, now in discharge of responsibilities, now in performing a generous act, the distant good is alone dwelt on and the proximate evil ignored. Consequences, pleasurable and painful, experienced by the actor forthwith, are of no importance; and they become of importance only when anticipated as occurring hereafter to the actor or to other persons. And further, future evils borne by the actor are considered of no account if they result from self-denial, and are emphasized only when they result from self-gratification. Obviously, estimates so framed are erroneous; and obviously, the pervading judgments of conduct based on such estimates must be distorted. Mark the anomalies of opinion produced.

If, as the sequence of a malady contracted in pursuit of illegitimate gratification, an attack of iritis injures vision, the mischief is to be counted among those entailed by immoral conduct; but if, regardless of protesting sensations, the eyes are used in study too soon after ophthalmia, and there follows blindness for years or for life, entailing not only personal unhappiness but a burden on others, moralists are silent. The broken leg which a drunkard's accident causes, counts among those miseries brought on self and family by intemperance, which form the ground for reprobating it; but if anxiety to fulfil duties prompts the continued use of a sprained knee spite of the pain, and brings on a chronic lameness involving lack of exercise, consequent ill-health, inefficiency, anxiety, and unhappiness, it is supposed that ethics has no verdict to give in the matter. A student who is plucked because he has spent in amusement the time and money that should have gone in study, is blamed for thus making parents unhappy and preparing for himself a miserable future; but another who, thinking exclusively of claims on him, reads night after night with hot or aching head, and, breaking down, cannot take his degree, but returns home shattered in health and unable to support himself, is named with pity only, as not subject to any moral judgment; or rather, the moral judgment passed is wholly favourable.

Thus recognizing the evils caused by some kinds of conduct only, men at large, and moralists as exponents of their beliefs, ignore the suffering and death daily caused around them by disregard of that guidance which has established itself in the course of evolution. Led by the tacit assumption, common to Pagan stoics and Christian ascetics, that we are so diabolically organized that pleasures

are injurious and pains beneficial, people on all sides
yield examples of lives blasted by persisting in actions
against which their sensations rebel. Here is one who,
drenched to the skin and sitting in a cold wind, pooh-poohs
his shiverings and gets rheumatic fever with subsequent
heart-disease, which makes worthless the short life remaining to him. Here is another who, disregarding painful
feelings, works too soon after a debilitating illness, and
establishes disordered health that lasts for the rest of his
days, and makes him useless to himself and others. Now
the account is of a youth who, persisting in gymnastic feats
spite of scarcely bearable straining, bursts a blood-vessel,
and, long laid on the shelf, is permanently damaged; while
now it is of a man in middle life who, pushing muscular
effort to painful excess, suddenly brings on hernia. In this
family is a case of aphasia, spreading paralysis, and death,
caused by eating too little and doing too much; in that,
softening of the brain has been brought on by ceaseless
mental efforts against which the feelings hourly protested;
and in others, less serious brain-affections have been contracted by over-study continued regardless of discomfort and
the cravings for fresh air and exercise.* Even without
accumulating special examples, the truth is forced on us by
the visible traits of classes. The careworn man of business
too long at his office, the cadaverous barrister poring half
the night over his briefs, the feeble factory hands and
unhealthy seamstresses passing long hours in bad air, the
anæmic, flat-chested school girls, bending over many lessons
and forbidden boisterous play, no less than Sheffield grinders
who die of suffocating dust, and peasants crippled with
rheumatism due to exposure, show us the wide-spread
miseries caused by persevering in actions repugnant to the
sensations and neglecting actions which the sensations
prompt. Nay the evidence is still more extensive and

---

* I can count up more than a dozen such cases among those personally
well known to me.

conspicuous. What are the puny malformed children, seen in poverty-stricken districts, but children whose appetites for food and desires for warmth have not been adequately satisfied? What are populations stinted in growth and prematurely aged, such as parts of France show us, but populations injured by work in excess and food in defect: the one implying positive pain the other negative pain? What is the implication of that greater mortality which occurs among people who are weakened by privations, unless it is that bodily miseries conduce to fatal illnesses? Or once more, what must we infer from the frightful amount of disease and death suffered by armies in the field, fed on scanty and bad provisions, lying on damp ground, exposed to extremes of heat and cold, inadequately sheltered from rain, and subject to exhausting efforts; unless it be the terrible mischiefs caused by continuously subjecting the body to treatment which the feelings protest against?

It matters not to the argument whether the actions entailing such effects are voluntary or involuntary. It matters not from the biological point of view, whether the motives prompting them are high or low. The vital functions accept no apologies on the ground that neglect of them was unavoidable, or that the reason for neglect was noble. The direct and indirect sufferings caused by nonconformity to the laws of life, are the same whatever induces the non-conformity; and cannot be omitted in any rational estimate of conduct. If the purpose of ethical inquiry is to establish rules of right living; and if the rules of right living are those of which the total results, individual and general, direct and indirect, are most conducive to human happiness; then it is absurd to ignore the immediate results and recognize only the remote results.

§ 38. Here might be urged the necessity for preluding the study of moral science, by the study of biological science. Here might be dwelt on the error men make in thinking they can understand those special phenomena of human life with which Ethics deals, while paying little or no attention to the general phenomena of human life, and while utterly ignoring the phenomena of life at large. And doubtless there would be truth in the inference that such acquaintance with the world of living things as discloses the part which pleasures and pains have played in organic evolution, would help to rectify these one-sided conceptions of moralists. It cannot be held, however, that lack of this knowledge is the sole cause, or the main cause, of their one-sidedness. For facts of the kind above instanced, which, duly attended to, would prevent such distortions of moral theory, are facts which it needs no biological inquiries to learn, but which are daily thrust before the eyes of all. The truth is, rather, that the general consciousness is so possessed by sentiments and ideas at variance with the conclusions necessitated by familiar evidence, that the evidence gets no attention. These adverse sentiments and ideas have several roots.

There is the theological root. As before shown, from the worship of cannibal ancestors who delighted in witnessing tortures, there resulted the primitive conception of deities who were propitiated by the bearing of pains, and, consequently, angered by the receipt of pleasures. Through the religions of the semi-civilized, in which this conception of the divine nature remains conspicuous, it has persisted, in progressively modified forms, down to our own times; and still colours the beliefs, both of those who adhere to the current creed and of those who nominally reject it.   There is another root in the primitive and stillsurviving militancy. While social antagonisms continue to generate war, which consists in endeavours to inflict pain and death while submitting to the risks of pain and death, and which necessarily involves great privations; it is needful that physical suffering, whether considered in itself or in the evils it bequeaths, should be thought little of, and that among pleasures recognized as most worthy should be those which victory brings.   Nor does partially-developed industrialism fail to furnish a root. With social evolution, which implies transition from the life of wandering hunters to the life of settled peoples engaged in labour, and which therefore entails activities widely unlike those to which the aboriginal constitution is adapted, there comes an under-exercise of faculties for which the social state affords no scope, and an over-taxing of faculties required for the social state : the one implying denial of certain pleasures and the other submission to certain pains. Hence, along 'with that growth of population which makes the struggle for existence intense, bearing of pains and sacrifice of pleasures is daily necessitated.

Now always and everywhere, there arises among men a theory conforming to their practice. The savage nature, originating the conception of a savage deity, evolves a theory of supernatural control sufficiently stringent and cruel to influence his conduct. With submission to despotic govern-.ment severe enough in its restraints to keep in order barbarous natures, there grows up a theory of divine right to rule, and the duty of absolute submission. Where war is made the business of life by the existence of warlike neighbours, virtues which are required for war come to be regarded as supreme virtues; while, contrariwise, when industrialism has grown predominant, the violence and the deception which warriors glory in come to be held criminal. In like manner, then, there arises a tolerable adjustment of the actually-accepted (not the nominally-accepted) theory of right living, to living as it is daily carried on. If the life is one that necessitates habitual denial of pleasures and bearing of pains, there grows up an answering ethical system under which the receipt of pleasures is tacitly disapproved and the bearing of pains avowedly approved. The mischiefs entailed by pleasures in excess are dwelt

7

on, while the benefits which normal pleasures bring are ignored; and the good results achieved by submission to pains are fully set forth while the evils are overlooked

But while recognizing the desirableness of, and indeed the necessity for, systems of ethics adapted, like religious systems and political systems, to their respective times and places; we have here to regard the first as, like the others, transitional. We must infer that like a purer creed and a better government, a truer ethics belongs to a more advanced social state. Led, *a priori*, to conclude that distortions must exist, we are enabled to recognize as such, the distortions we find: answering in nature, as these do, to expectation. And there is forced on us the truth that a scientific morality arises only as fast as the one-sided conceptions adapted to transitory conditions, are developed into both-sided conceptions. The science of right living has to take account of all consequences in so far as they affect happiness, personally or socially, directly or indirectly; and by as much as it ignores any class of consequences, by so much does it fail to be science.

§ 39. Like the physical view, then, the biological view corresponds with the view gained by looking at conduct in general from the stand-point of Evolution.

That which was physically defined as a moving equilibrium, we define biologically as a balance of functions. The implication of such a balance is that the several functions in their kinds, amounts, and combinations, are adjusted to the several activities which maintain and constitute complete life; and to be so adjusted is to have reached the goal towards which the evolution of conduct continually tends.

Passing to the feelings which accompany the performance of functions, we see that of necessity during the evolution of organic life, pleasures have become the concomitants of normal amounts of functions, while pains, positive and negative, have become the concomitants of excesses and defects of functions. And though in every species derangements of these relations are often caused by changes of conditions, they ever re-establish themselves: disappearance of the species being the alternative.

Mankind, inheriting from creatures of lower kinds, such adjustments between feelings and functions as concern fundamental bodily requirements; and daily forced by peremptory feelings to do the things which maintain life and avoid those which bring immediate death; has been subject to a change of conditions unusually great and involved. This has considerably deranged the guidance by sensations, and has deranged in a much greater degree the guidance by emotions. The result is that in many cases pleasures are not connected with actions which must be performed, nor pains with actions which must be avoided, but contrariwise.

Several influences have conspired to make men ignore the well-working of these relations between feelings and functions, and to observe whatever of ill-working is seen in them. Hence, while the evils which some pleasures entail are dilated upon, the benefits habitually accompanying receipt of pleasures are unnoticed; at the same time that the benefits achieved through certain pains are magnified while the immense mischiefs which pains bring are made little of.

The ethical theories characterized by these perversions, are products of, and are appropriate to, the forms of social life which the imperfectly-adapted constitutions of men produce. But with the progress of adaptation, bringing faculties and requirements into harmony, such incongruities of experience, and consequent distortions of theory, must diminish; until, along with complete adjustment of humanity to the social state, will go recognition of the truths that actions are completely right only when, besides being conducive to future happiness, special and general, they are immediately pleasurable, and that painfulness, not only ultimate but proximate, is the concomitant of actions which are wrong.

7 *

So that from the biological point of view, ethical science becomes a specification of the conduct of associated men who are severally so constituted that the various self-preserving activities, the activities required for rearing offspring, and those which social welfare demands, are fulfilled in the spontaneous exercise of duly proportioned faculties, each yielding when in action its quantum of pleasure; and who are, by consequence, so constituted that excess or defect in any one of these actions brings its quantum of pain, immediate and remote.

NOTE TO § 33. In his *Physical Ethics*, Mr. Alfred Barratt has expressed a view which here calls for notice. Postulating Evolution and its general laws, he refers to certain passages in the *Principles of Psychology* (1st Ed. Pt. III. ch. viii. pp. 395, sqq. cf. Pt. IV. ch. iv.) in which I have treated of the relation between irritation and contraction which "marks the dawn of sensitive life;" have pointed out that "the primordial tissue must be differently affected by contact with nutritive and with innutritive matters"—the two being for aquatic creatures respectively the soluble and the insoluble; and have argued that the contraction by which a protruded part of a rhizopod draws in a fragment of assimilable matter "is caused by a commencing absorption of the assimilable matter." Mr. Barratt, holding that consciousness "must be considered as an invariable property of animal life, and ultimately, in its elements, of the material universe" (p. 43), regards these responses of animal tissue to stimuli, as implying feeling of one or other kind. "Some kinds of impressed force," he says, "are followed by movements of retraction and withdrawal, others by such as secure a continuance of the impression. These two kinds of contraction are the phenomena and external marks of pain and pleasure respectively. Hence the tissue acts so as to secure pleasure and avoid pain by a law as truly physical and natural as that whereby a needle turns to the pole, or a tree to the light" (p. 52). Now without questioning that the raw material of consciousness is present even in undifferentiated protoplasm, and everywhere exists potentially in that Unknowable Power which, otherwise conditioned, is manifested in physical action (*Prin. of Psy.* § 272—3), I demur to the conclusion that it at first exists under the forms of pleasure and pain. These, I conceive, arise, as the more special feelings do, by a compounding of the ultimate elements of consciousness (*Prin. of Psy.* §§ 60, 61): being, indeed, general aspects of these more special feelings when they reach certain intensities. Considering that even in creatures which have developed nervous systems, a great part of the vital processes are carried on by unconscious reflex actions, I see no propriety in assuming the existence of what we understand by consciousness in creatures not only devoid of nervous systems but devoid of structures in general.

NOTE TO § 36. More than once in the *Emotions and the Will*, Dr. Bain insists on the connexion between pleasure and exaltation of vitality, and the connexion between pain and depression of vitality. As above shown, I concur in the view taken by him ; which is, indeed, put beyond dispute by general experience as well as by the more special experience of medical men.

When, however, from the invigorating and relaxing effects of pleasure and pain respectively, Dr. Bain derives the original tendencies to persist in acts which give pleasure and to desist from those which give pain, I find myself unable to go with him. He says—"We suppose movements spontaneously begun, and accidentally causing pleausure ; we then assume that with the pleasure there will be an increase of vital energy, in which increase the fortunate movements will share, and thereby increase the pleasure. Or, on the other hand, we suppose the spontaneous movements to give pain, and assume that, with the pain, there will be a decrease of energy, extending to the movements that cause the evil, and thereby providing a remedy " (3rd Ed. p. 315). This interpretation, implying that " the fortunate movements " merely *share* in the effects of augmented vital energy caused by the pleasure, does not seem to me congruous with observation. The truth appears rather to be that though there is a concomitant general increase of muscular tone, the muscles specially excited are those which, by their increased contraction, conduce to increased pleasure. Conversely, the implication that desistance from spontaneous movements which cause pain, is due to a general muscular relaxation shared in by the muscles causing these particular movements, seems to me at variance with the fact that the retractation commonly takes the form not of a passive lapse but of an active withdrawal. Further, it may be remarked that depressing as pain eventually is to the system at large, we cannot say that it at once depresses the muscular energies. Not simply, as Dr. Bain admits, does an acute smart produce spasmodic movements, but pains of all kinds, both sensational and emotional stimulate the muscles (*Essays* 1st series p. 360, 1, or 2nd ed. Vol. I. p. 211,12). Pain however (and also pleasure when very intense) simultaneously has an inhibitory effect on all the reflex actions ; and as the vital functions in general are carried on by reflex actions, this inhibition, increasing with the intensity of the pain, proportionately depresses the vital functions. Arrest of the heart's action and fainting is an extreme result of this inhibition; and the viscera at large feel its effects in degrees proportioned to the degrees of pain. Pain, therefore, while directly causing a discharge of muscular energy as pleasure does, eventually lowers muscular power by lowering those vital processes on which the supply of energy depends. Hence we cannot, I think, ascribe the prompt desistance from muscular movements causing pain, to decrease in the flow of energy ; for this decrease is felt only after an interval. Conversely, we cannot ascribe the persistence in a muscular act which yields pleasure to the resulting exaltation of energy ; but must, as indicated in § 33, ascribe it to the establishment of lines of discharge between the place of pleasurable stimulation and those contractile structures which maintain and increase the act causing the stimulation— connexions allied with the reflex, into which they pass by insensible gradations.

CHAPTER VII.

THE PSYCHOLOGICAL VIEW.

§ 40. The last chapter, in so far as it dealt with feelings in their relations to conduct, recognized only their physiological aspects: their psychological aspects were passed over. In this chapter, conversely, we are not concerned with the constitutional connexions between feelings, as incentives or deterrents, and physical benefits to be gained or mischiefs to be avoided; nor with the reactive effects of feelings on the state of the organism, as fitting or unfitting it for future action. Here we have to consider represented pleasures and pains, sensational and emotional, as constituting deliberate motives—as forming factors in the conscious adjustments of acts to ends.

§ 41. The rudimentary psychical act, not yet differentiated from a physical act, implies an excitation and a motion. In a creature of low type the touch of food excites prehension. In a somewhat higher creature the odour from nutritive matter sets up motion of the body towards the matter. And where rudimentary vision exists, sudden obscuration of light, implying the passage of something large, causes convulsive muscular movements which mostly carry the body away from the source of danger. In each of these cases we may distinguish four factors. There is (a), that property of the external object which primarily affects the organism—

the taste, smell, or opacity; and, connected with such
property, there is in the external object that character (*b*),
which renders seizure of it, or escape from it, beneficial.
Within the organism there is (*c*), the impression or sensation
which the property (*a*), produces, serving as stimulus; and
there is, connected with it, the motor change (*d*), by
which seizure or escape is effected.   Now Psychology is
chiefly concerned with the connexion between the relation
a b, and the relation *c d*, under all those forms which they
assume in the course of evolution.   Each of the factors, and
each of the relations, grows more involved as organization
advances.   Instead of being single, the identifying attribute
a, often becomes, in the environment of a superior animal,
a cluster of attributes; such as the size, form, colours,
motions, displayed by a distant creature that is dangerous.
The factor *b*, with which this combination of attributes is associated, becomes the congeries of characters,
powers, habits, which constitute it an enemy.   Of the
subjective factors, *c* becomes a complicated set of visual
sensations co-ordinated with one another and with the
ideas and feelings established by experience of such enemies,
and constituting the motive to escape; while *d* becomes the
intricate, and often prolonged, series of runs, leaps, doubles,
dives, &c., made in eluding the enemy.   In
human life we find the same four outer and inner
factors, still more multiform and entangled in their
compositions and connexions.   The entire assemblage of
physical attributes *a*, presented by an estate that is
advertized for sale, passes enumeration; and the assemblage
of various utilities, *b*, going along with these attributes,
is also beyond brief specification.   The perceptions and
ideas, likes and dislikes, *c*, set up by the aspect of
the estate, and which, compounded and re-compounded,
eventually form the motive for buying it, make a whole too
large and complex for description; and the transactions,
legal, pecuniary, and other, gone through in making the

purchase and taking possession, are scarcely less numerous and elaborate.   Nor must we overlook the fact that as evolution progresses, not only do the factors increase in complexity but also the relations among them. Originally, a is directly and simply connected with b, while c is directly and simply connected with d. But eventually, the connexions between a and b, and between c and d, become very indirect and involved. On the one hand, as the first illustration shows us, sapidity and nutritiveness are closely bound together; as are also the stimulation caused by the one and the contraction which utilizes the other. But, as we see in the last illustration, the connexion between the visible traits of an estate and those characters which constitute its value, is at once remote and complicated; while the transition from the purchaser's highly-composite motive to the numerous actions of sensory and motor organs, severally intricate, which effect the purchase, is though an entangled plexus of thoughts and feelings constituting his decision.

After this explanation will be apprehended a truth otherwise set forth in the *Principles of Psychology*. Mind consists of feelings and the relations among feelings. By composition of the relations, and ideas of relations, intelligence arises. By composition of the feelings, and ideas of feelings, emotion arises. And, other things equal, the evolution of either is great in proportion as the composition is great. One of the necessary implications is that cognition becomes higher in proportion as it is remoter from reflex action; while emotion becomes higher in proportion as it is remoter from sensation.

And now of the various corollaries from this broad view of psychological evolution, let us observe those which concern the motives and actions that are classed as moral and immoral.

§ 42. The mental process by which, in any case, the

adjustment of acts to ends is effected, and which, under its higher forms, becomes the subject-matter of ethical judgments, is, as above implied, divisible into the rise of a feeling or feelings constituting the motive, and the thought or thoughts through which the motive is shaped and finally issues in action. The first of these elements, originally an excitement, becomes a simple sensation; then a compound sensation; then a cluster of partially presentative and partially representative sensations, forming an incipient emotion; then a cluster of exclusively ideal or representative sensations, forming an emotion proper; then a cluster of such clusters, forming a compound emotion; and eventually becomes a still more involved emotion composed of the ideal forms of such compound emotions. The other element, beginning with that immediate passage of a single stimulus into a single motion, called reflex action, presently comes to be a set of associated discharges of stimuli producing associated motions, constituting instinct. Step by step arise more entangled combinations of stimuli, somewhat variable in their modes of union, leading to complex motions similarly variable in their adjustments; whence occasional hesitations in the sensori-motor processes. Presently is reached a stage at which the combined clusters of impressions, not all present together, issue in actions not all simultaneous; implying representation of results, or thought. After-wards follow stages in which various thoughts have time to pass before the composite motives produce the appropriate actions. Until at last arise those long deliberations during which the probabilities of various consequences are estimated, and the promptings of the correlative feelings balanced; constituting calm judgment. That under either of its aspects the later forms of this mental process are the higher, ethically considered as well as otherwise considered, will be readily seen.

For from the first, complication of sentiency has accompanied better and more numerous adjustments of acts to ends; as also has complication of movement, and complication of the co-ordinating or intellectual process uniting the two. Whence it follows that the acts characterized by the more complex motives and the more involved thoughts, have all along been of higher authority for guidance. Some examples will make this clear.

Here is an aquatic creature guided by the odour of organic matter towards things serving for food; but a creature which, lacking any other guidance, is at the mercy of larger creatures coming near. Here is another which, also guided to food by odour, possesses rudimentary vision; and so is made to start spasmodically away from a moving body which diffuses this odour, in those cases where it is large enough to produce sudden obscuration of light—usually an enemy. Evidently life will frequently be saved by conforming to the later and higher stimulus, instead of to the earlier and lower.   Observe at a more advanced stage a parallel conflict. This is a beast which pursues others for prey, and, either lacking experience or prompted by raging hunger, attacks one more powerful than itself and gets destroyed. Conversely, that is a beast which, prompted by a hunger equally keen, but either by individual experience or effects of inherited experience, made conscious of evil by the aspect of one more powerful than itself, is deterred from attacking, and saves its life by subordinating the primary motive, consisting of craving sensations, to the secondary motive, consisting of ideal feelings, distinct or vague.   Ascending at once from these examples of conduct in animals to examples of human conduct, we shall see that the contrasts between inferior and superior have habitually the same traits. The savage of lowest type devours all the food captured by to-day's chase; and, hungry on the morrow, has perhaps for days to bear the pangs of starvation. The superior savage, conceiving more vividly the entailed sufferings if no game is to be found, is deterred by his complex feeling from giving way entirely to his

simple feeling. Similarly are the two contrasted in the
inertness which goes along with lack of forethought, and the
activity which due forethought produces. The primitive man,
idly inclined, and ruled by the sensations of the moment,
will not exert himself until actual pains have to be
escaped; but the man somewhat advanced, able more distinctly to imagine future gratifications and sufferings, is
prompted by the thought of these to overcome his love of
ease: decrease of misery and mortality resulting from this
predominance of the representative feelings over the
presentative feelings. Without dwelling on the
fact that among the civilized, those who lead the life of the
senses are contrasted in the same way with those whose
lives are largely occupied with pleasures not of a sensual
kind, let me point out that there are analogous contrasts
between guidance by the less complex representative feelings, or lower emotions, and guidance by the more complex
representative feelings, or higher emotions. When led by
his acquisitiveness—a re-representative feeling which, acting
under due control, conduces to welfare—the thief takes
another man's property; his act is determined by certain
imagined proximate pleasures of relatively simple kinds,
rather than by less-clearly imagined possible pains that are
more remote and of relatively involved kinds. But in
the conscientious man, there is an adequate restraining
motive, still more re-representative in its nature, including
not only ideas of punishment, and not only ideas of lost
reputation and ruin, but including ideas of the claims of the
person owning the property, and of the pains which loss of
it will entail on him: all joined with a general aversion to
acts injurious to others, which arises from the inherited
effects of experience. And here at the end we see, as we
saw at the beginning, that guidance by the more complex
feeling, on the average conduces to welfare more than does
guidance by the simpler feeling.

The like holds with the intellectual co-ordinations through

which stimuli issue in motions. The lowest actions, called reflex, in which an impression made on an afferent nerve causes by discharge through an efferent nerve a contraction, shows us a very limited adjustment of acts to ends: the impression being simple, and the resulting motion simple, the internal co-ordination is also simple. Evidently when there are several senses which can be together affected by an outer object; and when, according as such object is discriminated as of one or other kind, the movements made in response are combined in one or other way; the intermediate co-ordinations are necessarily more involved. And evidently each further step in the evolution of intelligence, always instrumental to better self-preservation, exhibits this same general trait. The adjustments by which the more involved actions are made appropriate to the more involved circumstances, imply more intricate, and consequently more deliberate and conscious, co-ordinations; until, when we come to civilized men, who in their daily business taking into account many data and conditions adjust their proceedings to various consequences, we see that the intellectual actions, becoming of the kind we call judicial, are at once very elaborate and very deliberate.

Observe, then, what follows respecting the relative authorities of motives. Throughout the ascent from low creatures up to man, and from the lowest types of man up to the highest, self-preservation has been increased by the subordination of simple excitations to compound excitations—the subjection of immediate sensations to the ideas of sensations to come—the over-ruling of presentative feelings by representative feelings, and of representative feelings by re-representative feelings. As life has advanced, the accompanying sentiency has become increasingly ideal; and among feelings produced by the compounding of ideas, the highest, and those which have evolved latest, are the re-compounded or doubly ideal. Hence

it follows that as guides, the feelings have authorities
proportionate to the degrees in which they are removed by
their complexity and their ideality from simple sensations and appetites.   A further implication is
made clear by studying the intellectual sides of these
mental processes by which acts are adjusted to ends.
Where they are low and simple, these comprehend
the guiding only of immediate acts by immediate stimuli—the entire transaction in each case, lasting but a
moment, refers only to a proximate result. But with the
development of intelligence and the growing ideality of
the motives, the ends to which the acts are adjusted cease
to be exclusively immediate. The more ideal motives
concern ends that are more distant ; and with approach to
the highest types, present ends become increasingly subordinate to those future ends which the ideal motives have
for their objects. Hence there arises a certain presumption
in favour of a motive which refers to a remote good, in
comparison with one which refers to a proximate good.

§ 43. In the last chapter I hinted that besides the
several influences there named as fostering the ascetic
belief that doing things which are agreeable is detrimental
while bearing disagreeable things is beneficial, there
remained to be named an influence of deeper origin. This
is shadowed forth in the foregoing paragraphs.

For the general truth that guidance by such simple
pleasures and pains as result from fulfilling or denying
bodily desires, is, under one aspect, inferior to guidance by
those pleasures and pains which the complex ideal feelings
yield, has led to the belief that the promptings of bodily
desires should be disregarded. Further, the general truth
that pursuit of proximate satisfactions is, under one aspect,
inferior to pursuit of ultimate satisfactions, has led to the
belief that proximate satisfactions must not be valued.

In the early stages of every science, the generalizations

reached are not qualified enough.   The discriminating statements of the truths formulated, arise afterwards, by limitation
of the undiscriminating statements.   As with bodily vision,
which at first appreciates only the broadest traits of objects,
and so leads to rude classings which developed vision,
impressible by minor differences, has to correct; so with
mental vision in relation to general truths, it happens that
at first the inductions, wrongly made all-embracing, have
to wait for scepticism and critical observation to restrict
them, by taking account of unnoticed differences.   Hence,
we may expect to find the current ethical conclusions too
sweeping.   Let us note how, in three ways, these dominant
beliefs, alike of professed moralists and of people at large,
are made erroneous by lack of qualifications.

   In the first place, the authority of the lower feelings as
guides is by no means always inferior to the authority of
the higher feelings, but is often superior.   Daily occur
occasions on which sensations must be obeyed rather than
sentiments.   Let any one think of sitting all night naked in
a snowstorm, or going a week without food, or letting his
head be held under water for ten minutes, and he will see
that the pleasures and pains directly related to maintenance of life, may not be wholly subordinated to the
pleasures and pains indirectly related to maintenance of
life.   Though in many cases guidance by the simple feelings
rather than by the complex feelings is injurious, in other
cases guidance by the complex feelings rather than by the
simple feelings is fatal;   and throughout a wide range
of cases their relative authorities as guides are indeterminate.   Grant that in a man pursued, the protesting
feelings accompanying intense and prolonged effort, must,
to preserve life, be over-ruled by the fear of his pursuers;
it may yet happen that, persisting till he drops, the resulting
exhaustion causes death, though, the pursuit having been
abandoned, death would not otherwise have resulted.   Grant
that a widow left in poverty, must deny her appetite that

she may give enough food to her children to keep them
alive; yet the denial of her appetite pushed too far, may
leave them not only entirely without food but without
guardianship. Grant that, working his brain unceasingly
from dawn till dark, the man in pecuniary difficulties must
disregard rebellious bodily sensations in obedience to the
conscientious desire to liquidate the claims on him; yet he
may carry this subjection of simple feelings to complex
feelings to the extent of shattering his health, and failing
in that end which, with less of this subjection, he might
have achieved. Clearly, then, the subordination of lower
feelings must be a conditional subordination. The supremacy of higher feelings must be a qualified supremacy.

In another way does the generalization ordinarily made
err by excess. With the truth that life is high in proportion as the simple presentative feelings are under the
control of the compound representative feelings, it joins, as
though they were corollaries, certain propositions which
are not corollaries. The current conception is, not that the
lower must yield to the higher when the two conflict, but
that the lower must be disregarded even when there is no
conflict. This tendency which the growth of moral ideas
has generated, to condemn obedience to inferior feelings
when superior feelings protest, has begotten a tendency to
condemn inferior feelings considered intrinsically. " I really
think she does things because she likes to do them," once said
to me one lady concerning another : the form of expression
and the manner both implying the belief not only that such
behaviour is wrong, but also that every one must recognize
it as wrong. And there prevails widely a notion of this
kind. In practice, indeed, the notion is very generally
inoperative. Though it prompts various incidental asce-
ticisms, as of those who think it alike manly and salutary to
go without a great coat in cold weather, or to persevere
through the winter in taking an out-of-door plunge, yet,
generally, the pleasurable feelings accompanying due fulfil-

ment of bodily needs, are accepted: acceptance being, indeed, sufficiently peremptory. But oblivious of these contradictions in their practice, men commonly betray a vague idea that there is something degrading, or injurious, or both, in doing that which is agreeable and avoiding that which is disagreeable. "Pleasant but wrong," is a phrase frequently used in a way implying that the two are naturally connected. As above hinted, however, such beliefs result from a confused apprehension of the general truth that the more compound and representative feelings are, on the average, of higher authority than the simple and presentative feelings. Apprehended with discrimination, this truth implies that the authority of the simple, ordinarily less than that of the compound but occasionally greater, is habitually to be accepted when the compound do not oppose.

In yet a third way is this principle of subordination misconceived. One of the contrasts between the earlier-evolved feelings and the later-evolved feelings, is that they refer respectively to the more immediate effects of actions and to the more remote effects; and speaking generally, guidance by that which is near is inferior to guidance by that which is distant. Hence has resulted the belief that, irrespective of their kinds, the pleasures of the present must be sacrificed to the pleasures of the future. We see this in the maxim often impressed on children when eating their meals, that they should reserve the nicest morsel till the last: the check on improvident yielding to immediate impulse, being here joined with the tacit teaching that the same gratification becomes more valuable as it becomes more distant. Such thinking is traceable throughout daily conduct; by no means indeed in all, but in those who are distinguished as prudent and well regulated in their conduct. Hurrying over his breakfast that he may catch the train, snatching a sandwich in the middle of the day, and eating a late dinner when he is so worn out that he is incapacitated for evening recreation, the man of business pursues a life in which not only the satisfactions of bodily desires, but also those of higher tastes and feelings, are, as far as may be, disregarded, that distant ends may be achieved; and yet if you ask what are these distant ends, you find (in cases where there are no parental responsibilities) that they are included under the conception of more comfortable living in time to come. So ingrained is this belief that it is wrong to seek immediate enjoyments and right to seek remote ones only, that you may hear from a busy man who has been on a pleasure excursion, a kind of apology for his conduct. He deprecates the unfavourable judgments of his friends by explaining that the state of his health had compelled him to take a holiday. Nevertheless, if you sound him with respect to his future, you find that his ambition is by-and-by to retire and devote himself wholly to the relaxations which he is now somewhat ashamed of taking.

The general truth disclosed by the study of evolving conduct, sub-human and human, that for the better preservation of life the primitive, simple, presentative feelings must be controlled by the later-evolved, compound, and representative feelings, has thus come, in the course of civilization, to be recognized by men; but necessarily at first in too indiscriminate a way. The current conception, while it errs by implying that the authority of the higher over the lower is unlimited, errs also by implying that the rule of the lower must be resisted even when it does not conflict with the rule of the higher, and further errs by implying that a gratification which forms a proper aim if it is remote, forms an improper aim if it is proximate.

§ 44. Without explicitly saying so, we have been here tracing the genesis of the moral consciousness. For unquestionably the essential trait in the moral consciousness, is the control of some feeling or feelings by some other feeling or feelings.

Among the higher animals we may see, distinctly enough,

8

the conflict of feelings and the subjection of simpler to more compound; as when a dog is restrained from snatching food by fear of the penalties which may come if he yields to his appetite; or as when he desists from scratching at a hole lest he should lose his master, who has walked on. Here, however, though there is subordination, there is not conscious subordination—there is no introspection revealing the fact that one feeling has yielded to another. So is it even with human beings when little developed mentally. The pre-social man, wandering about in families and ruled by such sensations and emotions as are caused by the circumstances of the moment, though occasionally subject to conflicts of motives, meets with comparatively few cases in which the advantage of postponing the immediate to the remote is forced on his attention; nor has he the intelligence requisite for analyzing and generalizing such of these cases as occur. Only as social evolution renders the life more complex, the restraints many and strong, the evils of impulsive conduct marked, and the comforts to be gained by providing for the future tolerably certain, can there come experiences numerous enough to make familiar the benefit of subordinating the simpler feelings to the more complex ones. Only then, too, does there arise a sufficient intellectual power to make an induction from these experiences, followed by a sufficient massing of individual inductions into a public and traditional induction impressed on each generation as it grows up.

And here we are introduced to certain facts of profound significance. This conscious relinquishment of immediate and special good to gain distant and general good, while it is a cardinal trait of the self-restraint called moral, is also a cardinal trait of self-restraints other than those called moral—the restraints that originate from fear of the visible ruler, of the invisible ruler, and of society at large. Whenever the individual refrains from doing that which the passing desire prompts, lest he should afterwards suffer

legal punishment, or divine vengeance, or public reprobation, or all of them, he surrenders the near and
definite pleasure rather than risk the remote and greater,
though less definite, pains, which taking it may bring on
him; and, conversely, when he undergoes some present pain,
that he may reap some probable future pleasure, political,
religious, or social. But though all these four kinds of
internal control have the common character that the simpler
and less ideal feelings are consciously over-ruled by the
more complex and ideal feelings; and though, at first, they
are practically co-extensive and undistinguished; yet, in the
course of social evolution they differentiate; and, eventually,
the moral control with its accompanying conceptions and
sentiments, emerges as independent.   Let us glance at the
leading aspects of the process.

While, as in the rudest groups, neither political nor
religious rule exists, the leading check to the immediate
satisfaction of each desire as it arises, is consciousness of
the evils which the anger of fellow savages may entail, if
satisfaction of the desire is obtained at their cost.   In this
early stage the imagined pains which constitute the
governing motive, are those apt to be inflicted by beings
of like nature, undistinguished in power : the political,
religious, and social restraints, are as yet represented only
by this mutual dread of vengeance.   When special
strength, skill, or courage, makes one of them a leader in
battle, he necessarily inspires greater fear than any other ;
and there comes to be a more decided check on such
satisfactions of the desires as will injure or offend him.
Gradually as, by habitual war, chieftainship is established,
the evils thought of as likely to arise from angering the
chief, not only by aggression upon him but by disobedience to him, become distinguishable both from the smaller
evils which other personal antagonisms cause, and from
the more diffused evils thought of as arising from social
reprobation.   That is, political control begins to dif-

8 *

ferentiate from the more indefinite control of mutual dread. Meanwhile there has been developing the ghost-theory. In all but the rudest groups, the double of a deceased man, propitiated at death and afterwards, is conceived as able to injure the survivors. Consequently, as fast as the ghost-theory becomes established and definite, there grows up another kind of check on immediate satisfaction of the desires—a check constituted by ideas of the evils which ghosts may inflict if offended; and when political headship gets settled, and the ghosts of dead chiefs, thought of as more powerful and more relentless than other ghosts, are especially dreaded, there begins to take shape the form of restraint distinguished as religious. For a long time these three sets of restraints, with their correlative sanctions, though becoming separate in consciousness, remain co-extensive; and do so because they mostly refer to one end—success in war. The duty of blood-revenge is insisted on even while yet nothing to be called social organization exists. As the chief gains predominance, the killing of enemies becomes a political duty; and as the anger of the dead chief comes to be dreaded, the killing of enemies becomes a religious duty. Loyalty to the ruler while he lives and after he dies, is increasingly shown by holding life at his disposal for purposes of war. The earliest enacted punishments are those for insubordination and for breaches of observances which express subordination—all of them militant in origin. While the divine injunctions, originally traditions of the dead king's will, mainly refer to the destruction of peoples with whom he was at enmity; and divine anger or approval are conceived as determined by the degrees in which subjection to him is shown, directly by worship and indirectly by fulfilling these injunctions. The Fijian, who is said on entering the other world to commend himself by narrating his successes in battle, and who, when alive, is described as sometimes greatly distressed if he thinks he has not killed enemies enough to please his gods, shows us the resulting ideas and feelings; and reminds us of kindred ideas and feelings betrayed by ancient races.   To all which add that the control of social opinion, besides being directly exercised, as in the earliest stage, by praise of the brave and blame of the cowardly, comes to be indirectly exercised with a kindred general effect by applause of loyalty to the ruler and piety to the god. So that the three differentiated forms of control which grow up along with militant organization and action, while enforcing kindred restraints and incentives, also enforce one another; and their separate and joint disciplines have the common character that they involve the sacrifice of immediate special benefits to obtain more distant and general benefits.

At the same time there have been developing under the same three sanctions, restraints and incentives of another order, similarly characterized by subordination of the proximate to the remote. Joint aggressions upon men outside the society, cannot prosper if there are many aggressions of man on man within the society. War implies co-operation; and co-operation is prevented by antagonisms among those who are to co-operate. We saw that in the primitive ungoverned group, the main check on immediate satisfaction of his desires by each man, is the fear of other men's vengeance if they are injured by taking the satisfaction; and through early stages of social development, this dread of retaliation continues to be the chief motive to such forbearance as exists. But though long after political authority has become established the taking of personal satisfaction for injuries persists, the growth of political authority gradually checks it. The fact that success in war is endangered if his followers fight among themselves, forces itself on the attention of the ruler. He has a strong motive for restraining quarrels, and therefore for preventing the aggressions which cause quarrels; and as his power becomes greater he forbids the aggressions and inflicts punishments for disobedience.

Presently, political restraints of this class, like those of the preceding class, are enforced by religious restraints. The sagacious chief, succeeding in war partly because he thus enforces order among his followers, leaves behind him a tradition of the commands he habitually gave. Dread of his ghost tends to produce regard for these commands; and they eventually acquire sacredness. With further social evolution come, in like manner, further interdicts, checking aggressions of less serious kinds : until eventually there grows up a body of civil laws. And then in the way shown, arise beliefs concerning the divine disapproval of these minor, as well as of the major, civil offences : ending, occasionally, in a set of religious injunctions harmonizing with, and en-forcing, the political injunctions. While simultaneously there develops, as before, a social sanction for these rules of internal conduct, strengthening the political and religious sanctions.

But now observe that while these three controls, political, religious, and social, severally lead men to subordinate proximate satisfactions to remote satisfactions; and while they are in this respect like the moral control, which habi-tually requires the subjection of simple presentative feelings to complex representative feelings and postponement of present to future; yet they do not constitute the moral control, but are only preparatory to it—are controls within which the moral control evolves. The command of the political ruler is at first obeyed, not because of its perceived rectitude; but simply because it is his command, which there will be a penalty for disobeying. The check is not a mental representation of the evil consequences which the forbidden act will, in the nature of things, cause; but it is a mental representation of the factitious evil conse-quences. Down to our own time we trace in legal phrases, the original doctrine that the aggression of one citizen on another is wrong, and will be punished, not so much because of the injury done him, as because of the implied disregard of the king's will. Similarly, the sinfulness of breaking a divine injunction was universally at one time, and is still by many, held to consist in the disobedience to God, rather than in the deliberate entailing of injury; and even now it is a common belief that acts are right only if performed in conscious fulfilment of the divine will: nay; are even wrong if otherwise performed. The like holds, too, with that further control exercised by public opinion On listening to the remarks made respecting conformity to social rules, it is noticeable that breach of them is condemned not so much because of any essential impropriety as because the world's authority is ignored. How imperfectly the truly moral control is even now differentiated from these controls within which it has been evolving, we see in the fact that the systems of morality criticized at the outset, severally identify moral control with one or other of them. For moralists of one class derive moral rules from the commands of a supreme political power. Those of another class recognize no other origin for them than the revealed divine will. And though men who take social prescription for their guide do not formulate their doctrine, yet the belief, frequently betrayed, that conduct which society permits is not blameworthy, implies that there are those who think right and wrong can be made such by public opinion.

Before taking a further step we must put together the results of this analysis. The essential truths to be carried with us respecting these three forms of external control to which the social unit is subject, are these:—First, that they have evolved with the evolution of society, as means to social self-preservation, necessary under the conditions; and that, by implication, they are in the main congruous with one another. Second, that the correlative internal restraints generated in the social unit, are representations of remote results which are incidental rather than necessary—a legal penalty, a supernatural punishment, a social reprobation. Third, that these results, simpler and more directly wrought by personal agencies, can be more vividly conceived than can the results which, in the course of things, actions naturally entail; and the conceptions of them are therefore more potent over undeveloped minds. Fourth, that as with the restraints thus generated is always joined the thought of external coercion, there arises the notion of obligation; which so becomes habitually associated with the surrender of immediate special benefits for the sake of distant and general benefits. Fifth, that the moral control corresponds in large measure with the three controls thus originating, in respect of its injunctions; and corresponds, too, in the general nature of the mental processes producing conformity to those injunctions; but differs in their special nature.

§ 45. For now we are prepared to see that the restraints properly distinguished as moral, are unlike these restraints out of which they evolve, and with which they are long confounded, in this—they refer not to the extrinsic effects of actions but to their intrinsic effects. The truly moral deterrent from murder, is not constituted by a representation of hanging as a consequence, or by a representation of tortures in hell as a consequence, or by a representation of the horror and hatred excited in fellow men; but by a representation of the necessary natural results—the infliction of death-agony on the victim, the destruction of all his possibilities of happiness, the entailed sufferings to his belongings. Neither the thought of imprisonment, nor of divine anger, nor of social disgrace, is that which constitutes the moral check on theft; but the thought of injury to the person robbed, joined with a vague consciousness of the general evils caused by disregard of proprietary rights. Those who reprobate the adulterer on moral grounds, have their minds filled, not with ideas of an action for damages, or of future punishment following the breach of a commandment, or of loss of reputation; but they are occupied with ideas of unhappiness entailed on the aggrieved wife or husband, the damaged lives of children, and the diffused mischiefs which go along with disregard of the marriage tie. Conversely, the man who is moved by a moral feeling to help another in difficulty, does not picture to himself any reward here or hereafter; but pictures only the better condition he is trying to bring about. One who is morally prompted to fight against a social evil, has neither material benefit nor popular applause before his mind; but only the mischiefs he seeks to remove and the increased well-being which will follow their removal. Throughout, then, the moral motive differs from the motives it is associated with in this, that instead of being constituted by representations of incidental, collateral, non-necessary consequences of acts, it is constituted by representations of consequences which the acts naturally produce. These representations are not all distinct, though some of such are usually present; but they form an assemblage of indistinct representations accumulated by experience of the results of like acts in the life of the individual, super-posed on a still more indistinct but voluminous consciousness due to the inherited effects of such experiences in progenitors: forming a feeling that is at once massive and vague.

And now we see why the moral feelings and correlative restraints have arisen later than the feelings and restraints that originate from political, religious, and social authorities; and have so slowly, and even yet so incompletely, disentangled themselves. For only by these lower feelings and restraints could be maintained the conditions under which the higher feelings and restraints evolve. It is thus alike with the self-regarding feelings and with the other-regarding feelings. The pains which improvidence will bring, and the pleasures to be gained by storing up things for future use and by labouring to get such things, can be habitually contrasted in thought, only as fast as settled social arrangements make accumulation possible; and that there may arise such settled arrangements, fear of the seen ruler, of the unseen ruler, and of public opinion, must come into play. Only after political, religious, and social restraints have produced a stable community, can there be sufficient experience of the pains, positive and negative, sensational and emotional, which crimes of aggression cause, as to generate that moral aversion to them constituted by consciousness of their intrinsically evil results. And more manifest still is it that such a moral sentiment as that of abstract equity, which is offended not only by material injuries done to men but also by political arrangements that place them at a disadvantage, can evolve only after the social stage reached gives familiar experience both of the pains flowing directly from injustices and also of those flowing indirectly from the class-privileges which make injustices easy.

That the feelings called moral have the nature and origin alleged, is further shown by the fact that we associate the name with them in proportion to the degree in which they have these characters—firstly of being re-representative; secondly of being concerned with indirect rather than with direct effects, and generally with remote rather than immediate; and thirdly of referring to effects that are mostly general rather than special. Thus, though we condemn one man for extravagance and approve the economy shown by another man, we do not class their acts as respectively vicious and virtuous : these words are too strong : the present and future results here differ too little in concreteness and ideality to make the words fully applicable. Suppose, however, that the extravagance necessarily brings distress on wife and children—brings pains diffused over the lives of others as well as of self, and the viciousness of the extravagance becomes clear. Suppose, further, that prompted by the wish to relieve his family from the misery he has brought on them, the spendthrift forges a bill or commits some other fraud. Though, estimated apart, we characterize his overruling emotion as moral, and make allowance for him in consideration of it, yet his action taken as a whole we condemn as immoral: we regard as of superior authority, the feelings which respond to men's proprietary claims—feelings which are re-representative in a higher degree and refer to more remote diffused consequences. The difference, habitually recognized, between the relative elevations of justice and generosity, well illustrates this truth. The motive causing a generous act has reference to effects of a more concrete, special, and proximate kind, than has the motive to do justice; which, beyond the proximate effects, usually themselves less concrete than those that generosity contemplates, includes a consciousness of the distant, involved, diffused effects of maintaining equitable relations. And justice we hold to be higher generosity.

Comprehension of this long argument will be aided by here quoting a further passage from the before-named letter to Mr. Mill, following the passage already quoted from it.

"To make any position fully understood, it seems needful to add that, corresponding to the fundamental propositions of a developed Moral Science, there have been, and still are, developing in the race, certain fundamental moral intuitions; and that, though these moral intuitions are the results of accumulated experiences of Utility, gradually organized and inherited, they have come to be quite independent of conscious experience. Just in the same way that I believe the intuition of space, possessed by any living individual, to have arisen from organized and consolidated experiences of all antecedent individuals who bequeathed to him their slowly-developed nervous organizations—just as I believe that this intuition, requiring only to be made definite and complete by personal experiences, has practically become a form of thought, apparently quite independent of experience; so do I believe that the experiences of utility organized and consolidated through all past generations of the human race, have been producing corresponding nervous modifications, which, by continued transmission and accumulation, have become in us certain faculties of moral intuition—certain emotions responding to right and wrong conduct, which have no apparent basis in the individual experiences of utility. I also hold that just as the space-intuition responds to the exact demonstrations of Geometry, and has its rough conclusions interpreted and verified by them; so will moral intuitions respond to the demonstrations of Moral Science, and will have their rough conclusions interpreted and verified by them."

To this, in passing, I will add only that the evolution-hypothesis thus enables us to reconcile opposed moral theories, as it enables us to reconcile opposed theories of knowledge. For as the doctrine of innate forms of intellectual intuition falls into harmony with the experiential doctrine, when we recognize the production of intellectual faculties by inheritance of effects wrought by experience; so the doctrine of innate powers of moral perception becomes congruous with the utilitarian doctrine, when it is seen that preferences and aversions are rendered organic by inheritance of the effects of pleasurable and painful experiences in progenitors.

§ 46. One further question has to be answered—How does there arise the feeling of moral obligation in general? Whence comes the sentiment of duty, considered as distinct from the several sentiments which prompt temperance, providence, kindness, justice, truthfulness, &c. ? The answer is that it is an abstract sentiment generated in a manner analogous to that in which abstract ideas are generated.

The idea of each colour had originally entire concreteness given to it by an object possessing the colour; as some of the unmodified names, such as orange and violet, show us. The dissociation of each colour from the object specially associated with it in thought at the outset, went on as fast as the colour came to be associated in thought with objects unlike the first, and unlike one another. The idea of orange was conceived in the abstract more fully in proportion as the various orange-coloured objects remembered, cancelled one another's diverse attributes, and left outstanding their common attribute. So is it if we ascend a stage and note how there arises the abstract idea of colour apart from particular colours. Were all things red the conception of colour in the abstract could not exist. Imagine that every object was either red or green, and it is manifest that the mental habit would be to think of one or other of these two colours in connexion with anything named. But multiply the colours so that thought rambles undecidedly among the ideas of them that occur along with any object named, and there results the notion of indeterminate colour — the common property which objects possess of affecting us by light from their surfaces, as well as by their forms. For evidently the notion of this common property is that which remains constant while imagination is picturing every possible variety of colour. It is the uniform trait in all coloured things ; that is—colour in the abstract. Words referring to quantity furnish cases of more marked dissociation of abstract from concrete. Grouping various things as small in comparison either with those of their kind or with those of other kinds ; and similarly grouping some objects as comparatively great ; we get the opposite abstract notions of smallness and greatness. Applied as these are to innumerable very diverse things—not objects only, but forces, times, numbers, values,—they have become so little connected with concretes, that their abstract meanings are very vague. Further, we must note that an abstract idea thus formed often acquires an illusive independence ; as we may perceive in the case of motion, which, dissociated in thought from all particular bodies and velocities and directions, is sometimes referred to as though it could be conceived apart from something moving. Now all this holds of the subjective as well as of the objective ; and among other states of consciousness, holds of the emotions as known by introspection. By the grouping of those re-representative feelings above described, which, differing among themselves in other respects have a component in common ; and by the consequent mutual cancelling of their diverse components ; this common component is made relatively appreciable, and becomes an abstract feeling. Thus is produced the sentiment of moral obligation or duty. Let us observe its genesis.

We have seen that during the progress of animate existence, the later-evolved, more compound and more representative feelings, serving to adjust the conduct to more distant and general needs, have all along had an authority as guides superior to that of the earlier and simpler feelings —excluding cases in which these last are intense. This superior authority, unrecognizable by lower types of creatures which cannot generalize, and little recognizable by primitive men, who have but feeble powers of generalization, has become distinctly recognized as civilization and accompanying mental development have gone on. Accumulated experiences have produced the consciousness that guidance by feelings which refer to remote and general results, is usually more conducive to welfare than guidance by feelings to be immediately gratified. For what is the common character of the feelings that prompt honesty, truthfulness, diligence, providence, &c., which men habitually find to be better prompters than the appetites and simple impulses ? They are all complex, re-representative feelings, occupied with the future rather than the present. The idea of authoritativeness has therefore come to be connected with feelings having these traits : the implication being that the lower and simpler feelings are without authority. And this idea of authoritativeness is one element in the abstract consciousness of duty.

But there is another element—the element of coerciveness. This originates from experience of those several forms of restraint that have, as above described, established themselves in the course of civilization—the political, religious, and social. To the effects of punishments inflicted by law and public opinion on conduct of certain kinds, Dr. Bain ascribes the feeling of moral obligation. And I agree with him to the extent of thinking that by them is generated the sense of compulsion which the consciousness of duty includes, and which the word obligation indicates. The existence of an earlier and deeper element, generated as above described, is however, I think, implied by the fact that certain of the higher self-regarding feelings, instigating prudence and economy, have a moral authority in opposition to the simpler self-regarding feelings : showing that apart from any thought of factitious penalties on improvidence, the feeling constituted by representation of the natural penalties has acquired an acknowledged superiority. But accepting in the main the view that fears of the political and social penalties (to which, I think, the religious must be added) have generated that sense of coerciveness which goes along with the thought of postponing present to future and personal desires to the claims of others, it here chiefly concerns us to note that this sense of coerciveness becomes indirectly connected with the feelings distinguished as moral. For since the political, religious, and social restraining motives, are mainly formed of represented future results; and since the moral restraining motive is mainly formed of represented future results; it happens that the representations, having much in common, and being often aroused at the same time, the fear joined with three sets of them becomes, by association, joined with the fourth. Thinking of the extrinsic effects of a forbidden act, excites a dread which continues present while the intrinsic effects of the act are thought of; and being thus linked with these intrinsic effects causes a vague sense of moral compulsion. Emerging as the moral motive does but slowly from amidst the political, religious, and social motives, it long participates in that consciousness of subordination to some external agency which is joined with them; and only as it becomes distinct and predominant does it lose this associated consciousness—only then does the feeling of obligation fade.

This remark implies the tacit conclusion, which will be to most very startling, that the sense of duty or moral obligation is transitory, and will diminish as fast as moralization increases. Startling though it is, this conclusion may be satisfactorily defended. Even now progress towards the implied ultimate state is traceable. The observation is not

infrequent that persistence in performing a duty ends in
making it a pleasure; and this amounts to the admission
that while at first the motive contains an element of coercion,
at last this element of coercion dies out, and the act is
performed without any consciousness of being obliged to
perform it. The contrast between the youth on whom diligence is enjoined, and the man of business so absorbed in
affairs that he cannot be induced to relax, shows us how the
doing of work, originally under the consciousness that it
ought to be done, may eventually cease to have any such
accompanying consciousness. Sometimes, indeed, the relation
comes to be reversed; and the man of business persists in
work from pure love of it when told that he ought not.
Nor is it thus with self-regarding feelings only. That the
maintaining and protecting of wife by husband often result
solely from feelings directly gratified by these actions, without any thought of *must;* and that the fostering of children
by parents is in many cases made an absorbing occupation
without any coercive feeling of *ought;* are obvious truths
which show us that even now, with some of the fundamental
other-regarding duties, the sense of obligation has retreated
into the background of the mind. And it is in some degree
so with other-regarding duties of a higher kind. Conscien-
tiousness has in many out-grown that stage in which the
sense of a compelling power is joined with rectitude of
action. The truly honest man, here and there to be found,
is not only without thought of legal, religious, or social
compulsion, when he discharges an equitable claim on him;
but he is without thought of self-compulsion. He does
the right thing with a simple feeling of satisfaction in doing
it; and is, indeed, impatient if anything prevents him from
having the satisfaction of doing it.

Evidently, then, with complete adaptation to the social
state, that element in the moral consciousness which is expressed by the word obligation, will disappear. The higher
actions required for the harmonious carrying on of life,

will be as much matters of course as are those lower actions
which the simple desires prompt. In their proper times and
places and proportions, the moral sentiments will guide
men just as spontaneously and adequately as now do the
sensations. And though, joined with their regulating influence when this is called for, will exist latent ideas of the
evils which nonconformity would bring; these will occupy
the mind no more than do ideas of the evils of starvation
at the time when a healthy appetite is being satisfied by
a meal.

§ 47. This elaborate exposition, which the extreme complexity of the subject has necessitated, may have its leading
ideas re-stated thus :—

Symbolizing by *a* and *b*, related phenomena in the environment, which in some way concern the welfare of the
organism; and symbolizing by *c* and *d*, the impressions,
simple or compound, which the organism receives from the
one, and the motions, single or combined, by which its acts
are adapted to meet the other; we saw that psychology in
general is concerned with the connexion between the relation
a b and the relation *c d*. Further, we saw that by implication the psychological aspect of Ethics, is that aspect
under which the adjustment of *c d* to *a b*, appears, not as an
intellectual co-ordination simply, but as a co-ordination
in which pleasures and pains are alike factors and results.

It was shown that throughout Evolution, motive and
act become more complex, as the adaptation of inner
related actions to outer related actions extends in range
and variety. Whence followed the corollary that the
later-evolved feelings, more representative and re-representative in their constitution, and referring to remoter
and wider needs, have, on the average, an authority as
guides greater than have the earlier and simpler feelings.

After thus observing that even an inferior creature is
ruled by a hierarchy of feelings so constituted that general

welfare depends on a certain subordination of lower to higher, we saw that in man, as he passes into the social state, there arises the need for sundry additional subordinations of lower to higher : co-operation being made possible only by them. To the restraints constituted by mental representations of the intrinsic effects of actions, which, in their simpler forms, have been evolving from the beginning, are added the restraints caused by mental representations of extrinsic effects, in the shape of political, religious, and social penalties.

With the evolution of society, made possible by institutions maintaining order, and associating in men's minds the sense of obligation with prescribed acts and with desistances from forbidden acts, there arose opportunities for seeing the bad consequences naturally flowing from the conduct interdicted and the good consequences from the conduct required. Hence eventually grew up moral aversions and approvals : experience of the intrinsic effects necessarily here coming later than experience of the extrinsic effects, and therefore producing its results later.

The thoughts and feelings constituting these moral aversions and approvals, being all along closely connected with the thoughts and feelings constituting fears of political, religious, and social penalties, necessarily came to participate in the accompanying sense of obligation. The coercive element in the consciousness of duties at large, evolved by converse with external agencies which enforce duties, diffused itself by association through that consciousness of duty, properly called moral, which is occupied with intrinsic results instead of extrinsic results.

But this self-compulsion, which at a relatively-high stage becomes more and more a substitute for compulsion from without, must itself, at a still higher stage, practically disappear. If some action to which the special motive is insufficient, is performed in obedience to the feeling of moral obligation, the fact proves that the special faculty concerned is not yet equal to its function—has not acquired such strength that the required activity has become its normal activity, yielding its due amount of pleasure. With complete evolution then, the sense of obligation, not ordinarily present in consciousness, will be awakened only on those extraordinary occasions that prompt breach of the laws otherwise spontaneously conformed to.

And this brings us to the psychological aspect of that conclusion which, in the last chapter, was reached under its biological aspect. The pleasures and pains which the moral sentiments originate, will, like bodily pleasures and pains, become incentives and deterrents so adjusted in their strengths to the needs, that the moral conduct will be the natural conduct.

CHAPTER VIII.

THE SOCIOLOGICAL VIEW.

§ 48. Not for the human race only, but for every race, there are laws of right living. Given its environment and its structure, and there is for each kind of creature a set of actions adapted in their kinds, amounts, and combinations, to secure the highest conservation its nature permits. The animal, like the man, has needs for food, warmth, activity, rest, and so forth; which must be fulfilled in certain relative degrees to make its life whole. Maintenance of its race implies satisfaction of special desires, sexual and philoprogenitive, in due proportions. Hence there is a supposable formula for the activities of each species, which, could it be drawn out, would constitute a system of morality for that species. But such a system of morality would have little or no reference to the welfare of others than self and offspring. Indifferent to individuals of its own kind, as an inferior creature is, and habitually hostile to individuals of other kinds, the formula for its life could take no cognizance of the lives of those with which it came in contact; or rather, such formula would imply that maintenance of its life was at variance with maintenance of their lives.

But on ascending from beings of lower kinds to the highest kind of being, man; or, more strictly, on ascending

from man in his pre-social stage to man in his social stage;
the formula has to include an additional factor. Though
not peculiar to human life under its developed form, the
presence of this factor is still, in the highest degree,
characteristic of it. Though there are inferior species
displaying considerable degrees of sociality; and though
the formulas for their complete lives would have to take
account of the relations arising from union; yet our own
species is, on the whole, to be distinguished as having a
formula for complete life which specially recognizes the
relations of each individual to others, in presence of whom,
and in co-operation with whom, he has to live.

This additional factor in the problem of complete living,
is, indeed, so important that the necessitated modifications
of conduct have come to form a chief part of the code
of conduct. Because the inherited desires which directly
refer to the maintenance of individual life, are fairly
adjusted to the requirements, there has been no need to
insist on that conformity to them which furthers self-
conservation. Conversely, because these desires prompt
activities that often conflict with the activities of others;
and because the sentiments responding to other's claims
are relatively weak; moral codes emphasize those restraints
on conduct which the presence of fellow men entails.

From the sociological point of view, then, Ethics
becomes nothing else than a definite account of the forms
of conduct that are fitted to the associated state, in such
wise that the lives of each and all may be the greatest
possible, alike in length and breadth.

§ 49. But here we are met by a fact which forbids us thus
to put in the foreground the welfares of citizens, individually
considered, and requires us to put in the foreground the
welfare of the society as a whole. The life of the social
organism must, as an end, rank above the lives of its
units. These two ends are not harmonious at the outset;

and though the tendency is towards harmonization of them, they are still partially conflicting.

As fast as the social state establishes itself, the preservation of the society becomes a means of preserving its units. Living together arose because, on the average, it proved more advantageous to each than living apart; and this implies that maintenance of combination is maintenance of the conditions to more satisfactory living than the combined persons would otherwise have. Hence, social self-preservation becomes a proximate aim taking precedence of the ultimate aim, individual self-preservation.

This subordination of personal to social welfare is, however, contingent : it depends on the presence of antagonistic societies. So long as the existence of a community is endangered by the actions of communities around, it must remain true that the interests of individuals must be sacrificed to the interests of the community, as far as is needful for the community's salvation. But if this is manifest, it is, by implication, manifest, that when social antagonisms cease, this need for sacrifice of private claims to public claims ceases also ; or rather, there cease to be any public claims at variance with private claims. All along, furtherance of individual lives has been the ultimate end ; and if this ultimate end has been postponed to the proximate end of preserving the community's life, it has been so only because this proximate end was instrumental to the ultimate end. When the aggregate is no longer in danger, the final object of pursuit, the welfare of the units, no longer needing to be postponed, becomes the immediate object of pursuit.

Consequently, unlike sets of conclusions respecting human conduct emerge, according as we are concerned with a state of habitual or occasional war, or are concerned with a state of permanent and general peace. Let us glance at these alternative states and the alternative implications.

§ 50. At present the individual man has to carry on his

life with due regard to the lives of others belonging to the
same society; while he is sometimes called on to be
regardless of the lives of those belonging to other societies.
The same mental constitution having to fulfil both these
requirements, is necessarily incongruous; and the correlative
conduct, adjusted first to the one need and then to the other,
cannot be brought within any consistent ethical system.

Hate and destroy your fellow man, is now the command;
and then the command is, love and aid your fellow man. Use
every means to deceive, says the one code of conduct; while
the other code says, be truthful in word and deed. Seize
what property you can and burn all you cannot take away,
are injunctions which the religion of enmity countenances;
while by the religion of amity, theft and arson are condemned as crimes. And as conduct has to be made up of
parts thus at variance with one another, the theory of
conduct remains confused. There co-exists a
kindred irreconcilability between the sentiments answering
to the forms of co-operation required for militancy and
industrialism respectively. While social antagonisms are
habitual, and while, for efficient action against other societies,
there needs great subordination to men who command, the
virtue of loyalty and the duty of implicit obedience have to
be insisted on: disregard of the ruler's will is punished with
death. But when war ceases to be chronic, and growing
industrialism habituates men to maintaining their own
claims while respecting the claims of others, loyalty becomes
less profound, the authority of the ruler is questioned or
denied in respect of various private actions and beliefs.
State-dictation is in many directions successfully defied,
and the political independence of the citizen comes to be
regarded as a claim which it is virtuous to maintain and
vicious to yield up. Necessarily during the transition, these
opposite sentiments are incongruously mingled. So
is it, too, with domestic institutions under the two *regimes*.
While the first is dominant, ownership of a slave is honour-

able, and in the slave submission is praiseworthy; but as
the last grows dominant, slave-owning becomes a crime and
servile obedience excites contempt. Nor is it otherwise
in the family. The subjection of women to men, complete
while war is habitual but qualified as fast as peaceful occupations replace it, comes eventually to be thought wrong;
and equality before the law is asserted. At the same time
the opinion concerning paternal power changes. The once
unquestioned right of the father to take his children's lives is
denied; and the duty of absolute submission to him, long
insisted on, is changed into the duty of obedience within
reasonable limits.

Were the ratio between the life of antagonism with alien
societies, and the life of peaceful co-operation within each
society, a constant ratio, some permanent compromise between
the conflicting rules of conduct appropriate to the two lives
might be reached. But since this ratio is a variable one,
the compromise can never be more than temporary. Ever
the tendency is towards congruity between beliefs and
requirements. Either the social arrangements are gradually
changed until they come into harmony with prevailing ideas
and sentiments; or, if surrounding conditions prevent
change in the social arrangements, the necessitated habits
of life modify the prevailing ideas and sentiments to the
requisite extent. Hence, for each kind and degree of social
evolution determined by external conflict and internal
friendship, there is an appropriate compromise between
the moral code of enmity and the moral code of amity:
not, indeed, a definable, consistent compromise, but a compromise fairly well understood.

This compromise, vague, ambiguous, illogical, though it
may be, is nevertheless for the time being authoritative.
For if, as above shown, the welfare of the society
must take precedence of the welfares of its component
individuals, during those stages in which the individuals have
to preserve themselves by preserving their society; then

such temporary compromise between the two codes of conduct as duly regards external defence, while favouring internal co-operation to the greatest extent practicable, subserves the maintenance of life in the highest degree; and thus gains the ultimate sanction. So that the perplexed and inconsistent moralities of which each society and each age shows us a more or less different one, are severally justified as being approximately the best under the circumstances.

But such moralities are, by their definitions, shown to be long to incomplete conduct; not to conduct that is fully evolved. We saw that the adjustments of acts to ends which, while constituting the external manifestations of life conduce to the continuance of life, have been rising to a certain ideal form now approached by the civilized man. But this form is not reached so long as there continue aggressions of one society upon another. Whether the hindrances to complete living result from the trespasses of fellow-citizens, or from the trespasses of aliens, matters not: if they occur there does not yet exist the state defined. The limit to the evolution of conduct is arrived at by the members of each society only when, being arrived at by members of other societies also, the causes of international antagonism end simultaneously with the causes of antagonism between individuals.

And now having from the sociological point of view recognized the need for, and authority of, these changing systems of ethics, proper to changing ratios between warlike activities and peaceful activities, we have, from the same point of view, to consider the system of ethics proper to the state in which peaceful activities are undisturbed.

§ 51. If, excluding all thought of dangers or hindrances from causes external to a society, we set ourselves to specify those conditions under which the life of each person, and therefore of the aggregate, may be the greatest possible; we come upon certain simple ones which, as here stated, assume the form of truisms.

For, as we have seen, the definition of that highest life accompanying completely-evolved conduct, itself excludes all acts of aggression—not only murder, assault, robbery and the major offences generally, but minor offences, such as libel, injury to property and so forth. While directly deducting from individual life, these indirectly cause pertur-bations of social life. Trespasses against others rouse anta-gonisms in them; and if these are numerous the group loses coherence. Hence, whether the integrity of the group itself is considered as the end; or whether the end con-sidered is the benefit ultimately secured to its units by maintaining its integrity; or whether the immediate benefit of its units taken separately, is considered the end; the implication is the same : such acts are at variance with achievement of the end That these inferences are self-evident and trite (as indeed the first inferences drawn from the data of every science that reaches the deductive stage naturally are) must not make us pass lightly over the all-important fact that, from the sociological point of view, the leading moral laws are seen to follow as corollaries from the definition of complete life carried on under social conditions.

Respect for these primary moral laws is not enough, however. Associated men pursuing their several lives without injuring one another but without helping one another, reap no advantages from association beyond those of companionship. If, while there is no co-operation for defensive purposes (which is here excluded by the hypothesis) there is also no co-operation for satisfying wants, the social state loses its *raison d'être*—almost, if not entirely. There are, indeed, people who live in a condition little removed from this; as the Esquimaux. But though these, exhibiting none of the co-operation necessitated by war, which is unknown to them, lead lives such that each family is substantially independent of others, occasional co-operation occurs. And, indeed, that families should live in company without ever yielding mutual aid, is scarcely conceivable.

Nevertheless, whether actually existing or only approached, we must here recognize as hypothetically possible, a state in which these primary moral laws alone are conformed to ; for the purpose of observing, in their uncomplicated forms, what are the negative conditions to harmonious social life. Whether the members of a social group do or do not co-operate, certain limitations to their individual activities are necessitated by their association ; and after recognizing these as arising in the absence of co-operation, we shall be the better prepared to understand how conformity to them is effected when co-operation begins.

§ 52. For whether men live together in quite independent ways, careful only to avoid aggressing ; or whether, advancing from passive association to active association, they co-operate ; their conduct must be such that the achievement of ends by each shall at least not be hindered. And it becomes obvious that when they co-operate, there must not only be no resulting hindrance but there must be facilitation ; since in the absence of facilitation there can be no motive to co-operate. What shape, then, must the mutual restraints take when co-operation begins ? or rather— What, in addition to the primary mutual restraints already specified, are those secondary mutual restraints required to make co-operation possible ?

One who, living in an isolated way, expends effort in pursuit of an end, gets compensation for the effort by securing the end ; and so achieves satisfaction. If he expends the effort without achieving the end, there results dissatisfaction. The satisfaction and the dissatisfaction, are measures of success and failure in life-sustaining acts ; since that which is achieved by effort is something which directly or indirectly furthers life, and so pays for the cost of the effort ; while if the effort fails there is nothing to pay for the cost of it, and so much life is wasted.   What must result from this when men's efforts are joined ?   The reply will be made clearer if we take the successive forms of co-operation in the order of ascending complexity.   We may distinguish as homogeneous co-operation, (1), that in which like efforts are joined for like ends that are simultaneously enjoyed.   As co-operation that is not completely homogeneous, we may distinguish, (2), that in which like efforts are joined for like ends that are not simultaneously enjoyed.   A co-operation of which the heterogeneity is more distinct is, (3), that in which unlike efforts are joined for like ends.   And lastly comes the decidedly heterogeneous co-operation, (4), that in which unlike efforts are joined for unlike ends.

The simplest and earliest of these, in which men's powers, similar in kind and degree, are united in pursuit of a benefit which, when obtained, they all participate in, is most familiarly exemplified in the catching of game by primitive men : this simplest and earliest form of industrial co-operation being also that which is least differentiated from militant co-operation ; for the co-operators are the same, and the processes, both destructive of life, are carried on in analogous ways.   The condition under which such co-operation may be successfully carried on, is that the co-operators shall share alike in the produce.   Each thus being enabled to repay himself in food for the expended effort, and being further enabled to achieve other such desired ends as maintenance of family, obtains satisfaction : there is no aggression of one on another, and the co-operation is harmonious.   Of course the divided produce can be but roughly proportioned to the several efforts joined in obtaining it ; but there is actually among savages, as we see that for harmonious co-operation there must be, a recognition of the principle that efforts when combined shall severally bring equivalent benefits, as they would do if they were separate.   Moreover, beyond the taking equal shares in return for labours that are approximately equal, there is generally an   attempt

at proportioning benefit to achievement, by assigning something extra, in the shape of the best part or the trophy, to
the actual slayer of the game. And obviously, if there is a
wide departure from this system of sharing benefits when
there has been a sharing of efforts, the co-operation will
cease. Individual hunters will prefer to do the best they
can for themselves separately.

Passing from this simplest case of co-operation to a case
not quite so simple—a case in which the homogeneity is
incomplete—let us ask how a member of the group may be
led without dissatisfaction to expend effort in achieving a
benefit which, when achieved, is enjoyed exclusively by
another? Clearly he may do this on condition that the other
shall afterwards expend a like effort, the beneficial result of
which shall be similarly rendered up by him in return. This
exchange of equivalents of effort is the form which social co-
operation takes while yet there is little or no division of labour
save that between the sexes. For example, the Bodo and
Dhimals " mutually assist each other for the nonce, as well in
constructing their houses as in clearing their plots for culti-
vation." And this principle—I will help you if you will
help me—common in simple communities where the occupations are alike in kind, and occasionally acted upon in more
advanced communities, is one under which the relation
between effort and benefit, no longer directly maintained, is
maintained indirectly. For whereas when men's activities
are carried on separately, or are joined in the way
exemplified above, effort is immediately paid for by benefit,
in this form of co-operation the benefit achieved by effort is
exchanged for a like benefit to be afterwards received when
asked for. And in this case as in the preceding case, co-
operation can be maintained only by fulfilment of the tacit
agreements. For if they are habitually not fulfilled, there
will commonly be refusal to give aid when asked ; and each
man will be left to do the best he can by himself. All those
advantages to be gained by union of efforts in doing

things that are beyond the powers of the single individual, will be unachievable. At the outset, then, fulfilment of contracts that are implied if not expressed, becomes a condition to social co-operation; and therefore to social development.

From these simple forms of co-operation in which the labours men carry on are of like kinds, let us turn to the more complex forms in which they carry on labours of unlike kinds. Where men mutually aid in building huts or felling trees, the number of days' work now given by one to another, is readily balanced by an equal number of days' work afterwards given by the other to him. And no estimation of the relative values of the labours being required, a definite understanding is little needed. But when division of labour arises—when there come transactions between one who makes weapons and another who dresses skins for clothing, or between a grower of roots and a catcher of fish —neither the relative amounts nor the relative qualities of their labours admit of easy measure; and with the multiplication of businesses, implying numerous kinds of skill and power, there ceases to be anything like manifest equivalence between either the bodily and mental efforts set against one another, or between their products. Hence the arrangement cannot now be taken for granted, as while the things exchanged are like in kind: it has to be stated. If A allows B to appropriate a product of his special skill, on condition that he is allowed to appropriate a different product of B's special skill, it results that as equivalence of the two products cannot be determined by direct comparison of their quantities and qualities, there must be a distinct understanding as to how much of the one may be taken in consideration of so much of the other.

Only under voluntary agreement, then, no longer tacit and vague but overt and definite, can co-operation be harmoniously carried on when division of labour becomes established. And as in the simplest co-operation, where like efforts are joined to secure a common good, the dissatisfaction caused in those who, having expended their labours do not get their shares of the good, prompts them to cease co-operating; as in the more advanced co-operation, achieved by exchanging equal labours of like kind expended at different times, aversion to co-operate is generated if the expected equivalent of labour is not rendered; so in this developed co-operation, the failure of either to surrender to the other that which was avowedly recognized as of like value with the labour or product given, tends to prevent co-operation by exciting discontent with its results. And evidently, while antagonisms thus caused impede the lives of the units, the life of the aggregate is endangered by diminished cohesion.

§ 53. Beyond these comparatively direct mischiefs, special and general, there have to be noted indirect mischiefs. As already implied by the reasoning in the last paragraph, not only social integration but also social differentiation, is hindered by breach of contract.

In Part II of the *Principles of Sociology,* it was shown that the fundamental principles of organization are the same for an individual organism and for a social organism; because both consist of mutually-dependent parts. In the one case as in the other, the assumption of unlike activities by the component members, is possible only on condition that they severally benefit in due degrees by one another's activities. That we may the better see what are the implications in respect of social structures, let us first note the implications in respect of individual structures.

The welfare of a living body implies an approximate equilibrium between waste and repair. If the activities involve an expenditure not made good by nutrition, dwindling follows. If the tissues are enabled to take up from the blood enriched by food, fit substances enough to replace those used up in efforts made, the weight may be maintained. And if the gain exceeds the loss, growth results. That which is true of the whole in its relations to the external world, is no less true of the parts in their relations to one another. Each organ, like the entire organism, is wasted by performing its function, and has to restore itself from the materials brought to it. If the quantity of materials furnished by the joint agency of the other organs is deficient, the particular organ dwindles. If they are sufficient, it can maintain its integrity. If they are in excess, it is enabled to increase. To say that this arrangement constitutes the physiological contract, is to use a metaphor which, though not true in aspect is true in essence. For the relations of structures are actually such that, by the help of a central regulative system, each organ is supplied with blood in proportion to the work it does. As was pointed out (*Principles of Sociology*, § 254) well-developed animals are so constituted that each muscle or viscus, when called into action, sends to the vaso-motor centres through certain nerve-fibres, an impulse caused by its action; whereupon through other nerve-fibres, there comes an impulse causing dilatation of its blood-vessels. That is to say, all other parts of the organism when they jointly require it to labour, forthwith begin to pay it in blood. During the ordinary state of physiological equilibrium, the loss and the gain balance, and the organ does not sensibly change. If the amount of its function is increased within such moderate limits that the local blood-vessels can bring adequately-increased supplies, the organ grows : beyond replacing its losses by its gains, it makes a profit on its extra transactions; so being enabled by extra structures to meet extra demands. But if the demands made on it become so great that the supply of materials cannot keep pace with the expenditure, either because the local blood-vessels are not large enough or for any other reason; then the organ begins to decrease from excess of waste over repair : there sets in what is known as atrophy. Now since each of the organs has thus to be paid in nutriment for its services by the rest; it follows that the due balancing of their respective claims and payments is requisite, directly for the welfare of each organ, and indirectly for the welfare of the organism. For in a whole formed of mutually-dependent parts, anything which prevents due performance of its duty by one part reacts injuriously on all the parts.

With change of terms these statements and inferences hold of a society. That social division of labour which parallels in so many other respects the physiological division of labour, parallels it in this respect also. As was shown at large in the *Principles of Sociology*, Part II, each order of functionaries and each group of producers, severally performing some action or making some article not for direct satisfaction of their own needs but for satisfaction of the needs of fellow-citizens in general, otherwise occupied, can continue to do this only so long as the expenditures of effort and returns of profit are approximately equivalent. Social organs like individual organs remain stationary if there come to them normal proportions of the commodities produced by the society as a whole. If because the demands made on an industry or profession are unusually great, those engaged in it make excessive profits, more citizens flock to it and the social structure constituted by its members grows; while decrease of the demands and therefore of the profits, either leads its members to choose other careers or stops the accessions needful to replace those who die, and the structure dwindles. Thus is maintained that proportion among the powers of the component parts which is most conducive to the welfare of the whole.

And now mark that the primary condition to achievement of this result is fulfilment of contract. If from the members of any part payment is frequently withheld, or falls short of the promised amount, then, through ruin of some and abandonment of the occupation by others, the part diminishes; and if it was before not more than

10

competent to its duty, it now becomes incompetent, and the society suffers. Or if social needs throw on some part great increase of function, and the members of it are enabled to get for their services unusually high prices; fulfilment of the agreements to give them these high prices, is the only way of drawing to the part such additional number of members as will make it equal to the augmented demands. For citizens will not come to it if they find the high prices agreed upon are not paid.

Briefly, then, the universal basis of co-operation is the proportioning of benefits received to services rendered. Without this there can be no physiological division of labour; without this there can be no sociological division of labour. And since division of labour, physiological or sociological, profits the whole and each part; it results that on maintenance of the arrangements necessary to it, depend both special and general welfare. In a society such arrangements are maintained only if bargains, overt or tacit, are carried out. So that beyond the primary requirement to harmonious co-existence in a society, that its units shall not directly aggress on one another; there comes this secondary requirement, that they shall not indirectly aggress by breaking agreements.

§ 54. But now we have to recognize the fact that complete fulfilment of these conditions, original and derived, is not enough. Social co-operation may be such that no one is impeded in the obtainment of the normal return for effort, but contrariwise is aided by equitable exchange of services; and yet much may remain to be achieved. There is a theoretically-possible form of society, purely industrial in its activities, which, though approaching nearer to the moral ideal in its code of conduct than any society not purely industrial, does not fully reach it.

For while industrialism requires the life of each citizen to be such that it may be carried on without direct or indirect aggressions on other citizens, it does not require his life to be such that it shall directly further the lives of other citizens. It is not a necessary implication of industrialism, as thus far defined, that each, beyond the benefits given and received by exchange of services, shall give and receive other benefits. A society is conceivable formed of men leading perfectly inoffensive lives, scrupulously fulfilling their contracts, and efficiently rearing their offspring, who yet, yielding to one another no advantages beyond those agreed upon, fall short of that highest degree of life which the gratuitous rendering of services makes possible. Daily experiences prove that every one would suffer many evils and lose many goods, did none give him unpaid assistance. The life of each would be more or less damaged had he to meet all contingencies single-handed. Further, if no one did for his fellows anything more than was required by strict performance of contract, private interests would suffer from the absence of attention to public interests. The limit of evolution of conduct is consequently not reached, until, beyond avoidance of direct and indirect injuries to others, there are spontaneous efforts to further the welfare of others.

It may be shown that the form of nature which thus to justice adds beneficence, is one which adaptation to the social state produces. The social man has not reached that harmonization of constitution with conditions forming the limit of evolution, so long as there remains space for the growth of faculties which, by their exercise, bring positive benefit to others and satisfaction to self. If the presence of fellow-men, while putting certain limits to each man's sphere of activity, opens certain other spheres of activity in which feelings while achieving their gratifications, do not diminish but add to the gratifications of others, then such spheres will inevitably be occupied. Recognition of this truth does not, however, call on us to qualify greatly that conception of the industrial

10 *

state above set forth; since sympathy is the root of both justice and beneficence.

§ 55. Thus the sociological view of Ethics supplements the physical, the biological, and the psychological views, by disclosing those conditions under which only associated activities can be so carried on, that the complete living of each consists with, and conduces to, the complete living of all.

At first the welfare of social groups, habitually in antagonism with other such groups, takes precedence of individual welfare; and the rules of conduct which are authoritative for the time being, involve incompleteness of individual life that the general life may be maintained. At the same time the rules have to enforce the claims of individual life as far as may be; since on the welfare of the units the welfare of the aggregate largely depends.

In proportion as societies endanger one another less, the need for subordinating individual lives to the general life, decreases; and with approach to a peaceful state, the general life, having from the beginning had furtherance of individual lives as its ultimate purpose, comes to have this as its proximate purpose.

During the transitional stages there are necessitated successive compromises between the moral code which asserts the claims of the society *versus* those of the individual, and the moral code which asserts the claims of the individual *versus* those of the society. And evidently each such compromise, though for the time being authoritative, admits of no consistent or definite expression.

But gradually as war declines—gradually as the compulsory co-operation needful in dealing with external enemies becomes unnecessary, and leaves behind the voluntary co-operation which effectually achieves internal sustentation; there grows increasingly clear the code of conduct which voluntary co-operation implies. And this final permanent code alone admits of being definitely formulated, and so constituting ethics as a science in contrast with empirical ethics.

The leading traits of a code under which complete living through voluntary co-operation is secured, may be simply stated. The fundamental requirement is that the life-sustaining actions of each shall severally bring him the amounts and kinds of advantage naturally achieved by them; and this implies firstly that he shall suffer no direct aggressions on his person or property, and secondly that he shall suffer no indirect aggressions by breach of contract. Observance of these negative conditions to voluntary co-operation having facilitated life to the greatest extent by exchange of services under agreement, life is to be further facilitated by exchange of services beyond agreement: the highest life being reached only when, besides helping to complete one another's lives by specified reciprocities of aid, men otherwise help to complete one another's lives.

CHAPTER IX.

CRITICISMS AND EXPLANATIONS.

§ 56. Comparisons of the foregoing chapters with one another, suggest sundry questions which must be answered partially, if not completely, before anything can be done towards reducing ethical principles from abstract forms to concrete forms.

We have seen that to admit the desirableness of conscious existence, is to admit that conduct should be such as will produce a consciousness which is desirable—a consciousness which is as much pleasurable and as little painful as may be. We have also seen that this necessary implication corresponds with the *à priori* inference, that the evolution of life has been made possible only by the establishment of connexions between pleasures and beneficial actions and between pains and detrimental actions. But the general conclusion reached in both of these ways, though it covers the area within which our special conclusions must fall, does not help us to reach those special conclusions.

Were pleasures all of one kind, differing only in degree; were pains all of one kind, differing only in degree; and could pleasures be measured against pains with definite results; the problems of conduct would be greatly simplified. Were the pleasures and pains serving as incentives and deterrents, simultaneously present to consciousness with like vividness, or were they all immediately impending, or were they all equi-distant in time; the problems would be further simplified. And they would be still further simplified if the pleasures and pains were exclusively those of the actor. But both the desirable and the undesirable feelings are of various kinds, making quantitative comparisons difficult; some are present and some are future, increasing the difficulty of quantitative comparison; some are entailed on self and some are entailed on others; again increasing the difficulty. So that the guidance yielded by the primary principle reached, is of little service unless supplemented by the guidance of secondary principles.

Already, in recognizing the needful subordination of presentative feelings to representative feelings, and the implied postponement of present to future throughout a wide range of cases, some approach towards a secondary principle of guidance has been made. Already, too, in recognizing the limitations which men's associated state puts to their actions, with the implied need for restraining feelings of some kinds by feelings of other kinds, we have come in sight of another secondary principle of guidance. Still, there remains much to be decided respecting the relative claims of these guiding principles, general and special.

Some elucidation of the questions involved, will be obtained by here discussing certain views and arguments set forth by past and present moralists.

§ 57. Using the name hedonism for that ethical theory which makes happiness the end of action; and distinguishing hedonism into the two kinds, egoistic and universalistic, according as the happiness sought is that of the actor himself or is that of all, Mr. Sidgwick alleges its implied belief to be that pleasures and pains are commensurable. In his criticism on (empirical) egoistic hedonism he says:—

"The fundamental assumption of Hedonism, clearly stated, is that all feelings considered merely as feelings can be arranged in a certain scale of desirability, so that the desirability or pleasantness of each bears a definite ratio to that of all the others."—*Methods of Ethics*, 2nd ed. p. 115.

And asserting this to be its assumption, he proceeds to point out difficulties in the way of the hedonistic calculation; apparently for the purpose of implying that these difficulties tell against the hedonistic theory.

Now though it may be shown that by naming the intensity, the duration, the certainty, and the proximity, of a pleasure or a pain, as traits entering into the estimation of its relative value, Bentham has committed himself to the specified assumption; and though it is perhaps reasonably taken for granted that hedonism as represented by him, is identical with hedonism at large; yet it seems to me that the hedonist, empirical or other, is not necessarily committed to this assumption. That the greatest surplus of pleasures over pains ought to be the end of action, is a belief which he may still consistently hold after admitting that the valuations of pleasures and pains are commonly vague and often erroneous. He may say that though indefinite things do not admit of definite measurements, yet approximately true estimates of their relative values may be made when they differ considerably; and he may further say that even when their relative values are not determinable, it remains true that the most valuable should be chosen. Let us listen to him.

"A debtor who cannot pay me, offers to compound for his debt by making over one of sundry things he possesses— a diamond ornament, a silver vase, a picture, a carriage. Other questions being set aside, I assert it to be my pecuniary interest to choose the most valuable of these; but I cannot say which is the most valuable. Does the proposition that it is my pecuniary interest to choose the most valuable therefore become doubtful? Must I not choose as well as I can; and if I choose wrongly must I give up my ground of choice? Must I infer that in matters of business I may not act on the principle that, other things equal, the more profitable transaction is to be preferred; because in many cases I cannot say which is the more profitable, and have often chosen the less profitable? Because I believe that of many dangerous courses I ought to take the least dangerous, do I make 'the fundamental assumption' that courses can be arranged according to a scale of dangerousness; and must I abandon my belief if I cannot so arrange them? If I am not by consistency bound to do this, then I am no more by consistency bound to give up the principle that the greatest surplus of pleasures over pains should be the end of action, because the 'commensurability of pleasures and pains' cannot be asserted."

At the close of his chapters on empirical hedonism, Mr. Sidgwick himself says he does "not think that the common experience of mankind, impartially examined, really sustains the view that Egoistic Hedonism is necessarily suicidal;" adding, however, that the "uncertainty of hedonistic calculation cannot be denied to have great weight." But here the fundamental assumption of hedonism, that happiness is the end of action, is still supposed to involve the assumption that "feelings can be arranged in a certain scale of desirability." This we have seen it does not: its fundamental assumption is in no degree invalidated by proof that such arrangement of them is impracticable.

To Mr. Sidgwick's argument there is the further objection, no less serious, that to whatever degree it tells against egoistic hedonism, it tells in a greater degree against universalistic hedonism, or utilitarianism. He admits that it tells as much; saying "whatever weight is to be attached to the objections brought against this assumption [the commensurability of pleasures and pains] must of course tell against the present method." Not only does it tell, but it tells in a double way. I do not mean merely that, as he points out, the assumption becomes greatly complicated if we take all sentient beings into account, and if we include posterity along with existing individuals. I mean that, taking as the end to be achieved the greatest happiness of the existing individuals forming a single community, the set of difficulties standing in the way of egoistic hedonism, is compounded with another set of difficulties no less great, when we pass from it to universalistic hedonism. For if the dictates of universalistic hedonism are to be fulfilled, it must be under the guidance of individual judgments, or of corporate judgments, or of both. Now any one of such judgments issuing from a single mind, or from any aggregate of minds, necessarily embodies conclusions respecting the happinesses of other persons; few of them known, and the great mass never seen. All these persons have natures differing in countless ways and degrees from the natures of those who form the judgments; and the happinesses of which they are severally capable differ from one another, and differ from the happinesses of those who form the judgments. Consequently, if against the method of egoistic hedonism there is the objection that a man's own pleasures and pains, unlike in their kinds, intensities, and times of occurrence, are incommensurable ; then against the method of universalistic hedonism it may be urged that to the incommensurability of each judge's own pleasures and pains (which he must use as standards) has now to be added the much more decided incommensurability of the pleasures and pains which he conceives to be experienced by innumerable other persons, all differently constituted from himself and from one another.

Nay more—there is a triple set of difficulties in the way of universalistic hedonism. To the double indeterminateness of the end has to be added the indeterminateness of the means. If hedonism, egoistic or universalistic, is to pass from dead theory into living practice, acts of one or other kind must be decided on to achieve proposed objects ; and in estimating the two methods we have to consider how far the fitness of the acts respectively required can be judged. If, in pursuing his own ends, the individual is liable to be led by erroneous opinions to adjust his acts wrongly, much more liable is he to be led by erroneous opinions to

adjust wrongly more complex acts to the more complex ends
constituted by other men's welfares. It is so if he operates
singly to benefit a few others; and it is still more so if he
co-operates with many to benefit all. Making general
happiness the immediate object of pursuit, implies numerous
and complicated instrumentalities officered by thousands of
unseen and unlike persons, and working on millions of
other persons unseen and unlike. Even the few factors in
this immense aggregate of appliances and processes which
are known, are very imperfectly known; and the great mass
of them are unknown. So that even supposing valuation
of pleasures and pains for the community at large is more
practicable than, or even as practicable as, valuation of his
own pleasures and pains by the individual; yet the ruling of
conduct with a view to the one end is far more difficult than
the ruling of it with a view to the other. Hence if the
method of egoistic hedonism is unsatisfactory, far more unsatisfactory for the same and kindred reasons, is the method
of universalistic hedonism, or utilitarianism.

And here we come in sight of the conclusion which it
has been the purpose of the foregoing criticism to bring
into view. The objection made to the hedonistic method
contains a truth, but includes with it an untruth. For
while the proposition that happiness, whether individual or
general, is the end of action, is not invalidated by proof that
it cannot under either form be estimated by measurement
of its components; yet it may be admitted that guidance
in the pursuit of happiness by a mere balancing of pleasures
and pains, is, if partially practicable throughout a certain
range of conduct, futile throughout a much wider range. It
is quite consistent to assert that happiness is the ultimate
aim of action, and at the same time to deny that it can
be reached by making it the immediate aim. I go with
Mr. Sidgwick as far as the conclusion that "we must at least
admit the desirability of confirming or correcting the results
of such comparisons [of pleasures and pains] by any other

method upon which we may find reason to rely;" and I then go further, and say that throughout a large part of conduct guidance by such comparisons is to be entirely set aside and replaced by other guidance.

§ 58. The antithesis here insisted upon between the hedonistic end considered in the abstract, and the method which current hedonism, whether egoistic or universalistic, associates with that end ; and the joining acceptance of the one with rejection of the other; commits us to an overt discussion of these two cardinal elements of ethical theory. I may conveniently initiate this discussion by criticizing another of Mr. Sidgwick's criticisms on the method of hedonism.

Though we can give no account of those simple pleasures which the senses yield, because they are undecomposable, yet we distinctly know their characters as states of consciousness. Conversely, the complex pleasures formed by compounding and re-compounding the ideas of simple pleasures, though theoretically resolvable into their components, are not easy to resolve ; and in proportion as they are heterogeneous in composition, the difficulty of framing intelligible conceptions of them increases. This is especially the case with the pleasures which accompany our sports. Treating of these, along with the pleasures of pursuit in general, for the purpose of showing that "in order to get them one must forget them," Mr. Sidgwick remarks :—

"A man who maintains throughout an epicurean mood, fixing his aim on his own pleasure, does not catch the full spirit of the chase ; his eagerness never gets just the sharpness of edge which imparts to the pleasure its highest zest and flavour. Here comes into view what we may call the fundamental paradox of Hedonism, that the impulse towards pleasure, if too predominant, defeats its own aim. This effect is not visible, or at any rate is scarcely visible, in the case of passive sensual pleasures. But of our active enjoyments generally, whether the activities on which they attend are classed as 'bodily' or as 'intellectual' (as well as of many emotional pleasures), it may certainly be said that we cannot attain them, at least in their best form, so long as we concentrate our aim on them."—*Methods of Ethics*, 2nd ed. p. 41.

Now I think we shall not regard this truth as paradoxical

after we have duly analyzed the pleasure of pursuit. The chief components of this pleasure are;—first, a renewed consciousness of personal efficiency (made vivid by actual success and partially excited by impending success) which consciousness of personal efficiency, connected in experience with achieved ends of every kind, arouses a vague but massive consciousness of resulting gratifications; and, second, a representation of the applause which recognition of this efficiency by others has before brought, and will again bring. Games of skill show us this clearly. Considered as an end in itself, the good cannon which a billiard player makes yields no pleasure. Whence then does the pleasure of making it arise? Partly from the fresh proof of capability which the player gives to himself, and partly from the imagined admiration of those who witness the proof of his capability: the last being the chief, since he soon tires of making cannons in the absence of witnesses. When from games which, yielding the pleasures of success, yield no pleasure derived from the end considered intrinsically, we pass to sports in which the end has intrinsic value as a source of pleasure, we see substantially the same thing. Though the bird which the sportsman brings down is useful as food, yet his satisfaction arises mainly from having made a good shot, and from having added to the bag which will presently bring praise of his skill. The gratification of self-esteem he immediately experiences; and the gratification of receiving applause he experiences, if not immediately and in full degree, yet by representation; for the ideal pleasure is nothing else than a faint revival of the real pleasure. These two kinds of agreeable excitement present in the sportsman during the chase, constitute the mass of the desires stimulating him to continue it; for all desires are nascent forms of the feelings to be obtained by the efforts they prompt. And though while seeking more birds these representative feelings are not so vividly excited as by success just achieved, yet they are excited by

imaginations of further successes; and so make enjoyable
the activities constituting the pursuit. Recognizing, then,
the truth that the pleasures of pursuit are much more those
derived from the efficient use of means than those derived
from the end itself, we see that "the fundamental paradox
of hedonism" disappears.

These remarks concerning end and means, and the pleasure
accompanying use of the means as added to the pleasure
derived from the end, I have made for the purpose of
drawing attention to a fact of profound significance. During
evolution there has been a superposing of new and more
complex sets of means upon older and simpler sets of means;
and a superposing of the pleasures accompanying the
uses of these successive sets of means; with the result that
each of these pleasures has itself eventually become an end.
We begin with a simple animal which, without ancillary
appliances, swallows such food as accident brings in its way;
and so, as we may assume, stills some kind of craving.
Here we have the primary end of nutrition with its accompanying satisfaction, in their simple forms. We pass to
higher types having jaws for seizing and biting—jaws which
thus, by their actions, facilitate achievement of the primary
end. On observing animals furnished with these organs,
we get evidence that the use of them becomes in itself
pleasurable irrespective of the end: instance a squirrel, which,
apart from food to be so obtained, delights in nibbling everything it gets hold of. Turning from jaws to limbs we see
that these, serving some creatures for pursuit and others
for escape, similarly yield gratification by their exercise; as
in lambs which skip and horses which prance. How the
combined use of limbs and jaws, originally subserving the
satisfaction of appetite, grows to be in itself pleasurable, is
daily illustrated in the playing of dogs. For that throwing
down and worrying which, when prey is caught, precedes
eating, is, in their mimic fights, carried by each as far as he
dares. Coming to means still more remote from the end,

namely, those by which creatures chased are caught, we are again shown by dogs that when no creature is caught there is still a gratification in the act of catching. The eagerness with which a dog runs after stones, or dances and barks in anticipation of jumping into the water after a stick, proves that apart from the satisfaction of appetite, and apart even from the satisfaction of killing prey, there is a satisfaction in the successful pursuit of a moving object. Throughout, then, we see that the pleasure attendant on the use of means to achieve an end, itself becomes an end.

Now if we contemplate these as phenomena of conduct in general, some facts worthy of note may be discerned—facts which, if we appreciate their significance, will aid us in developing our ethical conceptions. One of them is that among the successive sets of means, the later are the more remote from the primary end; are, as co-ordinating earlier and simpler means, the more complex; and are accompanied by feelings which are more representative. Another fact is that each set of means, with its accompanying satisfactions, eventually becomes in its turn dependent on one originating later than itself. Before the gullet swallows, the jaws must lay hold; before the jaws tear out and bring within the grasp of the gullet a piece fit for swallowing, there must be that co-operation of limbs and senses required for killing the prey; before this co-operation can take place, there needs the much longer co-operation constituting the chase; and even before this there must be persistent activities of limbs, eyes, and nose, in seeking prey. The pleasure attending each set of acts, while making possible the pleasure attending the set of acts which follows, is joined with a representation of this subsequent set of acts and its pleasure, and of the others which succeed in order; so that along with the feelings accompanying the search for prey, are partially aroused the feelings accompanying the actual chase, the actual destruction, the actual devouring, and the eventual satisfaction of appetite. A third fact is that the use of each set of means in due order, constitutes an obligation. Maintenance of its life being regarded as the end of its conduct, the creature is obliged to use in succession the means of finding prey, the means of catching prey, the means of killing prey, the means of devouring prey. Lastly, it follows that though the assuaging of hunger, directly associated with sustentation, remains to the last the ultimate end; yet the successful use of each set of means in its turn is the proximate end—the end which takes temporary precedence in authoritativeness.

§ 59. The relations between means and ends thus traced throughout the earlier stages of evolving conduct, are traceable throughout later stages; and hold true of human conduct, up even to its highest forms. As fast as, for the better maintenance of life, the simpler sets of means and the pleasures accompanying the uses of them, come to be supplemented by the more complex sets of means and their pleasures, these begin to take precedence in time and in imperativeness. To use effectually each more complex set of means becomes the proximate end, and the accompanying feeling becomes the immediate gratification sought; though there may be, and habitually is, an associated consciousness of the remoter ends and remoter gratifications to be obtained. An example will make clear the parallelism.

Absorbed in his business the trader, if asked what is his main end, will say—making money. He readily grants that achievement of this end is desired by him in furtherance of ends beyond it. He knows that in directly seeking money he is indirectly seeking food, clothes, house-room, and the comforts of life for self and family. But while admitting that money is but a means to these ends, he urges that the money-getting actions precede in order of time and obligation, the various actions and concomitant pleasures subserved by them; and he testifies to the fact that making money has become itself an end, and success in it a source of satisfaction, apart from these more distant ends.   Again, on observing more closely the trader's proceedings, we find that though to the end of living comfortably he gets money, and though to the end of getting money he buys and sells at a profit, which so becomes a means more immediately pursued, yet he is chiefly occupied with means still more remote from ultimate ends, and in relation to which even the selling at a profit becomes an end. For leaving to subordinates the actual measuring out of goods and receiving of proceeds, he busies himself mainly with his general affairs— inquiries concerning markets, judgments of future prices, calculations, negotiations, correspondence : the anxiety from hour to hour being to do well each one of these things indirectly conducive to the making of profits. And these ends precede in time and obligation the effecting of profitable sales, just as the effecting of profitable sales precedes the end of money-making, and just as the end of money-making precedes the end of satisfactory living.   His book-keeping best exemplifies the principle at large. Entries to the debtor or creditor sides are being made all through the day ; the items are classified and arranged in such way that at a moment's notice the state of each account may be ascertained ; and then, from time to time, the books are balanced, and it is required that the result shall come right to a penny : satisfaction following proved correctness, and annoyance being caused by error. If you ask why all this elaborate process, so remote from the actual getting of money, and still more remote from the enjoyments of life, the answer is that keeping accounts correctly is fulfilling a condition to the end of money-making, and becomes in itself a proximate end—a duty to be discharged, that there may be discharged the duty of getting an income, that there may be discharged the duty of maintaining self, wife, and children.

11

Approaching as we here do to moral obligation, are we not shown its relations to conduct at large? Is it not clear that observance of moral principles is fulfilment of certain general conditions to the successful carrying on of special activities? That the trader may prosper, he must not only keep his books correctly, but must pay those he employs according to agreement, and must meet his engagements with creditors. May we not say, then, that conformity to the second and third of these requirements is, like conformity to the first, an indirect means to effectual use of the more direct means of achieving welfare? May we not say, too, that as the use of each more indirect means in due order becomes itself an end, and a source of gratification; so, eventually, becomes the use of this most indirect means? And may we not infer that though conformity to moral requirements precedes in imperativeness conformity to other requirements; yet that this imperativeness arises from the fact that fulfilment of the other requirements, by self or others or both, is thus furthered?

§ 60. This question brings us round to another side of the issue before raised. When alleging that empirical utilitarianism is but introductory to rational utilitarianism, I pointed out that the last does not take welfare for its immediate object of pursuit, but takes for its immediate object of pursuit conformity to certain principles which, in the nature of things, causally determine welfare. And now we see that this amounts to recognition of that law, traceable throughout the evolution of conduct in general, that each later and higher order of means takes precedence in time and authoritativeness of each earlier and lower order of means. The contrast between the ethical methods thus distinguished, made tolerably clear by the above illustrations, will be made still clearer by contemplating the two as put in opposition by the leading exponent of empirical utilitarianism. Treating of legislative aims, Bentham writes :—

" But justice, what is it that we are to understand by justice : and why not happiness but justice ? What happiness is, every man knows, because, what pleasure is, every man knows, and what pain is, every man knows. But what justice is,—this is what on every occasion is the subject-matter of dispute. Be the meaning of the word justice what it will, what regard is it entitled to otherwise than as a means of happiness."*

Let us first consider the assertion here made respecting the relative intelligibilities of these two ends; and let us afterwards consider what is implied by the choice of happiness instead of justice.

Bentham's positive assertion that "what happiness is every man knows, because, what pleasure is, every man knows," is met by counter-assertions equally positive. " Who can tell," asks Plato, " what pleasure really is, or know it in its essence, except the philosopher, who alone is conversant with realities."† Aristotle, too, after commenting on the different opinions held by the vulgar, by the political, by the contemplative, says of happiness that " to some it seems to be virtue, to others prudence, and to others a kind of wisdom: to some again, these, or some one of these, with pleasure, or at least, not without pleasure; others again include external prosperity."‡ And Aristotle, like Plato, comes to the remarkable conclusion that the pleasures of the intellect, reached by the contemplative life, constitute the highest happiness !§   How disagreements concerning the nature of happiness and the relative values of pleasures, thus exhibited in ancient times, continue down to modern times, is shown in Mr. Sidgwick's discussion of egoistic hedonism, above commented upon. Further, as was pointed out before, the indefiniteness attending the estimations of pleasures and pains, which stands in the way of egoistic hedonism as ordinarily conceived, is immensely increased on passing to universalistic hedonism as ordinarily conceived; since its

* *Constitutional Code*, chap. xvi, Supreme Legislative—Section vi, *Omnicompetence*.
† *Republic*, Bk. ix.   ‡ *Nicomachean Ethics*, Bk. i. chap. 8.   § Bk. x, chap. 7.

11 *

theory implies that the imagined pleasures and pains of
others are to be estimated by the help of these pleasures
and pains of self, already so difficult to estimate. And that
anyone after observing the various pursuits into which some
eagerly enter but which others shun, and after listening
to the different opinions concerning the likeableness of this
or that occupation or amusement, expressed at every table,
should assert that the nature of happiness can be fully
agreed upon, so as to render it a fit end for direct legislative
action, is surprising.

The accompanying proposition that justice is unintelligible as an end, is no less surprising. Though primitive
men have no words for either happiness or justice; yet
even among them an approach to the conception of justice
is traceable. The law of retaliation, requiring that a
death inflicted by one tribe on another, shall be balanced
by the death either of the murderer or some member of
his tribe, shows us in a vague shape that notion of equalness of treatment which forms an essential element in
it.   When we come to early races who have
given their thoughts and feelings literary form, we find
this conception of justice, as involving equalness of action,
becoming distinct. Among the Jews, David expressed in
words this association of ideas when, praying to God to "hear
the right," he said—"Let my sentence come forth from thy
presence; let thine eyes behold the things that are equal;"
as also, among early Christians, did Paul when to the Colos-
sians he wrote—"Masters, give unto your servants that which
is just and equal." Commenting on the different meanings
of justice, Aristotle concludes that "the just will therefore
be the lawful and the equal; and the unjust the unlawful
and the unequal. But since the unjust man is also one who
takes more than his share," &c. And that justice was similarly conceived by the Romans they proved by including
under it such meanings as exact, proportionate, impartial,
severally implying fairness of division; and still better

by identification of it with equity, which is a derivative of *æquus*: the word *æquus* itself having for one of its meanings just or impartial.   This coincidence of view among ancient peoples respecting the nature of justice, has extended to modern peoples; who by a general agreement in certain cardinal principles which their systems of law embody, forbidding direct aggressions, which are forms of unequal actions, and forbidding indirect aggressions by breaches of contract, which are other forms of unequal actions, one and all show us the identification of justice with equalness. Bentham, then, is wrong when he says— " But what justice is,—this is what on every occasion is the subject-matter of dispute." He is more wrong, indeed, than has thus far appeared. For, in the first place, he misrepresents utterly by ignoring the fact that in ninety-nine out of every hundred daily transactions between men, no dispute about justice arises; but the business done is recognized on both sides as justly done. And in the second place if, with respect to the hundredth transaction there is a dispute, the subject matter of it is not " what justice is," for it is admitted to be equity or equalness; but the subject matter of dispute always is— what, under these particular circumstances, constitutes equalness?—a widely different question.

It is not then self-evident, as Bentham alleges, that happiness is an intelligible end while justice is not; but, contrariwise, examination makes evident the greater intelligibility of justice as an end. And analysis shows why it is the more intelligible. For justice, or equity, or equalness, is concerned exclusively with *quantity* under *stated conditions;* whereas happiness is concerned with both *quantity* and *quality* under *conditions not stated.* When, as in case of theft, a benefit is taken while no equivalent benefit is yielded—when, as in case of adulterated goods bought or base coin paid, that which is agreed to be given in exchange as of equal value is not given, but something of less value—when, as in case of broken contract, the obligation on one side has been discharged while there has been no discharge, or incomplete discharge, of the obligation on the other; we see that, *the circumstances being specified,* the injustice complained of refers to the relative amounts of actions, or products, or benefits, the natures of which are recognized only so far as is needful for saying whether *as much* has been given, or done, or allowed, by each concerned, as was implied by tacit or overt understanding to be *an equivalent.* But when the end proposed is happiness, *the circumstances remaining unspecified,* the problem is that of estimating both quantities and qualities, unhelped by any such definite measures as acts of exchange imply, or as contracts imply, or as are implied by the differences between the doings of one aggressing and one aggressed upon. The mere fact that Bentham himself includes as elements in the estimation of each pleasure or pain, its intensity, duration, certainty, and proximity, suffices to show how difficult is this problem. And when it is remembered that all pleasures and pains, not felt in particular cases only but in the aggregate of cases, and severally regarded under these four aspects, have to be compared with one another and their relative values determined, simply by introspection; it will be manifest both that the problem is complicated by the addition of indefinite judgments of qualities to indefinite measures of quantities, and that it is further complicated by the multitudinousness of these vague estimations to be gone through and summed up.

But now passing over this assertion of Bentham that happiness is a more intelligible end than justice, which we find to be the reverse of truth, let us note the several implications of the doctrine that the supreme legislative body ought to make the greatest happiness of the greatest number its immediate aim.

It implies, in the first place, that happiness may be

compassed by methods framed directly for the purpose, without any previous inquiry respecting the conditions that must be fulfilled; and this pre-supposes a belief that there are no such conditions. For if there are any conditions without fulfilment of which happiness cannot be compassed, then the first step must be to ascertain these conditions with a view to fulfilling them; and to admit this is to admit that not happiness itself must be the immediate end, but fulfilment of the conditions to its attainment must be the immediate end. The alternatives are simple :—Either the achievement of happiness is not conditional, in which case one mode of action is as good as another, or it is conditional, in which case the required mode of action must be the direct aim and not the happiness to be achieved by it.

Assuming it conceded, as it will be, that there exist conditions which must be fulfilled before happiness can be attained, let us next ask what is implied by proposing modes of so controlling conduct as to further happiness, without previously inquiring whether any such modes are already known ? The implication is that human intelligence throughout the past, operating on experiences, has failed to discover any such modes ; whereas present human intelligence may be expected forthwith to discover them. Unless this be asserted, it must be admitted that certain conditions to the achievement of happiness have already been partially, if not wholly, ascertained; and if so, our first business should be to look for them. Having found them, our rational course is to bring existing intelligence to bear on these products of past intelligence, with the expectation that it will verify the substance of them while possibly correcting the form. But to suppose that no regulative principles for the conduct of associated human beings have thus far been established, and that they are now to be established *de novo*, is to suppose that man as he is differs from man as he was in an incredible degree.

Beyond ignoring the probability, or rather the certainty,

that past experience generalized by past intelligence, must
by this time have disclosed partially, if not wholly, some of
the essential conditions to the achievement of happiness,
Bentham's proposition ignores the formulated knowledge
of them actually existing.   For whence come the conception
of justice and the answering sentiment.   He will scarcely
say that they are meaningless, although his proposition
implies as much ; and if he admits that they have meanings, he must choose between two alternatives either of
which is fatal to his hypothesis.   Are they supernaturally-
caused modes of thinking and feeling, tending to make men
fulfil the conditions to happiness ?   If so their authority is
peremptory.   Are they modes of thinking and feeling
naturally caused in men by experience of these conditions ?   If so, their authority is no less peremptory.   Not
only, then, does Bentham fail to infer that certain principles of guidance must by this time have been ascertained,
but he refuses to recognize these principles as actually
reached and present to him.

And then after all, he tacitly admits that which he overtly
denies, by saying that—" Be the meaning of the word
justice what it will, what regard is it entitled to otherwise
than as a means to happiness ?"   For if justice is a means
having happiness as its end, then justice must take precedence of happiness, as every other means takes precedence
of every other end.   Bentham's own elaborate polity is a
means having happiness as its end, as justice is, by his
own admission, a means having happiness as an end.   If,
then, we may properly skip justice, and go directly to
the end happiness, we may properly skip Bentham's polity,
and go directly to the end happiness.   In short, we are
led to the remarkable conclusion that in all cases we
must contemplate exclusively the end and must disregard
the means.

§ 61   This relation of ends to means, underlying all ethical speculation, will be further elucidated if we join with some of the above conclusions, certain conclusions drawn in the last chapter. We shall see that while greatest happiness may vary widely in societies which, though ideally constituted, are subject to unlike physical circumstances, certain fundamental conditions to the achievement of this greatest happiness, are common to all such societies.

Given a people inhabiting a tract which makes nomadic habits necessary, and the happiness of each individual will be greatest when his nature is so moulded to the requirements of his life, that all his faculties find their due activities in daily driving and tending cattle, milking, migrating, and so forth. The members of a community otherwise similar, which is permanently settled, will severally achieve their greatest happiness when their natures have become such that a fixed habitat, and the occupations necessitated by it, supply the spheres in which each instinct and emotion is exercised and brings the concomitant pleasure. The citizens of a large nation industrially organized, have reached their possible ideal of happiness, when the producing, distributing, and other activities, are such in their kinds and amounts, that each citizen finds in them a place for all his energies and aptitudes, while he obtains the means of satisfying all his desires. Once more we may recognize as not only possible but probable, the eventual existence of a community, also industrial, the members of which, having natures similarly responding to these requirements, are also characterized by dominant æsthetic faculties, and achieve complete happiness only when a large part of life is filled with æsthetic activities. Evidently these different types of men, with their different standards of happiness, each finding the possibility of that happiness in his own society, would not find it if transferred to any of the other societies. Evidently though they might have in common such kinds of happiness as accompany the satisfaction of vital needs, they would not have in common sundry other kinds of happiness.

But now mark that while, to achieve greatest happiness in each of such societies, the special conditions to be fulfilled must differ from those to be fulfilled in the other societies, certain general conditions must be fulfilled in all the societies. Harmonious co-operation, by which alone in any of them the greatest happiness can be attained, is, as we saw, made possible only by respect for one another's claims: there must be neither those direct aggressions which we class as crimes against person and property, nor must there be those indirect aggressions constituted by breaches of contracts. So that maintenance of equitable relations between men, is the condition to attainment of greatest happiness in all societies; however much the greatest happiness attainable in each may differ in nature, or amount, or both.

And here a physical analogy may fitly be used to give the greatest definiteness to this cardinal truth. A mass of matter of whatever kind, maintains its state of internal equilibrium, so long as its component particles severally stand towards their neighbours in equi-distant positions. Accepting the conclusions of modern physicists, which imply that each molecule moves rhythmically, then a balanced state implies that each performs its movements within a space bounded by the like spaces required for the movements of those around. If the molecules have been so aggregated that the oscillations of some are more restrained than the oscillations of others, there is a proportionate instability. If the number of them thus unduly restrained is considerable, the instability is such that the cohesion in some part is liable to fail, and a crack results. If the excesses of restraint are great and multitudinous, a trifling disturbance causes the mass to break up into small fragments. To which add that the recognized remedy for this unstable state, is an exposure to such physical condition (ordinarily high temperature) as enables the molecules so to change their relative positions that their mutual restraints become equal on all sides. And now observe that this holds whatever be the natures of the molecules. They may be simple; they may be compound; they may be composed of this or that matter in this or that way. In other words, the special activities of each molecule, constituted by the relative movements of its units, may be various in their kinds and degrees; and yet, be they what they may, it remains true that to preserve internal equilibrium throughout the mass of molecules, the mutual limitations of their activities must be everywhere alike.

And this is the above-described pre-requisite to social equilibrium, whatever the special natures of the associated persons. Assuming that within each society such persons are of the same type, needing for the fulfilment of their several lives kindred activities, and though these activities may be of one kind in one society and of another kind in another, so admitting of indefinite variation, this condition to social equilibrium does not admit of variation. It must be fulfilled before complete life, that is greatest happiness, can be attained in any society; be the particular quality of that life, or that happiness, what it may.*

§ 62. After thus observing how means and ends in conduct stand to one another, and how there emerge certain conclusions respecting their relative claims, we may see a way to reconcile sundry conflicting ethical theories. These severally embody portions of the truth; and simply require combining in proper order to embody the whole truth.

The theological theory contains a part. If for the divine will, supposed to be supernaturally revealed, we substitute the naturally-revealed end towards which the Power manifested throughout Evolution works; then, since Evolution has been, and is still, working towards the highest life, it follows that conforming to those principles by which the highest life is achieved, is furthering that end. The doctrine

---

* This universal requirement it was which I had in view when choosing for my first work, published in 1850, the title *Social Statics*.

that perfection or excellence of nature should be the object
of pursuit, is in one sense true; for it tacitly recognizes
that ideal form of being which the highest life implies, and
to which Evolution tends. There is a truth, also, in the doctrine that virtue must be the aim; for this is another form
of the doctrine that the aim must be to fulfil the conditions
to achievement of the highest life. That the intuitions of a
moral faculty should guide our conduct, is a proposition in
which a truth is contained; for these intuitions are the slowly
organized results of experiences received by the race while
living in presence of these conditions. And that happiness is
the supreme end is beyond question true; for this is the
concomitant of that highest life which every theory of
moral guidance has distinctly or vaguely in view.

So understanding their relative positions, those ethical
systems which make virtue, right, obligation, the cardinal
aims, are seen to be complementary to those ethical systems
which make welfare, pleasure, happiness, the cardinal aims.
Though the moral sentiments generated in civilized men by
daily contact with social conditions and gradual adaptation
to them, are indispensable as incentives and deterrents;
and though the intuitions corresponding to these sentiments, have, in virtue of their origin, a general authority to
be reverently recognized; yet the sympathies and antipathies
hence originating, together with the intellectual expressions
of them, are, in their primitive forms, necessarily vague.
To make guidance by them adequate to all requirements,
their dictates have to be interpreted and made definite by
science; to which end there must be analysis of those
conditions to complete living which they respond to, and
from converse with which they have arisen. And such
analysis necessitates the recognition of happiness for each
and all, as the end to be achieved by fulfilment of these
conditions.

Hence, recognizing in due degrees all the various ethical
theories, conduct in its highest form will take as guides,

innate perceptions of right duly enlightened and made precise by an analytic intelligence ; while conscious that these guides are proximately supreme solely because they lead to the ultimately supreme end, happiness special and general.

CHAPTER X.

THE RELATIVITY OF PAINS AND PLEASURES.

§ 63. A truth of cardinal importance as a datum of Ethics, which was incidentally referred to in the last chapter, must here be set forth at full length. I mean the truth that not only men of different races, but also different men of the same race, and even the same men at different periods of life, have different standards of happiness. Though there is some recognition of this by moralists, the recognition is inadequate; and the far-reaching conclusions to be drawn when the relativity of happiness is fully recognized, are scarcely suspected.

It is a belief universal in early life—a belief which in most people is but partially corrected in later life, and in very few wholly dissipated—that there is something intrinsic in the pleasantness of certain things, while other things are intrinsically unpleasant. The error is analogous to, and closely allied with, the error crude realism makes. Just as to the uncultured mind it appears self-evident that the sweetness of sugar is inherent in sugar, that sound as we perceive it is sound as it exists in the external world, and that the warmth from a fire is in itself what it seems; so does it appear self-evident that the sweetness of sugar is necessarily grateful, that there is in a beautiful sound something that must be beautiful to all creatures, and that the agreeable feeling produced by warmth is a feeling which every other consciousness must find agreeable.

But as criticism proves the one set of conclusions to be wrong, so does it prove to be wrong the other set. Not only are the qualities of external things as intellectually apprehended by us, relative to our own organisms; but the pleasurableness or painfulness of the feelings which we associate with such qualities, are also relative to our own organisms. They are so in a double sense—they are relative to its structures, and they are relative to the states of its structures.

That we may not rest in a mere nominal acceptance of these general truths, but may so appreciate them as to see their full bearings on ethical theory, we must here glance at them as exemplified by animate creatures at large. For after contemplating the wide divergences of sentiency accompanying the wide divergences of organization which evolution in general has brought about, we shall be enabled the better to see the divergences of sentiency to be expected from the further evolution of humanity.

§ 64. Because they can be most quickly disposed of, let us first deal with pains: a further reason for first dealing with pains being that we may thus forthwith recognize, and then leave out of consideration, those sentient states the qualities of which may be regarded as absolute rather than relative.

The painfulness of the feelings produced by forces which tend to destroy organic structures, wholly or in part, is of course common to all creatures capable of feeling. We saw it to be inevitable that during evolution there must everywhere be established such connexions between external actions and the modes of consciousness they cause, that the injurious ones are accompanied by disagreeable feelings and the beneficial ones by agreeable feelings. Consequently, pressures or strains which tear or bruise, and heats which burn or scald, being in all cases partially or wholly destructive, are in all cases painful. But even here the relativity of the feelings may in one sense be asserted. For the effect of a force of given quantity or intensity, varies partly with the size and partly with the structure of the creature exposed to it. The weight which is scarcely felt by a large animal crushes a small one; the blow which breaks the limb of a mouse produces little effect on a horse; the weapon which lacerates a horse leaves a rhinoceros uninjured. And with these differences of injuriousness doubtless go differences of feeling. Merely glancing at the illustrations of this truth furnished by sentient beings in general, let us consider the illustrations mankind furnish.

Comparisons of robust labouring men with women or children, show us that degrees of mechanical stress which the first bear with impunity, produce on the others injuries and accompanying pains. The blistering of a tender skin by an amount of friction which does not even redden a coarse one, or the bursting of superficial bloodvessels, and consequent discolouration, caused in a person of lax tissues by a blow which leaves in well-toned tissues no trace, will sufficiently exemplify this contrast. Not only, however, are the pains due to violent incident forces, relative to the characters or constitutional qualities of the parts directly affected, but they are relative in equally marked ways, or even in more marked ways, to the characters of the nervous structures. The common assumption is that equal bodily injuries excite equal pains. But this is a mistake. Pulling out a tooth or cutting off a limb, gives to different persons widely different amounts of suffering: not the endurance only, but the feeling to be endured, varies greatly; and the variation largely depends on the degree of nervous development. This is well shown by the great insensibility of idiots—blows, cuts, and extremes of heat and cold, being borne by them with indifference.* The relation thus shown in the most marked manner where the development

* *On Idiocy and Imbecility,* by William W. Ireland, M.D., p. 255-6.

of the central nervous system is abnormally low, is shown
in a less marked manner where the development of the
central nervous system is normally low; namely, among
inferior races of men.   Many travellers have commented
on the strange callousness shown by savages who have
been mangled in battle or by accident; and surgeons in
India say that wounds and operations are better borne by
natives than by Europeans.   Further, there comes the
converse fact that among the higher types of men, larger-
brained and more sensitive to pain than the lower, the most
sensitive are those whose nervous developments, as shown
by their mental powers, are the highest: part of the evidence
being the relative intolerance of disagreeable sensations
common among men of genius,* and the general irritability
characteristic of them.

   That pain is relative not to structures only, but to their
states as well, is also manifest—more manifest indeed.
The sensibility of an external part depends on its temperature.   Cool it below a certain point and it becomes, as
we say, numb; and if by ether-spray it is made very cold,
it may be cut without any feeling being produced.   Conversely, heat the part so that its blood-vessels dilate, and
the pain which any injury or irritation causes is greater than
usual.   How largely the production of pain depends on the
condition of the part affected, we see in the extreme
tenderness of an inflamed surface—a tenderness such that
a slight touch causes shrinking, and such that rays from
the fire which ordinarily would be indifferent become
intolerable.   Similarly with the special senses.   A
light which eyes that are in good order bear without disagreeable feeling, cannot be borne by inflamed eyes.   And
beyond the local state, the state of the system as a whole,
and the state of the nervous centres, are both factors.
Those enfeebled by illness are distressed by noises which
those in health bear with equanimity; and men with over-

* For instances see *Fortnightly Review*, Vol. XXIV *(New Series)*, p. 712.

wrought brains are irritated in unusual degrees by annoyances, both physical and moral. Further, the temporary condition known as exhaustion enters into the relation. Limbs over-worn by prolonged exertion, cannot without aching perform acts which would at other times cause no appreciable feeling. After reading continuously for very many hours, even strong eyes begin to smart. And noises that can be listened to for a short time with indifference, become, if there is no cessation, causes of suffering.

So that though there is absoluteness in the relation between positive pains and actions that are positively injurious, in so far that wherever there is sentiency it exists; yet even here partial relativity may be asserted. For there is no fixed relation between the acting force and the produced feeling. The amount of feeling varies with the size of the organism, with the character of its outer structures, with the character of its nervous system; and also with the temporary states of the part affected, of the body at large, and of the nervous centres.

§ 65. The relativity of pleasures is far more conspicuous; and the illustrations of it furnished by the sentient world at large are innumerable.

It needs but to glance round at the various things which different creatures are prompted by their desires to eat and are gratified in eating—flesh for predaceous animals, grass for the herbivora, worms for the mole, flies for the swallow, seeds for the finch, honey for the bee, a decaying carcase for the maggot—to be reminded that the tastes for foods are relative to the structures of the creatures. And this truth, made conspicuous by a survey of animals in general, is forced on our attention even by a survey of different races of men. Here human flesh is abhorred, and there regarded as the greatest delicacy; in this country roots are allowed to putrefy before they are eaten, and in that the taint of decay produces disgust; the whale's blubber which one race devours with avidity, will in another by its very odour produce nausea. Nay, without looking abroad we may, in the common saying that "one man's meat is another man's poison," see the general admission that members of the same society so far differ, that a taste which is to these pleasurable is to those displeasurable. So is it with the other senses. Assafœtida which by us is singled out as typical of the disgusting in odour, ranks among the Esthonians as a favourite perfume; and even those around us vary so far in their likings that the scents of flowers grateful to some are repugnant to others. Analogous differences in the preferences for colours, we daily hear expressed. And in a greater or less degree the like holds with all sensations, down even to those of touch: the feeling yielded by velvet, which is to most agreeable, setting the teeth on edge in some.

It needs but to name appetite and satiety to suggest multitudinous facts showing that pleasures are relative not only to the organic structures but also to their states. The food which yields keen gratification when there is great hunger ceases to be grateful when hunger is satisfied; and if then forced on the eater is rejected with aversion. So, too, a particular kind of food, seeming when first tasted so delicious that daily repetition would be a source of endless enjoyment, becomes, in a few days, not only unenjoyable but repugnant. Brilliant colours which, falling on unaccustomed eyes give delight, pall on the sense if long looked at; and there is relief in getting away from the impressions they yield. Sounds sweet in themselves and sweet in their combinations, which yield to unfatigued ears intense pleasure, become, at the end of a long concert, not only wearisome but, if there is no escape from them, causes of irritation. The like holds down even to such simple sensations as those of heat and cold. The fire so delightful on a winter's day is, in hot weather, oppressive; and pleasure is then taken in the cold water from which, in winter, there would be

12 *

shrinking. Indeed, experiences lasting over but a few moments suffice to show how relative to the states of the structures are pleasurable sensations of these kinds; for it is observable that on dipping the cold hand into hot water, the agreeable feeling gradually diminishes as the hand warms.

These few instances will carry home the truth, manifest enough to all who observe, that the receipt of each agreeable sensation depends primarily on the existence of a structure which is called into play; and, secondarily, on the condition of that structure, as fitting it or unfitting it for activity.

§ 66. The truth that emotional pleasures are made possible, partly by the existence of correlative structures and partly by the states of those structures, is equally undeniable.

Observe the animal which, leading a life demanding solitary habits, has an adapted organization, and it gives no sign of need for the presence of its kind. Observe, conversely, a gregarious animal separated from the herd, and you see marks of unhappiness while the separation continues, and equally distinct marks of joy on joining its companions. In the one case there is no nervous structure which finds its sphere of action in the gregarious state; and in the other case such a structure exists. As was implied by instances cited in the last chapter for another purpose, animals leading lives involving particular kinds of activities, have become so constituted that pursuance of those activities, exercising the correlative structures, yields the associated pleasures. Beasts of prey confined in dens, show us by their pacings from side to side the endeavour to obtain, as well as they can, the satisfactions that accompany roaming about in their natural habitats; and that gratification in the expenditure of their locomotive energies shown us by porpoises playing round a vessel, is shown us by the similarly-unceasing excursions from end to end of its cell which a captured porpoise makes. The perpetual hoppings of the canary from bar to bar of its cage, and the ceaseless use of claws and bill in climbing about its perch by the parrot, are other activities which, severally related to the needs of the species, have severally themselves become sources of agreeable feelings. Still more clearly are we shown by the efforts which a caged beaver makes to build with such sticks and pieces of wood as are at hand, how dominant in its nature has become the building instinct; and how, apart from any advantage gained, its gets gratification by repeating, as well as it can, the processes of construction it is organized to carry on. The cat which, lacking something to tear with her claws, pulls at the mat with them, the confined giraffe which, in default of branches to lay hold of wears out the upper angles of the doors to its house by continually grasping them with its prehensile tongue, the rhinoceros which, having no enemy to fight, ploughs up the ground with his horn, all yield us analogous evidence. Clearly, these various actions performed by these various creatures are not intrinsically pleasurable; for they differ more or less in each species and are often utterly unlike. The pleasurableness is simply in the exercise of nervo-muscular structures adapted to the performance of the actions.

Though races of men are contrasted with one another so much less than genera and orders of animals are, yet, as we saw in the last chapter, along with visible differences there go invisible differences, with accompanying likings for different modes of life. Among some, as the Mantras, the love of unrestrained action and the disregard of companionship, are such that they separate if they quarrel, and hence live scattered; while among others, as the Damaras, there is little tendency to resist, but instead, an admiration for any one who assumes power over them. Already when exemplifying the indefiniteness of happiness as an end of action, I have referred to the unlike ideals of life pursued by the nomadic and the settled, the warlike and the peaceful,

—unlike ideals which imply unlikenesses of nervous structures caused by the inherited effects of unlike habits accumulating through generations. These contrasts, various in their kinds and degrees among the various types of mankind, everyone can supplement by analogous contrasts observable among those around. The occupations some delight in are to those otherwise constituted intolerable; and men's hobbies, severally appearing to themselves quite natural, often appear to their friends ludicrous and almost insane : facts which alone might make us see that the pleasurableness of actions of this or that kind, is due not to anything in the natures of the actions but to the existence of faculties which find exercise in them.

It must be added that each pleasurable emotion, like each pleasurable sensation, is relative not only to a certain structure but also to the state of that structure. The parts called into action must have had proper rest—must be in a condition fit for action; not in the condition which prolonged action produces. Be the order of emotion what it may, an unbroken continuity in the receipt of it eventually brings satiety. The pleasurable consciousness becomes less and less vivid, and there arises the need for a temporary cessation during which the parts that have been active may recover their fitness for activity; and during which also, the activities of other parts and receipt of the accompanying emotions may find due place.

§ 67. I have insisted on these general truths with perhaps needless iteration, to prepare the reader for more fully recognizing a corollary that is practically ignored. Abundant and clear as is the evidence, and forced though it is daily on everyone's attention, the conclusions respecting life and conduct which should be drawn, are not drawn; and so much at variance are these conclusions with current beliefs, that enunciation of them causes a stare of incredulity. Pervaded as all past thinking has been, and as

most present thinking is, by the assumption that the nature
of every creature has been specially created for it, and that
human nature, also specially created, is, like other natures,
fixed—pervaded too as this thinking has been, and is, by
the allied assumption that the agreeableness of certain
actions depends on their essential qualities, while other
actions are by their essential qualities made disagreeable;
it is difficult to obtain a hearing for the doctrine that the
kinds of action which are now pleasurable will, under
conditions requiring the change, cease to be pleasurable,
while other kinds of action will become pleasurable. Even
those who accept the doctrine of Evolution mostly hear
with scepticism, or at best with nominal faith, the inferences to be drawn from it respecting the humanity of
the future.

And yet as shown in myriads of instances indicated
by the few above given, those natural processes which
have produced multitudinous forms of structure adapted to
multitudinous forms of activity, have simultaneously made
these forms of activity pleasurable. And the inevitable
implication is that within the limits imposed by physical
laws, there will be evolved, in adaptation to any new
sets of conditions that may be established, appropriate
structures of which the functions will yield their respective
gratifications.

When we have got rid of the tendency to think that
certain modes of activity are necessarily pleasurable because
they give us pleasure, and that other modes which do not
please us are necessarily unpleasing; we shall see that the
re-moulding of human nature into fitness for the requirements of social life, must eventually make all needful
activities pleasurable, while it makes displeasurable all
activities at variance with these requirements. When we
have come fully to recognize the truth that there is nothing
intrinsically more gratifying in the efforts by which wild
animals are caught, than in the efforts expended in rearing

plants, and that the combined actions of muscles and senses in rowing a boat are not by their essential natures more productive of agreeable feeling than those gone through in reaping corn, but that everything depends on the co-operating emotions, which at present are more in accordance with the one than with the other; we shall infer that along with decrease of those emotions for which the social state affords little or no scope, and increase of those which it persistently exercises, the things now done with dislike from a sense of obligation will be done with immediate liking, and the things desisted from as a matter of duty will be desisted from because they are repugnant.

This conclusion, alien to popular beliefs and in ethical speculation habitually ignored, or at most recognized but partially and occasionally, will be thought by the majority so improbable that I must give further justification of it: enforcing the *à priori* argument by an *à posteriori* one. Small as is the attention given to the fact, yet is the fact conspicuous that the corollary above drawn from the doctrine of Evolution at large, coincides with the corollary which past and present changes in human nature force on us. The leading contrasts of character between savage and civilized, are just those contrasts to be expected from the process of adaptation.

The life of the primitive man is passed mainly in the pursuit of beasts, birds, and fish, which yields him a gratifying excitement; but though to the civilized man the chase gives gratification, this is neither so persistent nor so general. There are among us keen sportsmen; but there are many to whom shooting and fishing soon become wearisome; and there are not a few to whom they are altogether indifferent or even distasteful.   Conversely, the power of continued application which in the primitive man is very small, has among ourselves become considerable. It is true that most are coerced into industry by necessity ; but there are sprinkled throughout society men to whom active occupation is a need—men who are restless when away from business and miserable when they eventually give it up; men to whom this or that line of investigation is so attractive, that they devote themselves to it day after day, year after year; men who are so deeply interested in public affairs that they pass lives of labour in achieving political ends they think advantageous, hardly giving themselves the rest necessary for health.   Yet again, and still more strikingly, does the change become manifest when we compare undeveloped with developed humanity in respect of the conduct prompted by fellow feeling.   Cruelty rather than kindness is characteristic of the savage, and is in many cases a source of marked gratification to him; but though among the civilized are some in whom this trait of the savage survives, yet a love of inflicting pain is not general, and besides numbers who show benevolence, there are those who devote their whole time and much of their money to philanthropic ends, without thought of reward either here or hereafter.   Clearly these major, along with many minor, changes of nature, conform to the law set forth. Activities appropriate to their needs which give pleasures to savages have ceased to be pleasurable to many of the civilized; while the civilized have acquired capacities for other appropriate activities and accompanying pleasures which savages had no capacities for.

Now, not only is it rational to infer that changes like those which have been going on during civilization, will continue to go on, but it is irrational to do otherwise.   Not he who believes that adaptation will increase is absurd, but he who doubts that it will increase is absurd.   Lack of faith in such further evolution of humanity as shall harmonize its nature with its conditions, adds but another to the countless illustrations of inadequate consciousness of causation.   One who, leaving behind both primitive dogmas and primitive ways of looking at things, has, while accepting scientific conclusions acquired those habits of thought which science generates, will regard the conclusion above drawn as inevitable. He will find it impossible to believe that the processes which have heretofore so moulded all beings to the requirements of their lives that they get satisfactions in fulfilling them, will not hereafter continue so moulding them. He will infer that the type of nature to which the highest social life affords a sphere such that every faculty has its due amount, and no more than the due amount, of function and accompanying gratification, is the type of nature towards which progress cannot cease till it is reached. Pleasure being producible by the exercise of any structure which is adjusted to its special end, he will see the necessary implication to be that, supposing it consistent with maintenance of life, there is no kind of activity which will not become a source of pleasure if continued; and that therefore pleasure will eventually accompany every mode of action demanded by social conditions.

This corollary I here emphasize because it will presently play an important part in the argument.

CHAPTER XI.

EGOISM *VERSUS* ALTRUISM.

§ 68. If insistence on them tends to unsettle established systems of belief, self-evident truths are by most people silently passed over ; or else there is a tacit refusal to draw from them the most obvious inferences.

Of self-evident truths so dealt with, the one which here concerns us is that a creature must live before it can act. From this it is a corollary that the acts by which each maintains his own life must, speaking generally, precede in imperativeness all other acts of which he is capable. For if it be asserted that these other acts must precede in imperativeness the acts which maintain life; and if this, accepted as a general law of conduct, is conformed to by all; then by postponing the acts which maintain life to the other acts which life makes possible, all must lose their lives. That is to say, Ethics has to recognize the truth, recognized in unethical thought, that egoism comes before altruism. The acts required for continued self-preservation, including the enjoyment of benefits achieved by such acts, are the first requisites to universal welfare. Unless each duly cares for himself, his care for all others is ended by death ; and if each thus dies, there remain no others to be cared for.

This permanent supremacy of egoism over altruism, made

manifest by contemplating existing life, is further made manifest by contemplating life in course of evolution.

§ 69. Those who have followed with assent the recent course of thought, do not need telling that throughout past eras, the life, vast in amount and varied in kind, which has overspread the Earth, has progressed in subordination to the law that every individual shall gain by whatever aptitude it has for fulfilling the conditions to its existence. The uniform principle has been that better adaptation shall bring greater benefit; which greater benefit, while increasing the prosperity of the better adapted, shall increase also its ability to leave offspring inheriting more or less its better adaptation. And, by implication, the uniform principle has been that the ill-adapted, disadvantaged in the struggle for existence, shall bear the consequent evils: either disappearing when its imperfections are extreme, or else rearing fewer offspring, which, inheriting its imperfections, tend to dwindle away in posterity.

It has been thus with innate superiorities; it has been thus also with acquired ones. All along the law has been that increased function brings increased power; and that therefore such extra activities as aid welfare in any member of a race, produce in its structures greater ability to carry on such extra activities: the derived advantages being enjoyed by it to the heightening and lengthening of its life. Conversely, as lessened function ends in lessened structure, the dwindling of unused faculties has ever entailed loss of power to achieve the correlative ends: the result of inadequate fulfilment of the ends being diminished ability to maintain life. And by inheritance, such functionally-produced modifications have respectively furthered or hindered survival in posterity.

As already said, the law that each creature shall take the benefits and the evils of its own nature, be they those derived from ancestry or those due to self-produced modifications, has been the law under which life has evolved thus far; and it must continue to be the law however much further life may evolve. Whatever qualifications this natural course of action may now or hereafter undergo, are qualifications that cannot, without fatal results, essentially change it. Any arrangements which in a considerable degree prevent superiority from profiting by the rewards of superiority, or shield inferiority from the evils it entails—any arrangements which tend to make it as well to be inferior as to be superior; are arrangements diametrically opposed to the progress of organization and the reaching of a higher life.

But to say that each individual shall reap the benefits brought to him by his own powers, inherited and acquired, is to enunciate egoism as an ultimate principle of conduct. It is to say that egoistic claims must take precedence of altruistic claims.

§ 70. Under its biological aspect this proposition cannot be contested by those who agree in the doctrine of Evolution; but probably they will not at once allow that admission of it under its ethical aspect is equally unavoidable. While, as respects development of life, the well-working of the universal principle described is sufficiently manifest; the well-working of it as respects increase of happiness may not be seen at once. But the two cannot be disjoined.

Incapacity of every kind and of whatever degree, causes unhappiness directly and indirectly—directly by the pain consequent on the over-taxing of inadequate faculty, and indirectly by the non-fulfilment, or imperfect fulfilment, of certain conditions to welfare. Conversely, capacity of every kind sufficient for the requirement, conduces to happiness immediately and remotely—immediately by the pleasure accompanying the normal exercise of each power that is up to its work, and remotely by the pleasures which are furthered by the ends achieved. A creature that is weak or slow of foot, and so gets food only by exhausting efforts or escapes enemies with difficulty, suffers the pains of over-strained powers, of unsatisfied appetites, of distressed emotions; while the strong and swift creature of the same species delights in its efficient activities, gains more fully the satisfactions yielded by food as well as the renewed vivacity this gives, and has to bear fewer and smaller pains in defending itself against foes or escaping from them. Similarly with duller and keener senses, or higher and lower degrees of sagacity. The mentally-inferior individual of any race suffers negative and positive miseries; while the mentally-superior individual receives negative and positive gratifications. Inevitably, then, this law in conformity with which each member of a species takes the consequences of its own nature; and in virtue of which the progeny of each member, participating in its nature, also takes such consequences; is one that tends ever to raise the aggregate happiness of the species, by furthering the multiplication of the happier and hindering that of the less happy.

All this is true of human beings as of other beings. The conclusion forced on us is that the pursuit of individual happiness within those limits prescribed by social conditions, is the first requisite to the attainment of the greatest general happiness. To see this it needs but to contrast one whose self-regard has maintained bodily well-being, with one whose regardlessness of self has brought its natural results; and then to ask what must be the contrast between two societies formed of two such kinds of individuals.

Bounding out of bed after an unbroken sleep, singing or whistling as he dresses, coming down with beaming face ready to laugh on the smallest provocation, the healthy man of high powers, conscious of past successes and by his energy, quickness, resource, made confident of the future, enters on the day's business not with repugnance but with gladness; and from hour to hour experiencing satisfactions from work effectually done, comes home with an abundant surplus of energy remaining for hours of relaxation. Far otherwise is it with one who is enfeebled by great neglect of self. Already deficient, his energies are made more deficient by constant endeavours to execute tasks that prove beyond his strength, and by the resulting discouragement. Besides the depressing consciousness of the immediate future, there is the depressing consciousness of the remoter future, with its probability of accumulated difficulties and diminished ability to meet them. Hours of leisure which, rightly passed, bring pleasures that raise the tide of life and renew the powers of work, cannot be utilized: there is not vigour enough for enjoyments involving action, and lack of spirits prevents passive enjoyments from being entered upon with zest. In brief, life becomes a burden. Now if, as must be admitted, in a community composed of individuals like the first the happiness will be relatively great, while in one composed of individuals like the last there will be relatively little happiness, or rather much misery; it must be admitted that conduct causing the one result is good and conduct causing the other is bad.

But diminutions of general happiness are produced by inadequate egoism in several other ways. These we will successively glance at.

§ 71. If there were no proofs of heredity—if it were the rule that the strong are usually begotten by the weak while the weak usually descend from the strong, that vivacious children form the families of melancholy parents while fathers and mothers with overflowing spirits mostly have dull progeny, that from stolid peasants there ordinarily come sons of high intelligence while the sons of the cultured are commonly fit for nothing but following the plough—if there were no transmission of gout, scrofula, insanity, and did the diseased habitually give birth to the healthy and the healthy to the diseased, writers on Ethics might be justified in ignoring those effects of conduct which are felt by posterity through the natures they inherit.

As it is, however, the current ideas concerning the relative claims of egoism and altruism are vitiated by the omission of this all-important factor. For if health, strength and capacity, are usually transmitted ; and if disease, feebleness, stupidity, generally reappear in descendants; then a rational altruism requires insistance on that egoism which is shown by receipt of the satisfactions accompanying preservation of body and mind in the best state. The necessary implication is that blessings are provided for offspring by due self-regard, while disregard of self carried too far provides curses. When, indeed, we remember how commonly it is remarked that high health and overflowing spirits render any lot in life tolerable, while chronic ailments make gloomy a life most favourably circumstanced, it becomes amazing that both the world at large and writers who make conduct their study, should ignore the terrible evils which disregard of personal wellbeing inflicts on the unborn, and the incalculable good laid up for the unborn by attention to personal wellbeing. Of all bequests of parents to children the most valuable is a sound constitution. Though a man's body is not a property that can be inherited, yet his constitution may fitly be compared to an entailed estate ; and if he rightly understands his duty to posterity, he will see that he is bound to pass on that estate uninjured if not improved. To say this is to say that he must be egoistic to the extent of satisfying all those desires associated with the due performance of functions. Nay, it is to say more. It is to say that he must seek in due amounts the various pleasures which life offers. For beyond the effect these have in raising the tide of life and maintaining constitutional vigour, there is the effect they have in preserving and increasing a capacity for receiving enjoyment. Endowed with abundant energies and various tastes, some can get

gratifications of many kinds on opportunities hourly occurring; while others are so inert, and so uninterested in things
around, that they cannot even take the trouble to amuse themselves. And unless heredity be denied, the inference must be
that due acceptance of the miscellaneous pleasures life offers,
conduces to the capacity for enjoyment in posterity; and
that persistence in dull monotonous lives by parents,
diminishes the ability of their descendants to make the
best of what gratifications fall to them.

§ 72. Beyond the decrease of general happiness which
results in this indirect way if egoism is unduly subordinated,
there is a decrease of general happiness which results in a
direct way. He who carries self-regard far enough to keep
himself in good health and high spirits, in the first place
thereby becomes an immediate source of happiness to
those around, and in the second place maintains the
ability to increase their happiness by altruistic actions.
But one whose bodily vigour and mental health are under-
mined by self-sacrifice carried too far, in the first place
becomes to those around a cause of depression, and in the
second place renders himself incapable, or less capable, of
actively furthering their welfare.

In estimating conduct we must remember that there
are those who by their joyousness beget joy in others,
and that there are those who by their melancholy cast a
gloom on every circle they enter. And we must remember
that by display of overflowing happiness a man of the one
kind may add to the happiness of others more than by
positive efforts to benefit them; and that a man of the other
kind may decrease their happiness more by his presence
than he increases it by his actions. Full of vivacity, the one
is ever welcome. For his wife he has smiles and jocose
speeches; for his children stores of fun and play; for his
friends pleasant talk interspersed with the sallies of wit that
come from buoyancy. Contrariwise, the other is shunned.

The irritability resulting now from ailments, now from failures caused by feebleness, his family has daily to bear. Lacking adequate energy for joining in them, he has at best but a tepid interest in the amusements of his children; and he is called a wet blanket by his friends. Little account as our ethical reasonings take note of it, yet is the fact obvious that since happiness and misery are infectious, such regard for self as conduces to health and high spirits is a benefaction to others, and such disregard of self as brings on suffering, bodily or mental, is a malefaction to others. The duty of making one's self agreeable by seeming to be pleased, is, indeed, often urged; and thus to gratify friends is applauded so long as self-sacrificing effort is implied. But though display of real happiness gratifies friends far more than display of sham happiness, and has no drawback in the shape either of hypocrisy or strain, yet it is not thought a duty to fulfil the conditions which favour the display of real happiness. Nevertheless, if quantity of happiness produced is to be the measure, the last is more imperative than the first.

And then, as above indicated, beyond this primary series of effects produced on others there is a secondary series of effects. The adequately egoistic individual retains those powers which make altruistic activities possible. The individual who is inadequately egoistic, loses more or less of his ability to be altruistic. The truth of the one proposition is self-evident; and the truth of the other is daily forced on us by examples. Note a few of them. Here is a mother who, brought up in the insane fashion usual among the cultivated, has a physique not strong enough for suckling her infant, but who, knowing that its natural food is the best, and anxious for its welfare, continues to give it milk for a longer time than her system will bear. Eventually the accumulating reaction tells. There comes exhaustion running, it may be, into illness caused by depletion; occasionally ending in death, and often entailing chronic weakness. She becomes, perhaps for a time, perhaps permanently, incapable of carrying on household affairs; her other children suffer from the loss of maternal attention; and where the income is small, payments for nurse and doctor tell injuriously on the whole family.   Instance, again, what not unfrequently happens with the father. Similarly prompted by a high sense of obligation, and misled by current moral theories into the notion that self-denial may rightly be carried to any extent, he daily continues his office-work for long hours regardless of hot head and cold feet; and debars himself from social pleasures, for which he thinks he can afford neither time nor money. What comes of this entirely unegoistic course? Eventually a sudden collapse, sleeplessness, inability to work. That rest which he would not give himself when his sensations prompted, he has now to take in long measure. The extra earnings laid by for the benefit of his family, are quickly swept away by costly journeys in aid of recovery, and by the many expenses which illness entails. Instead of increased ability to do his duty by his offspring, there comes now inability. Life-long evils on them replace hoped-for goods.   And so is it, too, with the social effects of inadequate egoism. All grades furnish examples of the mischiefs, positive and negative, inflicted on society by excessive neglect of self. Now the case is that of a labourer who, conscientiously continuing his work under a broiling sun, spite of violent protest from his feelings, dies of sunstroke; and leaves his family a burden to the parish. Now the case is that of a clerk whose eyes permanently fail from over-straining, or who, daily writing for hours after his fingers are painfully cramped, is attacked with "scrivener's palsy," and, unable to write at all, sinks with aged parents into poverty which friends are called on to mitigate. And now the case is that of a man devoted to public ends who, shattering his health by ceaseless application, fails to achieve all he might have achieved by a more

13 *

reasonable apportionment of his time between labour on behalf of others and ministration to his own needs.

§ 73. In one further way is the undue subordination of egoism to altruism injurious. Both directly and indirectly unselfishness pushed to excess generates selfishness.

Consider first the immediate effects. That one man may yield up to another a gratification, it is needful that the other shall accept it; and where the gratification is of a kind to which their respective claims are equal, or which is no more required by the one than by the other, acceptance implies a readiness to get gratification at another's cost. The circumstances and needs of the two being alike, the transaction involves as much culture of egoism in the last as it involves culture of altruism in the first. It is true that not unfrequently, difference between their means or difference between their appetites for a pleasure which the one has had often and the other rarely, divests the acceptance of this character; and it is true that in other cases the benefactor manifestly takes so much pleasure in giving pleasure, that the sacrifice is partial, and the reception of it not wholly selfish. But to see the effect above indicated we must exclude such inequalities, and consider what happens where wants are approximately alike and where the sacrifices, not reciprocated at intervals, are perpetually on one side. So restricting the inquiry all can name instances verifying the alleged result. Everyone can remember circles in which the daily surrender of benefits by the generous to the greedy, has caused increase of greediness; until there has been produced an unscrupulous egoism intolerable to all around. There are obvious social effects of kindred nature. Most thinking people now recognize the demoralization caused by indiscriminate charity. They see how in the mendicant there is, besides destruction of the normal relation between labour expended and benefit obtained, a genesis of the expectation that others shall minister to his needs; showing itself sometimes in the venting of curses on those who refuse.

Next consider the remote results. When the egoistic claims are so much subordinated to the altruistic as to produce physical mischief, the tendency is towards a relative decrease in the number of the altruistic, and therefore an increased predominance of the egoistic. Pushed to extremes, sacrifice of self for the benefit of others, leads occasionally to death before the ordinary period of marriage; leads sometimes to abstention from marriage, as in sisters of charity; leads sometimes to an ill-health or a loss of attractiveness which prevents marriage; leads sometimes to non-acquirement of the pecuniary means needed for marriage; and in all these cases, therefore, the unusually altruistic leave no descendants. Where the postponement of personal welfare to the welfare of others has not been carried so far as to prevent marriage, it yet not unfrequently occurs that the physical degradation resulting from years of self-neglect causes infertility; so that again the most altruistically-natured leave no like-natured posterity. And then in less marked and more numerous cases, the resulting enfeeblement shows itself by the production of relatively weak offspring; of whom some die early, while the rest are less likely than usual to transmit the parental type to future generations. Inevitably, then, by this dying out of the especially unegoistic, there is prevented that desirable mitigation of egoism in the average nature which would else have taken place. Such disregard of self as brings down bodily vigour below the normal level, eventually produces in the society a counterbalancing excess of regard for self.

§ 74. That egoism precedes altruism in order of imperativeness, is thus clearly shown. The acts which make continued life possible, must, on the average, be more peremptory than all those other acts which life makes possible; including the acts which benefit others. Turning from life as existing to life as evolving, we are equally shown this. Sentient beings have progressed from low to high types, under the law that the superior shall profit by their superiority and the inferior shall suffer from their inferiority. Conformity to this law has been, and is still, needful, not only for the continuance of life but for the increase of happiness ; since the superior are those having faculties better adjusted to the requirements—faculties, therefore, which bring in their exercise greater pleasure and less pain.

More special considerations join these more general ones in showing us this truth. Such egoism as preserves a vivacious mind in a vigorous body furthers the happiness of descendants, whose inherited constitutions make the labours of life easy and its pleasures keen ; while, conversely, unhappiness is entailed on posterity by those who bequeath them constitutions injured by self-neglect. Again, the individual whose well-conserved life shows itself in over-flowing spirits, becomes, by his mere existence, a source of pleasure to all around; while the depression which commonly accompanies ill-health diffuses itself through family and among friends. A further contrast is that whereas one who has been duly regardful of self retains the power of being helpful to others, there results from self-abnegation in excess, not only an inability to help others but the infliction of positive burdens on them. Lastly, we come upon the truth that undue altruism increases egoism ; both directly in contemporaries and indirectly in posterity.

And now observe that though the general conclusion enforced by these special conclusions, is at variance with nominally-accepted beliefs, it is not at variance with actually-accepted beliefs. While opposed to the doctrine which men are taught should be acted upon, it is in harmony with the doctrine which they do act upon and dimly see must be acted upon. For omitting such abnormalities of conduct as are instanced above, everyone, alike by deed and word, implies that in the business of life personal welfare is the primary consideration. The labourer looking for wages in return for work done, no less than the merchant who sells goods at a profit, the doctor who expects fees for advice, the priest who calls the scene of his ministrations "a living," assumes as beyond question the truth that selfishness, carried to the extent of enforcing his claims and enjoying the returns his efforts bring, is not only legitimate but essential. Even persons who avow a contrary conviction prove by their acts that it is inoperative. Those who repeat with emphasis the maxim—"Love your neighbour as yourself," do not render up what they possess so as to satisfy the desires of all as much as they satisfy their own desires. Nor do those whose extreme maxim is—"Live for others," differ appreciably from people around in their regards for personal welfare, or fail to appropriate their shares of life's pleasures. In short, that which is above set forth as the belief to which scientific ethics leads us, is that which men do really believe, as distinguished from that which they believe they believe.

Finally it may be remarked that a rational egoism, so far from implying a more egoistic human nature, is consistent with a human nature that is less egoistic. For excesses in one direction do not prevent excesses in the opposite direction; but rather, extreme deviations from the mean on one side lead to extreme deviations on the other side. A society in which the most exalted principles of self-sacrifice for the benefit of neighbours are enunciated, may be a society in which unscrupulous sacrifice of alien fellow-creatures is not only tolerated but applauded. Along with professed anxiety to spread these exalted principles among heathens, there may go the deliberate fastening of a quarrel upon them with a view to annexing their territory. Men who every Sunday have listened approvingly to injunctions carrying the regard for other men to an impracticable extent, may yet hire themselves out to slay, at the word of command, any people in any part of the world, utterly indifferent to the right or wrong of the matter fought about. And as in these cases transcendent altruism in theory co-exists with brutal egoism in practice, so, conversely, a more qualified altruism may have for its concomitant a greatly moderated egoism. For asserting the due claims of self, is, by implication, drawing a limit beyond which the claims are undue; and is, by consequence, bringing into greater clearness the claims of others.

CHAPTER XII.

ALTRUISM *VERSUS* EGOISM.

§ 75. If we define altruism as being all action which, in the normal course of things, benefits others instead of benefiting self, then, from the dawn of life, altruism has been no less essential than egoism. Though primarily it is dependent on egoism, yet secondarily egoism is dependent on it.

Under altruism in this comprehensive sense, I take in the acts by which offspring are preserved and the species maintained. Moreover, among these acts must be included not such only as are accompanied by consciousness, but also such as conduce to the welfare of offspring without mental representation of the welfare—acts of automatic altruism as we may call them. Nor must there be left out those lowest altruistic acts which subserve race-maintenance without implying even automatic nervous processes —acts not in the remotest sense psychical, but in a literal sense physical. Whatever action, unconscious or conscious, involves expenditure of individual life to the end of increasing life in other individuals, is unquestionably altruistic in a sense, if not in the usual sense ; and it is here needful to understand it in this sense that we may see how conscious altruism grows out of unconscious altruism.

The simplest beings habitually multiply by spontaneous

fission. Physical altruism of the lowest kind, differentiating from physical egoism, may in this case be considered as not yet independent of it. For since the two halves which before fission constituted the individual, do not on dividing disappear, we must say that though the individuality of the parent infusorium or other protozoon is lost in ceasing to be single, yet the old individual continues to exist in each of the new individuals. When, however, as happens generally with these smallest animals, an interval of quiescence ends in the breaking up of the whole body into minute parts, each of which is the germ of a young one, we see the parent entirely sacrificed in forming progeny.

Here might be described how among creatures of higher grades, by fission or gemmation, parents bequeath parts of their bodies, more or less organized, to form offspring at the cost of their own individualities   Numerous examples might also be given of the ways in which the development of ova is carried to the extent of making the parental body little more than a receptacle for them : the implication being that the accumulations of nutriment which parental activities have laid up, are disposed of for the benefit of posterity. And then might be dwelt on the multitudinous cases where, as generally throughout the insect-world, maturity having been reached and a new generation provided for, life ends : death follows the sacrifices made for progeny.

But leaving these lower types in which the altruism is physical only, or in which it is physical and automatically-psychical only, let us ascend to those in which it is also, to a considerable degree, conscious.   Though in birds and mammals such parental activities as are guided by instinct, are accompanied by either no representations or but vague representations of the benefits which the young receive ; yet there are also in them actions which we may class as altruistic in the higher sense. The agitation which creatures of these classes show when their young are in danger, joined often with efforts on their behalf, as well as the grief displayed after loss of their young, make it manifest that in them parental altruism has a concomitant of emotion.

Those who understand by altruism only the conscious sacrifice of self to others among human beings, will think it strange, or even absurd, to extend its meaning so widely. But the justification for doing this is greater than has thus far appeared. I do not mean merely that in the course of evolution, there has been a progress through infinitesimal gradations from purely physical and unconscious sacrifices of the individual for the welfare of the species, up to sacrifices consciously made. I mean that from first to last the sacrifices are, when reduced to their lowest terms, of the same essential nature : to the last, as at first, there is involved a loss of bodily substance. When a part of the parental body is detached in the shape of gemmule, or egg, or fœtus, the material sacrifice is conspicuous ; and when the mother yields milk by absorbing which the young one grows, it cannot be questioned that there is also a material sacrifice. But though a material sacrifice is not manifest when the young are benefited by activities on their behalf ; yet, as no effort can be made without an equivalent waste of tissue, and as the bodily loss is proportionate to the expenditure that takes place without reimbursement in food consumed, it follows that efforts made in fostering offspring do really represent a part of the parental substance ; which is now given indirectly instead of directly.

Self-sacrifice, then, is no less primordial than self-preservation. Being in its simple physical form absolutely necessary for the continuance of life from the beginning ; and being extended under its automatic form, as indispensable to maintenance of race in types considerably advanced ; and being developed to its semi-conscious and conscious forms, along with the continued and complicated attendance by which the offspring of superior creatures are brought to maturity ; altruism has been evolving simultaneously with egoism. As was pointed out in an early chapter, the same superiorities which have enabled the individual to preserve itself better, have enabled it better to preserve the individuals derived from it; and each higher species, using its improved faculties primarily for egoistic benefit, has spread in proportion as it has used them secondarily for altruistic benefit.

The imperativeness of altruism as thus understood, is, indeed, no less than the imperativeness of egoism was shown to be in the last chapter. For while, on the one hand, a falling short of normal egoistic acts entails enfeeblement or loss of life, and therefore loss of ability to perform altruistic acts; on the other hand, such defect of altruistic acts as causes death of offspring or inadequate development of them, involves disappearance from future generations of the nature that is not altruistic enough—so decreasing the average egoism. In short, every species is continually purifying itself from the unduly egoistic individuals, while there are being lost to it the unduly altruistic individuals.

§ 76. As there has been an advance by degrees from unconscious parental altruism to conscious parental altruism of the highest kind, so has there been an advance by degrees from the altruism of the family to social altruism.

A fact to be first noted is that only where altruistic relations in the domestic group have reached highly-developed forms, do there arise conditions making possible full development of altruistic relations in the political group. Tribes in which promiscuity prevails or in which the marital relations are transitory, and tribes in which polyandry entails in another way indefinite relationships, are incapable of much organization. Nor do peoples who are habitually polygamous, show themselves able to take on those high forms of social co-operation which demand due subordination of self to others. Only where monogamic marriage has become general and eventually universal— only where there have consequently been established the

closest ties of blood—only where family altruism has been
most fostered, has social altruism become conspicuous.   It
needs but to recall the compound forms of the Aryan family
as described by Sir Henry Maine and others, to see that
family feeling, first extending itself to the gens and the
tribe, and afterwards to the society formed of related tribes,
prepared the way for fellow feeling among citizens not
of the same stock.

Recognizing this natural transition, we are here chiefly
concerned to observe that throughout the latter stages of
the progress, as throughout the former, increase of egoistic
satisfactions has depended on growth of regard for the
satisfactions of others.   On contemplating a line of successive parents and offspring, we see that each, enabled while
young to live by the sacrifices predecessors make for it, itself
makes, when adult, equivalent sacrifices for successors; and
that in default of this general balancing of benefits received
by benefits given, the line dies out.   Similarly, it is manifest
that in a society each generation of members, indebted for
such benefits as social organization yields them to preceding generations, who have by their sacrifices elaborated
this organization, are called on to make for succeeding
generations such kindred sacrifices as shall at least maintain this organization, if they do not improve it : the alternative being decay and eventual dissolution of the society,
implying gradual decrease in the egoistic satisfactions of its
members.

And now we are prepared to consider the several ways in
which, under social conditions, personal welfare depends on
due regard for the welfare of others.   Already the conclusions to be drawn have been foreshadowed.   As in the
chapter on the biological view were implied the inferences
definitely set forth in the last chapter ; so in the chapter on
the sociological view were implied the inferences to be
definitely set forth here.   Sundry of these are trite enough;

but they must nevertheless be specified, since the statement would be incomplete without them.

§ 77. First to be dealt with comes that negative altruism implied by such curbing of the egoistic impulses as prevents direct aggression.

As before shown, if men instead of living separately are to unite for defence or for other purposes, they must severally reap more good than evil from the union. On the average, each must lose less from the antagonisms of those with whom he is associated, than he gains by the association. At the outset, therefore, that increase of egoistic satisfactions which the social state brings, can be purchased only by altruism sufficient to cause some recognition of others' claims: if not a voluntary recognition, still, a compulsory recognition.

While the recognition is but of that lowest kind due to dread of retaliation, or of prescribed punishment, the egoistic gain from association is small; and it becomes considerable only as the recognition becomes voluntary— that is, more altruistic. Where, as among some of the wild Australians, there exists no limit to the right of the strongest, and the men fight to get possession of women while the wives of one man fight among themselves about him, the pursuit of egoistic satisfactions is greatly impeded. Besides the bodily pain occasionally given to each by conflict, and the more or less of subsequent inability to achieve personal ends, there is the waste of energy entailed in maintaining readiness for self-defence, and there is the accompanying occupation of consciousness by emotions that are on the average of cases disagreeable. Moreover, the primary end of safety in presence of external foes is ill-attained in proportion as there are internal animosities; such furtherance of satisfactions as industrial co-operation brings cannot be had; and there is little motive to labour for extra benefits when the products of labour are insecure. And from this early stage to comparatively late stages, we may trace in the wearing of arms, in the carrying on of family feuds, and in the taking of daily precautions for safety, the ways in which the egoistic satisfactions of each are diminished by deficiency of that altruism which checks overt injury of others.

The private interests of the individual are on the average better subserved, not only in proportion as he himself refrains from direct aggression, but also, on the average, in proportion as he succeeds in diminishing the aggressions of his fellows on one another. The prevalance of antagonisms among those around, impedes the activities carried on by each in pursuit of satisfactions; and by causing disorder makes the beneficial results of activities more doubtful. Hence, each profits egoistically from the growth of an altruism which leads each to aid in preventing or diminishing others' violence.

The like holds when we pass to that altruism which restrains the undue egoism displayed in breaches of contract. General acceptance of the maxim that honesty is the best policy, implies general experience that gratification of the self-regarding feelings is eventually furthered by such checking of them as maintains equitable dealings. And here, as before, each is personally interested in securing good treatment of his fellows by one another. For in countless ways evils are entailed on each by the prevalence of fraudulent transactions. As everyone knows, the larger the number of a shopkeeper's bills left unpaid by some customers, the higher must be the prices which other customers pay. The more manufacturers lose by defective raw materials or by carelessness of workmen, the more must they charge for their fabrics to buyers. The less trustworthy people are, the higher rises the rate of interest, the larger becomes the amount of capital hoarded, the greater are the impediments to industry. The further traders and people in general go beyond their means, and hypothecate the property of others in speculation, the more serious are those commercial panics which bring disasters on multitudes and injuriously affect all.

This introduces us to yet a third way in which such personal welfare as results from the proportioning of benefits gained to labours given, depends on the making of certain sacrifices for social welfare. The man who, expending his energies wholly on private affairs refuses to take trouble about public affairs, pluming himself on his wisdom in minding his own business, is blind to the fact that his own business is made possible only by maintenance of a healthy social state, and that he loses all round by defective governmental arrangements. Where there are many likeminded with himself—where, as a consequence, offices come to be filled by political adventurers and opinion is swayed by demagogues—where bribery vitiates the administration of the law and makes fraudulent State-transactions habitual; heavy penalties fall on the community at large, and, among others, on those who have thus done everything for self and nothing for society. Their investments are insecure; recovery of their debts is difficult; and even their lives are less safe than they would otherwise have been.

So that on such altruistic actions as are implied, firstly in being just, secondly in seeing justice done between others, and thirdly in upholding and improving the agencies by which justice is administered, depend, in large measure, the egoistic satisfactions of each.

§ 78. But the identification of personal advantage with the advantage of fellow-citizens is much wider than this. In various other ways the well-being of each rises and falls with the well-being of all.

A weak man left to provide for his own wants, suffers by getting smaller amounts of food and other necessaries than he might get were he stronger. In a community formed of

weak men, who divide their labours and exchange the products, all suffer evils from the weakness of their fellows.
The quantity of each kind of product is made deficient by
the deficiency of labouring power; and the share each
gets for such share of his own product as he can afford
to give, is relatively small. Just as the maintenance of
paupers, hospital patients, inmates of asylums, and others
who consume but do not produce, leaves to be divided·
among producers a smaller stock of commodities than would
exist were there no incapables; so must there be left a
smaller stock of commodities to be divided, the greater the
number of inefficient producers, or the greater the average
deficiency of producing power. Hence, whatever decreases
the strength of men in general restricts the gratifications of
each by making the means to them dearer.

More directly, and more obviously, does the bodily well-
being of his fellows concern him; for their bodily ill-being,
when it takes certain shapes, is apt to bring similar bodily
ill-being on him. If he is not himself attacked by cholera,
or small-pox, or typhus, when it invades his neighbourhood,
he often suffers a penalty through his belongings. Under
conditions spreading it, his wife catches diphtheria, or his
servant is laid up with scarlet fever, or his children take now
this and now that infectious disorder. Add together the
immediate and remote evils brought on him year after year
by epidemics, and it becomes manifest that his egoistic
satisfactions are greatly furthered by such altruistic activities
as render disease less prevalent.

With the mental, as well as with the bodily, states of fellow-
citizens, his enjoyments are in multitudinous ways bound up.
Stupidity like weakness raises the cost of commodities.
Where farming is unimproved, the prices of food are higher
than they would else be; where antiquated routine maintains
itself in trade, the needless expense of distribution weighs on
all; where there is no inventiveness, everyone loses the benefits which improved appliances diffuse. Other than economic

14

evils come from the average unintelligence—periodically
through the manias and panics that arise because traders
rush in herds all to buy or all to sell; and habitually through
the mal-administration of justice, which people and rulers
alike disregard while pursuing this or that legislative will-o'-
the-wisp. Closer and clearer is the dependence of his personal
satisfactions on others' mental states, which each experiences
in his household. Unpunctuality and want of system are
perpetual sources of annoyance. The unskilfulness of the
cook causes frequent vexation and occasional indigestion.
Lack of forethought in the housemaid leads to a fall over a
bucket in a dark passage. And inattention to a message
or forgetfulness in delivering it, entails failure in an
important engagement. Each, therefore, benefits egoistically
by such altruism as aids in raising the average intelligence.
I do not mean such altruism as taxes ratepayers that
children's minds may be filled with dates, and names, and
gossip about kings, and narratives of battles, and other
useless information, no amount of which will make them
capable workers or good citizens; but I mean such altruism
as helps to spread a knowledge of the nature of things and
to cultivate the power of applying that knowledge.

Yet again, each has a private interest in public morals
and profits by improving them. Not in large ways only,
by aggressions and breaches of contract, by adulterations
and short measures, does each suffer from the general
unconscientiousness; but in more numerous small ways.
Now it is through the untruthfulness of one who gives a
good character to a bad servant; now it is by the reckless-
ness of a laundress who, using bleaching agents to save
trouble in washing, destroys his linen; now it is by the
acted falsehood of railway passengers who, by dispersed
coats, make him believe that all the seats in a compart-
ment are taken when they are not. Yesterday the
illness of his child due to foul gases, led to the discovery
of a drain that had become choked because it was ill-made

by a dishonest builder under supervision of a careless or bribed surveyor. To-day workmen employed to rectify it bring on him cost and inconvenience by dawdling; and their low standard of work, determined by the unionist principle that the better workers must not discredit the worse by exceeding them in efficiency, he may trace to the immoral belief that the unworthy should fare as well as the worthy. To-morrow it turns out that business for the plumber has been provided by damage which the bricklayers have done.

Thus the improvement of others, physically, intellectually, and morally, personally concerns each; since their imperfections tell in raising the cost of all the commodities he buys, in increasing the taxes and rates he pays, and in the losses of time, trouble, and money, daily brought on him by others' carelessness, stupidity, or unconscientiousness.

§ 79. Very obvious are certain more immediate connexions between personal welfare and ministration to the welfare of those around. The evils suffered by those whose behaviour is unsympathetic, and the benefits to self which unselfish conduct brings, show these.

That anyone should have formulated his experience by saying that the conditions to success are a hard heart and a sound digestion, is marvellous considering the many proofs that success, even of a material kind, greatly depending as it does on the good offices of others, is furthered by whatever creates goodwill in others. The contrast between the prosperity of those who to but moderate abilities join natures which beget friendships by their kindliness, and the adversity of those who, though possessed of superior faculties and greater acquirements, arouse dislikes by their hardness or indifference, should force upon all the truth that egoistic enjoyments are aided by altruistic actions.

This increase of personal benefit achieved by benefiting others, is but partially achieved where a selfish motive

14 *

prompts the seemingly-unselfish act: it is fully achieved only where the act is really unselfish. Though services rendered with the view of some time profiting by reciprocated services, answer to a certain extent; yet, ordinarily, they answer only to the extent of bringing equivalents of reciprocated services. Those which bring more than equivalents are those not prompted by any thoughts of equivalents. For obviously it is the spontaneous outflow of good nature, not in the larger acts of life only but in all its details, which generates in those around the attachments prompting unstinted benevolence.

Besides furthering prosperity, other-regarding actions conduce to self-regarding gratifications by generating a genial environment. With the sympathetic being everyone feels more sympathy than with others. All conduct themselves with more than usual amiability to a person who hourly discloses a lovable nature. Such a one is practically surrounded by a world of better people than one who is less attractive. If we contrast the state of a man possessing all the material means to happiness, but isolated by his absolute egoism, with the state of an altruistic man relatively poor in means but rich in friends, we may see that various gratifications not to be purchased by money, come in abundance to the last and are inaccessible to the first.

While, then, there is one kind of other-regarding action, furthering the prosperity of fellow-citizens at large, which admits of being deliberately pursued from motives that are remotely self-regarding—the conviction being that personal well-being depends in large measure on the well-being of society—there is an additional kind of other-regarding action having in it no element of conscious self-regard, which nevertheless conduces greatly to egoistic satisfactions.

§ 80. Yet other modes exist in which egoism unqualified by altruism habitually fails. It diminishes the totality of egoistic pleasure by diminishing in several directions the capacity for pleasure.

Self-gratifications, considered separately or in the aggregate, lose their intensities by that too great persistence in them which results if they are made the exclusive objects of pursuit. The law that function entails waste, and that faculties yielding pleasure by their action cannot act incessantly without exhaustion and accompanying satiety, has the implication that intervals during which altruistic activities absorb the energies, are intervals during which the capacity for egoistic pleasure is recovering its full degree. The sensitiveness to purely personal enjoyments is maintained at a higher pitch by those who minister to the enjoyments of others, than it is by those who devote themselves wholly to personal enjoyments.

This which is manifest even while the tide of life is high, becomes still more manifest as life ebbs. It is in maturity and old age that we especially see how, as egoistic pleasures grow faint, altruistic actions come in to revive them in new forms. The contrast between the child's delight in the novelties daily revealed, and the indifference which comes as the world around grows familiar, until in adult life there remain comparatively few things that are greatly enjoyed, draws from all the reflection that as years go by pleasures pall. And to those who think, it becomes clear that only through sympathy can pleasures be indirectly gained from things that have ceased to yield pleasures directly. In the gratifications derived by parents from the gratifications of their offspring, this is conspicuously shown. Trite as is the remark that men live afresh in their children, it is needful here to set it down as reminding us of the way in which, as the egoistic satisfactions in life fade, altruism renews them while it transfigures them.

We are thus introduced to a more general consideration —the egoistic aspect of altruistic pleasure. Not, indeed, that this is the place for discussing the question whether the egoistic element can be excluded from altruism; nor is it the place for distinguishing between the altruism which is pursued with a foresight of the pleasurable feeling to be achieved through it, and the altruism which, though it achieves this pleasurable feeling, does not make pursuit of it a motive. Here we are concerned with the fact that, whether knowingly or unknowingly gained, the state of mind accompanying altruistic action, being a pleasurable state, is to be counted in the sum of pleasures which the individual can receive; and in this sense cannot be other than egoistic. That we must so regard it is proved on observing that this pleasure, like pleasures in general, conduces to the physical prosperity of the ego. As every other agreeable emotion raises the tide of life, so does the agreeable emotion which accompanies a benevolent deed. As it cannot be denied that the pain caused by the sight of suffering, depresses the vital functions—sometimes even to the extent of arresting the heart's action, as in one who faints on seeing a surgical operation; so neither can it be denied that the joy felt in witnessing others' joy exalts the vital functions. Hence, however much we may hesitate to class altruistic pleasure as a higher kind of egoistic pleasure, we are obliged to recognize the fact that its immediate effects in augmenting life and so furthering personal well-being, are like those of pleasures that are directly egoistic. And the corollary drawn must be that pure egoism is, even in its immediate results, less successfully egoistic than is the egoism duly qualified by altruism, which, besides achieving additional pleasures, achieves also, through raised vitality, a greater capacity for pleasures in general.

That the range of æsthetic gratifications is wider for the altruistic nature than for the egoistic nature, is also a truth not to be overlooked. The joys and sorrows of human beings form a chief element in the subject-matter of art;

and evidently the pleasures which art gives increase as the fellow-feeling with these joys and sorrows strengthens. If we contrast early poetry occupied mainly with war and gratifying the savage instincts by descriptions of bloody victories, with the poetry of modern times, in which the sanguinary forms but a small part while a large part, dealing with the gentler affections, enlists the feelings of readers on behalf of the weak ; we are shown that with the development of a more altruistic nature, there has been opened a sphere of enjoyment inaccessible to the callous egoism of barbarous times. So, too, between the fiction of the past and the fiction of the present, there is the difference that while the one was almost exclusively occupied with the doings of the ruling classes, and found its plots in their antagonisms and deeds of violence, the other, chiefly taking stories of peaceful life for its subjects, and to a considerable extent the life of the humbler classes, discloses a new world of interest in the every-day pleasures and pains of ordinary people. A like contrast exists between early and late forms of plastic art. When not representing acts of worship, the wall-sculptures and wall-paintings of the Assyrians and Egyptians, or the decorations of temples among the Greeks, represented deeds of conquest; whereas in modern times, while the works which glorify destructive activities are less numerous, there are an increasing number of works gratifying to the kindlier sentiments of spectators. To see that those who care nothing about the feelings of other beings are, by implication, shut out from a wide range of æsthetic pleasures, it needs but to ask whether men who delight in dog-fights may be expected to appreciate Beethoven's *Adelaida,* or whether Tennyson's *In Memoriam* would greatly move a gang of convicts.

§ 81. From the dawn of life, then, egoism has been dependent upon altruism as altruism has been dependent upon egoism; and in the course of evolution the reciprocal services of the two have been increasing.

The physical and unconscious self-sacrifice of parents to form offspring, which the lowest living things display from hour to hour, shows us in its primitive form the altruism which makes possible the egoism of individual life and growth. As we ascend to higher grades of creatures, this parental altruism becomes a direct yielding up of only part of the body, joined with an increasing contribution from the remainder in the shape of tissue wasted in efforts made on behalf of progeny. This indirect sacrifice of substance, replacing more and more the direct sacrifice as parental altruism becomes higher, continues to the last to represent also altruism which is other than parental; since this, too, implies loss of substance in making efforts that do not bring their return in personal aggrandisement.

After noting how among mankind parental altruism and family altruism pass into social altruism, we observed that a society, like a species, survives only on condition that each generation of its members shall yield to the next, benefits equivalent to those it has received from the last. And this implies that care for the family must be supplemented by care for the society.

Fulness of egoistic satisfactions in the associated state, depending primarily on maintenance of the normal relation between efforts expended and benefits obtained, which underlies all life, implies an altruism which both prompts equitable conduct and prompts the enforcing of equity. The well-being of each is involved with the well-being of all in sundry other ways. Whatever conduces to their vigour concerns him; for it diminishes the cost of everything he buys. Whatever conduces to their freedom from disease concerns him; for it diminishes his own liability to disease. Whatever raises their intelligence concerns him; for inconveniences are daily entailed on him by others' ignorance or folly. Whatever raises their moral characters concerns him; for at every turn he suffers from the average unconscientiousness.

Much more directly do his egoistic satisfactions depend on those altruistic activities which enlist the sympathies of others. By alienating those around, selfishnesses loses the unbought aid they can render; shuts out a wide range of social enjoyments; and fails to receive those exaltations of pleasure and mitigations of pain, which come from men's fellow-feeling with those they like.

Lastly, undue egoism defeats itself by bringing on an incapacity for happiness. Purely egoistic gratifications are rendered less keen by satiety, even in the earlier part of life, and almost disappear in the later; the less satiating gratifications of altruism are missed throughout life, and especially in that latter part when they largely replace egoistic gratifications; and there is a lack of susceptibility to æsthetic pleasures of the higher orders.

An indication must be added of the truth, scarcely at all recognized, that this dependence of egoism upon altruism ranges beyond the limits of each society, and tends ever towards universality. That within each society it becomes greater as social evolution, implying increase of mutual dependence, progresses, needs not be shown; and it is a corollary that as fast as the dependence of societies on one another is increased by commercial intercourse, the internal welfare of each becomes a matter of concern to the others. That the impoverishment of any country, diminishing both its producing and consuming powers, tells detrimentally on the people of countries trading with it, is a commonplace of political economy. Moreover, we have had of late years, abundant experience of the industrial derangements through which distress is brought on nations not immediately concerned, by wars between other nations. And if each community has the egoistic satisfactions of its members diminished by aggressions of neighbouring communities on one another, still more does it have them diminished by its own aggressions.   One who marks how, in various parts of the world, the unscrupulous greed of conquest cloaked by pretences of spreading the blessings of British rule and British religion, is now reacting to the immense detriment of the industrial classes at home, alike by increasing expenditure and paralyzing trade, may see that these industrial classes, absorbed in questions about capital and labour, and thinking themselves unconcerned in our doings abroad, are suffering from lack of that wide-reaching altruism which should insist on just dealings with other peoples, civilized or savage.   And he may also see that beyond these immediate evils, they will for a generation to come suffer the evils that must flow from resuscitating the type of social organization which aggressive activities produce, and from the lowered moral tone which is its accompaniment.

CHAPTER XIII.

TRIAL AND COMPROMISE.

§ 82. In the foregoing two chapters the case on behalf of Egoism and the case on behalf of Altruism have been stated. The two conflict; and we have now to consider what verdict ought to be given.

If the opposed statements are severally valid, or even if each of them is valid in part, the inference must be that pure egoism and pure altruism are both illegitimate. If the maxim—"Live for self," is wrong, so also is the maxim—"Live for others." Hence a compromise is the only possibility.

This conclusion, though already seeming unavoidable, I do not here set down as proved. The purpose of this chapter is to justify it in full; and I enunciate it at the outset because the arguments used will be better understood, if the conclusion to which they converge is in the reader's view.

How shall we so conduct the discussion as most clearly to bring out this necessity for a compromise? Perhaps the best way will be that of stating one of the two claims in its extreme form, and observing the implied absurdities. To deal thus with the principle of pure selfishness, would be to waste space. Every one sees that an unchecked satisfaction of personal desires from moment to moment, in absolute disregard of all other beings, would cause universal conflict and social dissolution. The principle of pure unselfishness, less obviously mischievous, may therefore better be chosen.

There are two aspects under which the doctrine that others' happiness is the true ethical aim presents itself. The "others" may be conceived personally, as individuals with whom we stand in direct relations; or they may be conceived impersonally, as constituting the community. In so far as the self-abnegation implied by pure altruism is concerned, it matters not in which sense "others" is used. But criticism will be facilitated by distinguishing between these two forms of it. We will take the last form first.

§ 83. This commits us to an examination of "the greatest happiness principle," as enunciated by Bentham and his followers. The doctrine that "the general happiness" ought to be the object of pursuit, is not, indeed, overtly identified with pure altruism. But as, if general happiness is the proper end of action, the individual actor must regard his own share of it simply as a unit in the aggregate, no more to be valued by him than any other unit, it results that since this unit is almost infinitesimal in comparison with the aggregate, his action, if directed exclusively to achievement of general happiness, is, if not absolutely altruistic, as nearly so as may be. Hence the theory which makes general happiness the immediate object of pursuit, may rightly be taken as one form of the pure altruism to be here criticized.

Both as justifying this interpretation and as furnishing a definite proposition with which to deal, let me set out by quoting a passage from Mr. Mill's *Utilitarianism*.

"The Greatest-Happiness Principle," he says, "is a mere form of words without rational signification, unless one person's happiness, supposed equal in degree (with the proper allowance made for kind), is counted for exactly as much as another's. Those conditions being supplied, Bentham's dictum, 'everybody to count for one, nobody for more than one,' might be written under the principle of utility as an explanatory commentary" (p. 91.)

Now though the meaning of "greatest happiness" as an

end, is here to a certain degree defined, the need for
further definition is felt the moment we attempt to decide
on ways of regulating conduct so as to attain the end.   The
first question which arises is—Must we regard this "greatest
happiness principle" as a principle of guidance for the
community in its corporate capacity, or as a principle of
guidance for its members separately considered, or both ?
If the reply is that the principle must be taken as a guide
for governmental action rather than for individual action,
we are at once met by the inquiry,—What is to be the
guide for individual action?   If individual action is not
to be regulated solely for the purpose of achieving " the
greatest happiness of the greatest number," some other
principle of regulation for individual action is required ;
and " the greatest happiness principle" fails to furnish the
needful ethical standard.   Should it be rejoined that the
individual in his capacity of political unit, is to take furtherance of general happiness as his end, giving his vote or
otherwise acting on the legislature with a view to this end,
and that in so far guidance is supplied to him, there comes
the further inquiry—Whence is to come guidance for
the remainder of individual conduct, constituting by far
the greater part of it ?   If this private part of individual
conduct is not to have general happiness as its direct aim,
then an ethical standard other than that offered has still to
be found.

Hence, unless pure altruism as thus formulated confesses
its inadequacy, it must justify itself as a sufficient rule
for all conduct, individual and social.   We will first deal
with it as the alleged right principle of public policy ; and
then as the alleged right principle of private action.

§ 84. On trying to understand precisely the statement
that when taking general happiness as an end, the rule
must be—"everybody to count for one, nobody for more than
one," there arises the idea of distribution.   We can form

no idea of distribution without thinking of something distributed and recipients of this something. That we may clearly conceive the proposition we must clearly conceive both these elements of it. Let us take first the recipients.

"Everybody to count for one, nobody for more than one." Does this mean that, in respect of whatever is portioned out, each is to have the same share whatever his character, whatever his conduct? Shall he if passive have as much as if active? Shall he if useless have as much as if useful? Shall he if criminal have as much as if virtuous? If the distribution is to be made without reference to the natures and deeds of the recipients, then it must be shown that a system which equalizes, as far as it can, the treatment of good and bad, will be beneficial. If the distribution is not to be indiscriminate, then the formula disappears. The something distributed must be apportioned otherwise than by equal division. There must be adjustment of amounts to deserts; and we are left in the dark as to the mode of adjustment—we have to find other guidance.

Let us next ask what is the something to be distributed? The first idea which occurs is that happiness itself must be divided out among all. Taken literally, the notions that the greatest happiness should be the end sought, and that in apportioning it everybody should count for one and nobody for more than one, imply that happiness is something that can be cut up into parts and handed round. This, however, is an impossible interpretation. But after recognizing the impossibility of it, there returns the question—What is it in respect of which everybody is to count for one and nobody for more than one?

Shall the interpretation be that the concrete means to happiness are to be equally divided? Is it intended that there shall be distributed to all in equal portions the necessaries of life, the appliances to comfort, the facilities for amusement? As a conception simply, this is more defensible.

But passing over the question of policy—passing over the question whether greatest happiness would *ultimately* be secured by such a process (which it obviously would not) it turns out on examination that greatest happiness could not even *proximately* be so secured.   Differences of age, of growth, of constitutional need, differences of activity and consequent expenditure, differences of desires and tastes, would entail the inevitable result that the material aids to happiness which each received would be more or less un-adapted to his requirements.   Even if purchasing power were equally divided, the greatest happiness would not be achieved if everybody counted for one and nobody for more than one; since, as the capacities for utilizing the purchased means to happiness would vary both with the constitution and the stage of life, the means which would approximately suffice to satisfy the wants of one would be extremely insufficient to satisfy the wants of another, and so the greatest total of happiness would not be obtained : means might be unequally apportioned in a way that would produce a greater total.

But now if happiness itself cannot be cut up and distributed equally, and if equal division of the material aids to happiness would not produce greatest happiness, what is the thing to be thus apportioned ?—what is it in respect of which everybody is to count for one and nobody for more than one ?   There seems but a single possibility. There remain to be equally distributed nothing but the conditions under which each may pursue happiness.   The limitations to action—the degrees of freedom and restraint, shall be alike for all.   Each shall have as much liberty to pursue his ends as consists with maintaining like liberties to pursue their ends by others ; and one as much as another shall have the enjoyment of that which his efforts, carried on within these limits, obtain.   But to say that in respect of these conditions everybody shall count for one and nobody for more than one, is simply to say that equity shall be enforced.

Thus, considered as a principle of public policy, Bentham's principle, when analyzed, transforms itself into the principle he slights. Not general happiness becomes the ethical standard by which legislative action is to be guided, but universal justice. And so the altruistic theory under this form collapses.

§ 85. From examining the doctrine that general happiness should be the end of public action, we pass now to examine the doctrine that it should be the end of private action.

It is contended that from the stand-point of pure reason, the happiness of others has no less a claim as an object of pursuit for each than personal happiness. Considered as parts of a total, happiness felt by self and like happiness felt by another, are of equal values ; and hence it is inferred that, rationally estimated, the obligation to expend effort for others' benefit, is as great as the obligation to expend effort for one's own benefit. Holding that the utilitarian system of morals, rightly understood, harmonizes with the Christian maxim—" Love your neighbour as yourself," Mr. Mill says that " as between his own happiness and that of others, utilitarianism requires him to be as strictly impartial as a disinterested and benevolent spectator." (p. 24) Let us. consider the alternative interpretations which may be given to this statement.

Suppose, first, that a certain quantum of happiness has in some way become available, without the special instrumentality of A, B, C, or D, constituting the group concerned. Then the proposition is that each shall be ready to have this quantum of happiness as much enjoyed by one or more of the others as by himself. The disinterested and benevolent spectator would clearly, in such a case, rule that no one ought to have more of the happiness than another. But here, assuming as we do that the quantum of happiness has become available without the agency of any among the group, simple equity dictates as much. No one having in any way established a claim different from

the claims of others, their claims are equal; and due regard
for justice by each will not permit him to monopolize the
happiness.

Now suppose a different case. Suppose that the quantum
of happiness has been made available by the efforts of one
member of the group. Suppose that A has acquired by
labour some material aid to happiness. He decides to act
as the disinterested and benevolent spectator would direct.
What will he decide?—what would the spectator direct?
Let us consider the possible suppositions; taking first the
least reasonable.

The spectator may be conceived as deciding that the
labour expended by A in acquiring this material aid to
happiness, originates no claim to special use of it; but
that it ought to be given to B, C, or D, or that it ought
to be divided equally among B, C, and D, or that it ought
to be divided equally among all members of the group,
including A who has laboured for it. And if the spectator is conceived as deciding thus to-day, he must be conceived as deciding thus day after day; with the result that
one of the group expends all the effort, getting either none
of the benefit or only his numerical share, while the others
get their shares of the benefit without expending any efforts.
That A might conceive the disinterested and benevolent
spectator to decide in this way, and might feel bound to
act in conformity with the imagined decision, is a strong
supposition; and probably it will be admitted that such
kind of impartiality, so far from being conducive to the
general happiness, would quickly be fatal to everyone. But
this is not all. Action in pursuance of such a decision
would in reality be negatived by the very principle enunciated. For not only A, but also B, C, and D, have to act
on this principle. Each of them must behave as he conceives an impartial spectator would decide. Does B conceive the impartial spectator as awarding to him, B, the
product of A's labour? Then the assumption is that B

15

conceives the impartial spectator as favouring himself, B, more than A conceives him as favouring himself, A; which is inconsistent with the hypothesis. Does B, in conceiving the impartial spectator, exclude his own interests as completely as A does? Then how can he decide so much to his own advantage, so partially, as to allow him to take from A an equal share of the benefit gained by A's labour, towards which he and the rest have done nothing?

Passing from this conceivable, though not credible, decision of the spectator, here noted for the purpose of observing that habitual conformity to it would be impossible, there remains to be considered the decision which a spectator really impartial would give. He would say that the happiness, or material aid to happiness, which had been purchased by A's labour, was to be taken by A. He would say that B, C, and D had no claims to it, but only to such happiness, or aids to happiness, as their respective labours had purchased. Consequently, A, acting as the imaginary impartial spectator would direct, is, by this test, justified in appropriating such happiness or aid to happiness as his own efforts have achieved.

And so under its special form as under its general form, the principle is true only in so far as it embodies a disguised justice. Analysis again brings out the result that making "general happiness" the end of action, really means maintaining what we call equitable relations among individuals. Decline to accept in its vague form "the greatest-happiness principle," and insist on knowing what is the implied conduct, public or private, and it turns out that the principle is meaningless save as indirectly asserting that the claims of each should be duly regarded by all. The utilitarian altruism becomes a duly qualified egoism.

§ 86. Another point of view from which to judge the altruistic theory may now be taken. If, assuming the proper object of pursuit to be general happiness, we proceed rationally, we must ask in what different ways the aggregate, general happiness, may be composed ; and must then ask what composition of it will yield the largest sum.

Suppose that each citizen pursues his own happiness independently, not to the detriment of others but without active concern for others ; then their united happinesses constitute a certain sum—a certain general happiness. Now suppose that each, instead of making his own happiness the object of pursuit, makes the happiness of others the object of pursuit ; then, again, there results a certain sum of happiness. This sum must be less than, or equal to, or greater than, the first. If it is admitted that this sum is either less than the first or only equal to it, the altruistic course of action is confessedly either worse than, or no better than, the egoistic. The assumption must be that the sum of happiness obtained is greater. Let us observe what is involved in this assumption.

If each pursues exclusively the happiness of others ; and if each is also a recipient of happiness (which he must be, for otherwise no aggregate happiness can be formed out of their individual happinesses) ; then the implication is that each gains the happiness due to altruistic action exclusively ; and that in each this is greater in amount than the egoistic happiness obtainable by him, if he devoted himself to pursuit of it. Leaving out of consideration for a moment these relative amounts of the two, let us note the conditions to the receipt of altruistic happiness by each. The sympathetic nature gets pleasure by giving pleasure ; and the proposition is that if the general happiness is the object of pursuit, each will be made happy by witnessing others' happiness. But what in such case constitutes the happiness of others ? These others are also, by the hypothesis, pursuers and receivers of altruistic pleasure. The genesis of altruistic pleasure in each is to depend on the display of pleasures by others ; which is again to depend on the display of pleasures by others ; and so on perpetually. Where, then, is the pleasure

15*

to begin? Obviously there must be egoistic pleasure some-where, before there can be the altruistic pleasure caused by sympathy with it. Obviously, therefore, each must be egoistic in due amount, even if only with the view of giving others the possibility of being altruistic. So far from the sum of happiness being made greater if all make greatest happiness the exclusive end, the sum disappears entirely.

How absurd is the supposition that the happiness of all can be achieved without each pursuing his own happiness, will be best shown by a physical simile. Suppose a cluster of bodies, each of which generates heat; and each of which is, therefore, while a radiator of heat to those around, also a receiver of heat from them. Manifestly each will have a certain proper heat irrespective of that which it gains from the rest; and, each will have a certain heat gained from the rest irrespective of its proper heat. What will happen? So long as each of the bodies continues to be a generator of heat, each continues to maintain a temperature partly derived from itself and partly derived from others. But if each ceases to generate heat for itself and depends on the heat radiated to it by the rest, the entire cluster becomes cold. Well, the self-generated heat stands for egoistic pleasure; the heat radiated and received stands for sympathetic pleasure; and the disappearance of all heat if each ceases to be an originator of it, corresponds to the disappearance of all pleasure if each ceases to originate it egoistically.

A further conclusion may be drawn. Besides the im-plication that before altruistic pleasure can exist, egoistic pleasure must exist, and that if the rule of conduct is to be the same for all, each must be egoistic in due degree; there is the implication that, to achieve the greatest sum of happiness, each must be more egoistic than altruistic. For, speaking generally, sympathetic pleasures must ever con-tinue less intense than the pleasures with which there is sympathy. Other things equal, ideal feelings cannot be as vivid as real feelings. It is true that those having strong imaginations may, especially in cases where the affections are engaged, feel the moral pain if not the physical pain of another, as keenly as the actual sufferer of it, and may participate with like intensity in another's pleasure : sometimes even mentally representing the received pleasure as greater than it really is, and so getting reflex pleasure greater than the recipients' direct pleasure. Such cases, however, and cases in which even apart from exaltation of sympathy caused by attachment, there is a body of feeling sympathetically aroused equal in amount to the original feeling, if not greater, are necessarily exceptional. For in such cases the total consciousness includes many other elements besides the mentally-represented pleasure or pain—notably the luxury of pity and the luxury of goodness ; and genesis of these can occur but occasionally: they could not be habitual concomitants of sympathetic pleasures if all pursued these from moment to moment. In estimating the possible totality of sympathetic pleasures, we must include nothing beyond the representations of the pleasures others experience. And unless it be asserted that we can have other's states of consciousness perpetually re-produced in us more vividly than the kindred states of consciousness are aroused in ourselves by their proper personal causes, it must be admitted that the totality of altruistic pleasures cannot become equal to the totality of egoistic pleasures. Hence, beyond the truth that before there can be altruistic pleasures there must be the egoistic pleasures from sympathy with which they arise, there is the truth that, to obtain the greatest sum of altruistic pleasures, there must be a greater sum of egoistic pleasures.

§ 87. That pure altruism is suicidal may be yet otherwise demonstrated. A perfectly moral law must be one which becomes perfectly practicable as human nature becomes perfect. If its practicableness decreases as human nature improves; and if an ideal human nature necessitates its impracticability; it cannot be the moral law sought.

Now opportunities for practising altruism are numerous and great in proportion as there is weakness, or incapacity, or imperfection. If we pass beyond the limits of the family, in which a sphere for self-sacrificing activities must be preserved as long as offspring have to be reared; and if we ask how there can continue a social sphere for self-sacrificing activities; it becomes obvious that the continued existence of serious evils, caused by prevalent defects of nature, is implied. As fast as men adapt themselves to the requirements of social life, so fast will the demands for efforts on their behalf diminish. And with arrival at finished adaptation, when all persons are at once completely self-conserved and completely able to fulfil the obligations which society imposes on them, those occasions for postponement of self to others which pure altruism contemplates, disappear.

Such self-sacrifices become, indeed, doubly impracticable. Carrying on successfully their several lives, men not only cannot yield to those around the opportunities for giving aid, but aid cannot ordinarily be given them without interfering with their normal activities, and so diminishing their pleasures. Like every inferior creature, led by its innate desires spontaneously to do all that its life requires, man, when completely moulded to the social state, must have desires so adjusted to his needs that he fulfils the needs in gratifying the desires. And if his desires are severally gratified by the performance of required acts, none of these can be performed for him without balking his desires. Acceptance from others of the results of their activities can take place only on condition of relinquishing the pleasures derived from his own activities. Diminution rather than increase of happiness would result, could altruistic action in such case be enforced.

And here, indeed, we are introduced to another baseless assumption which the theory makes.

§ 88. The postulate of utilitarianism as formulated in the statements above quoted, and of pure altruism as otherwise expressed, involves the belief that it is possible for happiness, or the means to happiness, or the conditions to happiness, to be transferred. Without any specified limitation the proposition taken for granted is, that happiness in general admits of detachment from one and attachment to another—that surrender to any extent is possible by one and appropriation to any extent is possible by another. But a moment's thought shows this to be far from the truth. On the one hand, surrender carried to a certain point is extremely mischievous and to a further point fatal; and on the other hand, much of the happiness each enjoys is self-generated and can neither be given nor received.

To assume that egoistic pleasures may be relinquished to any extent, is to fall into one of those many errors of ethical speculation which result from ignoring the truths of biology. When taking the biological view of ethics we saw that pleasures accompany normal amounts of functions, while pains accompany defects or excesses of functions; further, that complete life depends on complete discharge of functions, and therefore on receipt of the correlative pleasures. Hence, to yield up normal pleasures is to yield up so much life; and there arises the question—to what extent may this be done? If he is to continue living, the individual *must* take certain amounts of those pleasures which go along with fulfilment of the bodily functions, and *must* avoid the pains which entire non-fulfilment of them entails. Complete abnegation means death; excessive abnegation means illness; abnegation less excessive means physical degradation and consequent loss of power to fulfil obligations, personal and other. When, therefore, we attempt to specialize the proposal to live not for self-satisfaction but for the satisfaction of others, we meet with the difficulty that beyond a certain limit this cannot be done. And when we have decided what decrease of bodily welfare, caused by sacrifice of pleasures and acceptance of pains, it is proper for the individual to make, there is forced on us the fact that the portion of happiness, or means to happiness, which it is possible for him to yield up for redistribution, is a limited portion.

Even more rigorous on another side is the restriction put upon the transfer of happiness, or the means to happiness. The pleasures gained by efficient action—by successful pursuit of ends, cannot by any process be parted with, and cannot in any way be appropriated by another. The habit of arguing about general happiness sometimes as though it were a concrete product to be portioned out, and sometimes as though it were co-extensive with the use of those material aids to pleasure which may be given and received, has caused inattention to the truth that the pleasures of achievement are not transferable. Alike in the boy who has won a game of marbles, the athlete who has performed a feat, the statesman who has gained a party triumph, the inventor who has devised a new machine, the man of science who has discovered a truth, the novelist who has well delineated a character, the poet who has finely rendered an emotion, we see pleasures which must, in the nature of things, be enjoyed exclusively by those to whom they come. And if we look at all such occupations as men are not impelled to by their necessities—if we contemplate the various ambitious which play so large a part in life; we are reminded that so long as the consciousness of efficiency remains a dominant pleasure, there will remain a dominant pleasure which cannot be pursued altruistically but must be pursued egoistically.

Cutting off, then, at the one end, those pleasures which are inseparable from maintenance of the physique in an uninjured state; and cutting off at the other end the pleasures of successful action; the amount that remains is so greatly diminished, as to make untenable the assumption that happiness at large admits of distribution after the manner which utilitarianism assumes.

§ 89. In yet one more way may be shown the inconsistency of this transfigured utilitarianism which regards its doctrine as embodying the Christian maxim—"Love your neighbour as yourself," and of that altruism which, going still further, enunciates the maxim—"Live for others."

A right rule of conduct must be one which may with advantage be adopted by all. "Act according to that maxim only, which you can wish, at the same time, to become a universal law," says Kant. And clearly, passing over needful qualifications of this maxim, we may accept it to the extent of admitting that a mode of action which becomes impracticable as it approaches universality, must be wrong. Hence, if the theory of pure altruism, implying that effort should be expended for the benefit of others and not for personal benefit, is defensible, it must be shown that it will produce good results when acted upon by all. Mark the consequences if all are purely altruistic.

First, an impossible combination of moral attributes is implied. Each is supposed by the hypothesis to regard self so little and others so much, that he willingly sacrifices his own pleasures to give pleasures to them. But if this is a universal trait, and if action is universally congruous with it, we have to conceive each as being not only a sacrificer but also one who accepts sacrifices. While he is so unselfish as willingly to yield up the benefit for which he has laboured, he is so selfish as willingly to let others yield up to him the benefits they have laboured for. To make pure altruism possible for all, each must be at once extremely unegoistic and extremely egoistic. As a giver, he must have no thought for self; as a receiver, no thought for others. Evidently, this implies an inconceivable mental constitution. The sympathy which is so solicitous for others as willingly to injure self in benefiting them, cannot at the same time be so regardless of others as to accept benefits which they injure themselves in giving.

The incongruities that emerge if we assume pure altruism to be universally practised, may be otherwise exhibited thus. Suppose that each, instead of enjoying such pleasures as come to him, or such consumable appliances to pleasure as he has worked for, or such occasions for pleasure as reward his efforts, relinquishes these to a single other, or adds them to a common stock from which others benefit; what will result? Different answers may be given according as we assume that there are, or are not, additional influences brought into play.   Suppose there are no additional influences. Then, if each transfers to another his happiness, or means to happiness, or occasions for happiness, while some one else does the like to him, the distribution of happiness is, on the average, unchanged; or if each adds to a common stock his happiness, or means to happiness, or occasions for happiness, from which common stock each appropriates his portion, the average state is still, as before, unchanged. The only obvious effect is that transactions must be gone through in the redistribution; and loss of time and labour must result.   Now suppose some additional influence which makes the process beneficial; what must it be? The totality can be increased only if the acts of transfer increase the quantity of that which is transferred. The happiness, or that which brings it, must be greater to one who derives it from another's efforts, than it would have been had his own efforts procured it; or otherwise, supposing a fund of happiness, or of that which brings it, has been formed by contributions from each, then each, in appropriating his share, must find it larger than it would have been had no such aggregation and dispersion taken place. To justify belief in such increase two conceivable assumptions may be made. One is that though the sum of pleasures, or of pleasure-yielding things, remains the same yet the kind of pleasure, or of pleasure-yielding things, which each receives in exchange from another, or from the aggregate of others, is one which he appreciates more than that for which he laboured. But to assume this is to assume that each labours directly for the thing which he enjoys less, rather than for the thing which he enjoys more, which is absurd. The other assumption is that while the exchanged or redistributed pleasure of the egoistic kind, remains the same in amount for each, there is added to it the altruistic pleasure accompanying the exchange. But this assumption is clearly inadmissible if, as is implied, the transaction is universal—is one through which each becomes giver and receiver to equal extents. For if the transfer of pleasures, or of pleasure-yielding things, from one to another or others, is always accompanied by the consciousness that there will be received from him or them an equivalent; there results merely a tacit exchange, either direct or roundabout. Each becomes altruistic in no greater degree than is implied by being equitable; and each, having nothing to exalt his happiness, sympathetically or otherwise, cannot be a source of sympathetic happiness to others.

§ 90. Thus, when the meanings of its words are inquired into, or when the necessary implications of its theory are examined, pure altruism, in whatever form expressed, commits its adherents to various absurdities.

If "the greatest happiness of the greatest number," or in other words, "the general happiness," is the proper end of action, then not only for all public action but for all private action, it must be the end; because, otherwise, the greater part of action remains unguided. Consider its fitness for each. If corporate action is to be guided by the principle, with its interpreting comment—"everybody to count for one, nobody for more than one"— there must be an ignoring of all differences of character and conduct, merits and demerits, among citizens, since no discrimination is provided for; and moreover, since that in respect of which all are to count alike cannot be happiness itself, which is indistributable, and since equal sharing of the concrete means to happiness, besides failing ultimately would fail proximately to produce the greatest happiness; it results that equal distribution of the conditions under which happiness may be pursued is the only tenable meaning : we discover in the principle nothing but a round-about insistance on equity. If, taking happiness at large as the aim of private action, the individual is required to judge between his own happiness and that of others as an impartial spectator would do, we see that no supposition concerning the spectator save one which suicidally ascribes partiality to him, can bring out any other result than that each shall enjoy such happiness, or appropriate such means to happiness, as his own efforts gain : equity is again the sole content. When, adopting another method, we consider how the greatest sum of happiness may be composed, and, recognizing the fact that equitable egoism will produce a certain sum, ask how pure altruism is to produce a greater sum ; we are shown that if all, exclusively pursuing altruistic pleasures, are so to produce a greater sum of pleasures, the implication is that altruistic pleasures, which arise from sympathy, can exist in the absence of egoistic pleasures with which there may be sympathy—an impossibility ; and another implication is that if, the necessity for egoistic pleasures being admitted, it is said that the greatest sum of happiness will be attained if all individuals are more altruistic than egoistic, it is indirectly said that as a general truth, representative feelings are stronger than presentative feelings—another impossibility. Again, the doctrine of pure altruism assumes that happiness may be to any extent transferred or redistributed; whereas the fact is that pleasures of one order cannot be transferred in large measure without results which are fatal or extremely injurious, and that pleasures of another order cannot be transferred in any degree. Further, pure altruism presents this fatal anomaly; that while a right principle of action must be more and more practised as men improve, the altruistic principle becomes less and less practicable as men approach an ideal form, because the sphere for practising it continually decreases. Finally, its self-destructiveness is made manifest on observing that for all to adopt it as a principle of action, which they must do if it is a sound principle, implies that all are at once extremely unegoistic and extremely egoistic—ready to injure self for others' benefit, and ready to accept benefit at the cost of injury to others: traits which cannot co-exist.

The need for a compromise between egoism and altruism is thus made conspicuous. We are forced to recognize the claims which his own well-being has on the attention of each by noting how, in some directions we come to a deadlock, in others to contradictions, and in others to disastrous results, if they are ignored. Conversely, it is undeniable that disregard of others by each, carried to a great extent is fatal to society, and carried to a still greater extent is fatal to the family, and eventually to the race. Egoism and altruism are therefore co-essential.

§ 91. What form is the compromise between egoism and altruism to assume? how are their respective claims to be satisfied in due degrees?

It is a truth insisted on by moralists and recognized in common life, that the achievement of individual happiness is not proportionate to the degree in which individual happiness is made the object of direct pursuit; but there has not yet become current the belief that, in like manner, the achievement of general happiness is not proportionate to the degree in which general happiness is made the object of direct pursuit. Yet failure of direct pursuit in the last case is more reasonably to be expected than in the first.

When discussing the relations of means and ends, we saw

that as individual conduct evolves, its principle becomes more and more that of making fulfilment of means the proximate end, and leaving the ultimate end, welfare or happiness, to come as a result. And we saw that when general welfare or happiness is the ultimate end, the same principle holds even more rigorously ; since the ultimate end under its impersonal form, is less determinate than under its personal form, and the difficulties in the way of achieving it by direct pursuit still greater. Recognizing, then, the fact that corporate happiness still more than individual happiness, must be pursued not directly but indirectly, the first question for us is—What must be the general nature of the means through which it is to be achieved.

It is admitted that self-happiness is, in a measure, to be obtained by furthering the happiness of others. May it not be true that, conversely, general happiness is to be obtained by furthering self-happiness ? If the well-being of each unit is to be reached partly through his care for the well-being of the aggregate, is not the well-being of the aggregate to be reached partly through the care of each unit for himself? Clearly, our conclusion must be that general happiness is to be achieved mainly through the adequate pursuit of their own happinesses by individuals ; while, reciprocally, the happinesses of individuals are to be achieved in part by their pursuit of the general happiness.

And this is the conclusion embodied in the progressing ideas and usages of mankind. This compromise between egoism and altruism has been slowly establishing itself ; and towards recognition of its propriety, men's actual beliefs, as distinguished from their nominal beliefs, have been gradually approaching. Social evolution has been bringing about a state in which the claims of the individual to the proceeds of his activities, and to such satisfactions as they bring, are more and more positively asserted ; at the same time that insistance on others' claims, and habitual respect for them, have been increasing. Among the rudest savages personal interests are very vaguely distinguished from the interests of others. In early stages of civilization, the proportioning of benefits to efforts is extremely rude: slaves and serfs get for work, arbitrary amounts of food and shelter: exchange being infrequent, there is little to develop the idea of equivalence. But as civilization advances and status passes into contract, there comes daily experience of the relation between advantages enjoyed and labour given: the industrial system maintaining, through supply and demand, a due adjustment of the one to the other. And this growth of voluntary co-operation—this exchange of services under agreement, has been necessarily accompanied by decrease of aggressions one upon another, and increase of sympathy: leading to exchange of services beyond agreement. That is to say, the more distinct assertions of individual claims and more rigorous apportioning of personal enjoyments to efforts expended, has gone hand in hand with growth of that negative altruism shown in equitable conduct and that positive altruism shown in gratuitous aid.

A higher phase of this double change has in our own times becomes conspicuous. If, on the one hand, we note the struggles for political freedom, the contests between labour and capital, the judicial reforms made to facilitate enforcement of rights, we see that the tendency still is towards complete appropriation by each of whatever benefits are due to him, and consequent exclusion of his fellows from such benefits. On the other hand, if we consider what is meant by the surrender of power to the masses, the abolition of class-privileges, the efforts to diffuse knowledge, the agitations to spread temperance, the multitudinous philanthropic societies; it becomes clear that regard for the well-being of others is increasing *pari passu* with the taking of means to secure personal well-being.

What holds of the relations within each society holds to

some extent, if to a less extent, of the relations between
societies.   Though to maintain national claims, real or
imaginary, often of a trivial kind, the civilized still make
war on one another; yet their several nationalities are more
respected than in past ages.   Though by victors portions of
territory are taken and money compensations exacted; yet
conquest is not now, as of old, habitually followed by entire
appropriation of territories and enslavement of peoples.
The individualities of societies are in a larger measure
preserved.   Meanwhile the altruistic intercourse is greater:
aid is rendered on occasions of disaster by flood, by fire, by
famine, or otherwise.   And in international arbitration as
lately exemplified, implying the recognition of claims by one
nation upon another, we see a further progress in this wider
altruism.   Doubtless there is much to be said by way of
set-off; for in the dealings of the civilized with the uncivilized, little of this progress can be traced.   It may be
urged that the primitive rule—"Life for life," has been
developed by us into the rule—"For one life many lives,"
as in the cases of Bishop Patteson and Mr. Birch; but
then there is the qualifying fact that we do not torture our
prisoners or mutilate them.   If it be said that as the
Hebrews thought themselves warranted in seizing the lands
God promised to them, and in some cases exterminating
the inhabitants, so we, to fulfil the "manifest intention of
Providence," dispossess inferior races whenever we want
their territories; it may be replied that we do not kill
many more than seems needful, and tolerate the existence
of those who submit.   And should any one point out that as
Attila, while conquering or destroying peoples and nations,
regarded himself as "the scourge of God," punishing men
for their sins, so we, as represented by a High Commis-
sioner and a priest he quotes, think ourselves called on to
chastise with rifles and cannon, heathens who practise poly-
gamy; there is the rejoinder that not even the most ferocious
disciple of the teacher of mercy would carry his vengeance

so far as to depopulate whole territories and erase scores of cities. And when, on the other hand, we remember that there is an Aborigines Protection Society, that there are Commissioners in certain colonies appointed to protect native interests, and that in some cases the lands of natives have been purchased in ways which, however unfair, have implied some recognition of their claims; we may say that little as the compromise between egoism and altruism has progressed in international affairs, it has still progressed somewhat in the direction indicated.

CHAPTER XIV.

CONCILIATION.

§ 92. As exhibited in the last chapter, the compromise between the claims of self and the claims of others seems to imply permanent antagonism between the two. The pursuit by each of his own happiness while paying due regard to the happiness of his fellows, apparently necessitates the ever-recurring question—how far must the one end be sought and how far the other: suggesting, if not discord in the life of each, still, an absence of complete harmony. This is not the inevitable inference however.

When, in the *Principles of Sociology*, Part III, the phenomena of race-maintenance among living things at large were discussed, that the development of the domestic relations might be the better understood, it was shown that during evolution there has been going on a conciliation between the interests of the species, the interests of the parents, and the interests of the offspring. Proof was given that as we ascend from the lowest forms of life to the highest, race-maintenance is achieved with a decreasing sacrifice of life, alike of young individuals and of adult individuals, and also with a decreasing sacrifice of parental lives to the lives of offspring. We saw that, with the progress of civilization, like changes go on among human beings; and that the highest domestic relations are those in which the conciliation of welfares within the family becomes greatest, while the welfare of the society is best subserved. Here it remains to be shown that a kindred conciliation has been, and is, taking place between the interests of each citizen and the interests of citizens at large; tending ever towards a state in which the two become merged in one, and in which the feelings answering to them respectively, fall into complete concord.

In the family group, even as we observe it among many inferior vertebrates, we see that the parental sacrifice, now become so moderate in amount as to consist with long-continued parental life, is not accompanied by consciousness of sacrifice; but, contrariwise, is made from a direct desire to make it: the altruistic labours on behalf of young are carried on in satisfaction of parental instincts. If we trace these relations up through the grades of mankind, and observe how largely love rather than obligation prompts the care of children, we see the conciliation of interests to be such that achievement of parental happiness coincides with securing the happiness of offspring: the wish for children among the childless, and the occasional adoption of children, showing how needful for attainment of certain egoistic satisfactions are these altruistic activities. And further evolution, causing along with higher nature diminished fertility, and therefore smaller burdens on parents, may be expected to bring a state in which, far more than now, the pleasures of adult life will consist in raising offspring to perfection while simultaneously furthering the immediate happiness of offspring.

Now though altruism of a social kind, lacking certain elements of parental altruism, can never attain the same level; yet it may be expected to attain a level at which it will be like parental altruism in spontaneity—a level such that ministration to others' happiness will become a daily need—a level such that the lower egoistic satisfactions will be continually subordinated to this higher egoistic satisfaction, not by any effort to subordinate them, but by the

16 *

preference for this higher egoistic satisfaction whenever it can be obtained.

Let us consider how the development of sympathy, which must advance as fast as conditions permit, will bring about this state.

§ 93. We have seen that during the evolution of life, pleasures and pains have necessarily been the incentives to and deterrents from, actions which the conditions of existence demanded and negatived. An implied truth to be here noted is, that faculties which, under given conditions, yield partly pain and partly pleasure, cannot develop beyond the limit at which they yield a surplus of pleasure : if beyond that limit more pain than pleasure results from exercise of them, their growth must be arrested.

Through sympathy both these forms of feeling are excited. Now a pleasurable consciousness is aroused on witnessing pleasure ; now a painful consciousness is aroused on witnessing pain. Hence, if beings around him habitually manifest pleasure and but rarely pain, sympathy yields to its possessor a surplus of pleasure ; while, contrariwise, if little pleasure is ordinarily witnessed and much pain, sympathy yields a surplus of pain to its possessor. The average development of sympathy must, therefore, be regulated by the average manifestations of pleasure and pain in others. If the life usually led under given social conditions is such that suffering is daily inflicted, or is daily displayed by associates, sympathy cannot grow : to assume growth of it is to assume that the constitution will modify itself in such way as to increase its pains and therefore depress its energies ; and is to ignore the truth that bearing any kind of pain gradually produces insensibility to that pain, or callousness. On the other hand, if the social state is such that manifestations of pleasure predominate, sympathy will increase ; since sympathetic pleasures, adding to the totality of pleasures enhancing vitality, conduce to the physical prosperity of the most sympathetic, and since the pleasures of sympathy exceeding its pains in all, lead to an exercise of it which strengthens it.

The first implication is one already more than once indicated. We have seen that along with habitual militancy and under the adapted type of social organization, sympathy cannot develop to any considerable height. The destructive activities carried on against external enemies sear it; the state of feeling maintained causes within the society itself frequent acts of aggression or cruelty; and further, the compulsory co-operation characterizing the militant *régime* necessarily represses sympathy—exists only on condition of an unsympathetic treatment of some by others.

But even could the militant *régime* forthwith end, the hindrances to development of sympathy would still be great. Though cessation of war would imply increased adaptation of man to social life, and decrease of sundry evils, yet there would remain much non-adaptation and much consequent unhappiness. In the first place, that form of nature which has generated and still generates wars, though by implication raised to a higher form, would not at once be raised to so high a form that there would cease all injustices and the pains they cause. For a considerable period after predatory activities had ended, the defects of the predatory nature would continue: entailing their slowly-diminishing evils. In the second place, the ill-adjustment of the human constitution to the pursuits of industrial life, must long persist, and may be expected to survive in a measure the cessation of wars: the required modes of activity must remain for innumerable generations in some degree displeasurable. And in the third place, deficiencies of self-control such as the improvident show us, as well as those many failures of conduct due to inadequate foresight of consequences, though less marked than now, could not fail still to produce suffering.

Nor would even complete adaptation, if limited to

disappearance of the non-adaptations just indicated, remove all sources of those miseries which, to the extent of their manifestation, check the growth of sympathy. For while the rate of multiplication continues so to exceed the rate of mortality as to cause pressure on the means of subsistence, there must continue to result much unhappiness; either from balked affections or from over-work and stinted means. Only as fast as fertility diminishes, which we have seen it must do along with further mental development (*Principles of Biology*, § § 367—377), can there go on such diminution of the labours required for efficiently supporting self and family, that they will not constitute a displeasurable tax on the energies.

Gradually then, and only gradually, as these various causes of unhappiness become less can sympathy become greater. Life would be intolerable if, while the causes of misery remained as they now are, all men were not only in a high degree sensitive to the pains, bodily and mental, felt by those around and expressed in the faces of those they met, but were unceasingly conscious of the miseries everywhere being suffered as consequences of war, crime, misconduct, misfortune, improvidence, incapacity. But, as the moulding and re-moulding of man and society into mutual fitness progresses, and as the pains caused by unfitness decrease, sympathy can increase in presence of the pleasures that come from fitness. The two changes are indeed so related that each furthers the other. Such growth of sympathy as conditions permit, itself aids in lessening pain and augmenting pleasure; and the greater surplus of pleasure that results makes possible further growth of sympathy.

§ 94. The extent to which sympathy may develop when the hindrances are removed, will be better conceived after observing the agencies through which it is excited, and setting down the reasons for expecting those agencies to

become more efficient. Two factors have to be considered
—the natural language of feeling in the being sympathized
with, and the power of interpreting that language in the
being who sympathizes. We may anticipate development of
both.

Movements of the body and facial changes are visible
effects of feeling which, when the feeling is strong, are
uncontrollable. When the feeling is less strong however,
be it sensational or emotional, they may be wholly or partially repressed; and there is a habit, more or less constant,
of repressing them : this habit being the concomitant of a
nature such that it is often undesirable that others
should see what is felt. So necessary with our existing
characters and conditions are concealments thus prompted,
that they have come to form a part of moral duty; and
concealment for its own sake is often insisted upon as an
element in good manners. All this is caused by the prevalence
of feelings at variance with social good—feelings which
cannot be shown without producing discords or estrange-
ments. But in proportion as the egoistic desires fall
more under control of the altruistic, and there come fewer
and slighter impulses of a kind to be reprobated, the need
for keeping guard over facial expression and bodily movement will decrease, and these will with increasing clearness
convey to spectators the mental state. Nor is this all.
Restrained as its use is, this language of the emotions is at
present prevented from growing. But as fast as the emotions become such that they may be more candidly displayed,
there will go, along with the habit of display, development
of the means of display; so that besides the stronger
emotions, the more delicate shades and smaller degrees
of emotion will visibly exhibit themselves : the emotional
language will become at once more copious, more varied,
more definite. And obviously sympathy will be proportionately facilitated.

An equally important, if not a more important, advance of

kindred nature, is to be anticipated. The vocal signs of sentient states will simultaneously evolve further. Loudness of tone, pitch of tone, quality of tone, and change of tone, are severally marks of feeling; and, combined in different ways and proportions, serve to express different amounts and kinds of feelings. As elsewhere pointed out, cadences are the comments of the emotions on the propositions of the intellect.* Not in excited speech only, but in ordinary speech, we show by ascending and descending intervals, by degrees of deviation from the medium tone, as well as by place and strength of emphasis, the kind of sentiency which accompanies the thought expressed. Now the manifestation of feeling by cadence, like its manifestation by visible changes, is at present under restraint : the motives for repression act in the one case as they act in the other. A double effect is produced. This audible language of feeling is not used up to the limit of its existing capacity; and it is to a considerable degree misused, so as to convey other feelings than those which are felt. The result of this disuse and misuse is to check that evolution which normal use would cause. We must infer, then, that as moral adaptation progresses, and there is decreasing need for concealment of the feelings, their vocal signs will develop much further. Though it is not to be supposed that cadences will ever convey emotions as exactly as words convey thoughts, yet it is quite possible that the emotional language of the future may rise as much above our present emotional language, as our intellectual language has already risen above the intellectual language of the lowest races.

A simultaneous increase in the power of interpreting both visible and audible signs of feeling must be taken into account. Among those around we see differences both of ability to perceive such signs and of ability to conceive the implied mental states and their causes : here, a stolidity un-

---

* See Essay on " The Origin and Function of Music."

impressed by a slight facial change or altered tone of voice, or else unable to imagine what is felt; and there, a quick observation and a penetrating intuition, making instantly comprehensible the state of mind and its origin. If we suppose both these faculties exalted— both a more delicate perception of the signs and a strengthened constructive imagination—we shall get some idea of the deeper and wider sympathy that will hereafter arise. More vivid representations of the feelings of others, implying ideal excitements of feelings approaching to real excitements, must imply a greater likeness between the feelings of the sympathizer and those of the sympathized with : coming near to identity.

By simultaneous increase of its subjective and objective factors, sympathy may thus, as the hindrances diminish, rise above that now shown by the sympathetic as much as in them it has risen above that which the callous show.

§ 95. What must be the accompanying evolution of conduct? What must the relations between egoism and altruism become as this form of nature is neared?

A conclusion drawn in the chapter on the relativity of pleasures and pains, and there emphasized as one to be borne in mind, must now be recalled. It was pointed out that, supposing them to be consistent with continuance of life, there are no activities which may not become sources of pleasure, if surrounding conditions require persistence in them. And here it is to be added, as a corollary, that if the conditions require any class of activities to be relatively great, there will arise a relatively great pleasure accompanying that class of activities. What bearing have these general inferences on the special question before us?

That alike for public welfare and private welfare sympathy is essential, we have seen. We have seen that co-operation and the benefits which it brings to each and all, become high in proportion as the altruistic, that is the sympathetic, interests extend. The actions prompted by fellow-feeling are thus to be counted among those demanded by social conditions. They are actions which maintenance and further development of social organization tend ever to increase; and therefore actions with which there will be joined an increasing pleasure. From the laws of life it must be concluded that unceasing social discipline will so mould human nature, that eventually sympathetic pleasures will be spontaneously pursued to the fullest extent advantageous to each and all. The scope for altruistic activities will not exceed the desire for altruistic satisfactions.

In natures thus constituted, though the altruistic gratifications must remain in a transfigured sense egoistic, yet they will not be egoistically pursued—will not be pursued from egoistic motives. Though pleasure will be gained by giving pleasure, yet the thought of the sympathetic pleasure to be gained will not occupy consciousness, but only the thought of the pleasure given. To a great extent this is so now. In the truly sympathetic, attention is so absorbed with the proximate end, others' happiness, that there is none given to the prospective self-happiness which may ultimately result. An analogy will make the relation clear.

A miser accumulates money, not deliberately saying to himself—"I shall by doing this get the delight which possession gives." He thinks only of the money and the means of getting it; and he experiences incidentally the pleasure that comes from possession. Owning property is that which he revels in imagining, and not the feeling which owning property will cause. Similarly, one who is sympathetic in the highest sense, is mentally engaged solely in representing pleasure as experienced by another; and pursues it for the benefit of that other, forgetting any participation he will have in it. Subjectively considered, then, the conciliation of egoism and altruism will eventually become such that though the altruistic pleasure, as being a part of the consciousness of one who experiences it, can never be other than egoistic, it will not be consciously egoistic.

Let us now ask what must happen in a society composed of persons constituted in this manner.

§ 96. The opportunities for that postponement of self to others which constitutes altruism as ordinarily conceived, must, in several ways, be more and more limited as the highest state is approached.

Extensive demands on the benevolent, presuppose much unhappiness. Before there can be many and large calls on some for efforts on behalf of others, there must be many others in conditions needing help—in conditions of comparative misery. But, as we have seen above, the development of fellow-feeling can go on only as fast as misery decreases. Sympathy can reach its full height only when there have ceased to be frequent occasions for anything like serious self-sacrifice.

Change the point of view, and this truth presents itself under another aspect. We have already seen that with the progress of adaptation each becomes so constituted that he cannot be helped without in some way arresting a pleasurable activity. There cannot be a beneficial interference between faculty and function when the two are adjusted. Consequently, in proportion as mankind approach complete adjustment of their natures to social needs, there must be fewer and smaller opportunities for giving aid.

Yet again, as was pointed out in the last chapter, the sympathy which prompts efforts for others' welfare must be pained by self-injury on the part of others; and must, therefore, cause aversion to accept benefits derived from their self-injuries. What is to be inferred? While each when occasion offers is ready, anxious even, to surrender egoistic satisfactions; others, similarly-natured, cannot but resist the surrender. If anyone, proposing to treat himself more hardly than a disinterested spectator would direct, refrains

from appropriating that which is due, others, caring for him
if he will not care for himself, must necessarily insist that
he shall appropriate it.   General altruism then, in its
developed form, must inevitably resist individual excesses
of altruism.   The relation at present familiar to us will be
inverted; and instead of each maintaining his own claims,
others will maintain his claims for him: not, indeed, by
active efforts, which will be needless, but by passively resist-
ing any undue yielding up of them.   There is nothing in
such behaviour which is not even now to be traced in our
daily experiences as beginning.   In business transactions
among honourable men, there is usually a desire on either
side that the other shall treat himself fairly.   Not unfrequently, there is a refusal to take something regarded
as the other's due, but which the other offers to give up.
In social intercourse, too, the cases are common in which
those who would surrender their shares of pleasure are not
permitted by the rest to do so.   Further development of
sympathy cannot but make this mode of behaving increasingly general and increasingly genuine.

Certain complex restraints on excesses of altruism exist,
which, in another way, force back the individual upon a
normal egoism.   Two may here be noted.   In the first
place, self-abnegations often repeated imply on the part of the
actor a tacit ascription of relative selfishness to others who
profit by the self-abnegations.   Even with men as they are,
there occasionally arises a feeling among those for whom
sacrifices are frequently made, that they are being insulted
by the assumption that they are ready to receive them ; and
in the mind of the actor also, there sometimes grows up a
recognition of this feeling on their part, and a consequent
check on his too great or too frequent surrenders of pleasure.
Obviously in more developed natures, this kind of check must
act still more promptly.   In the second place, when, as
the hypothesis implies, altruistic pleasures have reached a
greater intensity than they now possess, each person will be

debarred from undue pursuit of them by the consciousness that other persons, too, desire them, and that scope for others' enjoyment of them must be left. Even now may be observed among groups of friends, where some competition in amiability is going on, relinquishments of opportunities for self-abnegation that others may have them. "Let her give up the gratification, she will like to do so;" "Let him undertake the trouble, it will please him;" are suggestions which from time to time illustrate this consciousness. The most developed sympathy will care for the sympathetic satisfactions of others as well as for their selfish satisfactions. What may be called a higher equity will refrain from trespassing on the spheres of others' altruistic activities, as a lower equity refrains from trespassing on the spheres of their egoistic activities. And by this checking of what may be called an egoistic altruism, undue sacrifices on the part of each must be prevented.

What spheres, then, will eventually remain for altruism as it is commonly conceived? There are three. One of them must to the last continue large in extent; and the others must progressively diminish, though they do not disappear. The first is that which family-life affords. Always there must be a need for subordination of self-regarding feelings to other-regarding feelings in the rearing of children. Though this will diminish with diminution in the number to be reared, yet it will increase with the greater elaboration and prolongation of the activities on their behalf. But as shown above, there is even now partially effected a conciliation such that those egoistic satisfactions which parenthood yields are achieved through altruistic activities—a conciliation tending ever towards completeness. An important developement of family-altruism must be added : the reciprocal care of parents by children during old age—a care becoming lighter and better fulfilled, in which a kindred conciliation may be looked for. Pursuit of social welfare at large must afford hereafter, as it does now, scope for the postponement of selfish interests to unselfish interests, but a continually lessening scope; because as adaptation to the social state progresses, the needs for those regulative actions by which social life is made harmonious become less. And here the amount of altruistic action which each undertakes must inevitably be kept within moderate bounds by others; for if they are similarly altruistic, they will not allow some to pursue public ends to their own considerable detriment that the rest may profit. In the private relations of men, opportunities for self sacrifice prompted by sympathy, must ever in some degree, though eventually in a small degree, be afforded by accidents, diseases, and misfortunes in general; since, however near to completeness the adaptation of human nature to the conditions of existence at large, physical and social, may become, it can never reach completeness. Flood, fire, and wreck must to the last yield at intervals opportunities for heroic acts; and in the motives to such acts, anxiety for others will be less alloyed with love of admiration than now. Extreme, however, as may be the eagerness for altruistic action on the rare occasions hence arising, the amount falling to the share of each must, for the reasons given, be narrowly limited. But though in the incidents of ordinary life, postponements of self to others in large ways must become very infrequent, daily intercourse will still furnish multitudinous small occasions for the activity of fellow feeling. Always each may continue to further the welfare of others by warding off from them evils they cannot see, and by aiding their actions in ways unknown to them; or, conversely putting it, each may have, as it were, supplementary eyes and ears in other persons, which perceive for him things he cannot perceive himself: so perfecting his life in numerous details, by making its adjustments to environing actions complete.

§ 97. Must it then follow that eventually, with this diminution of the spheres for it, altruism must diminish in total amount? By no means. Such a conclusion implies a misconception.

Naturally, under existing conditions, with suffering widely diffused and so much of effort demanded from the more fortunate in succouring the less fortunate, altruism is understood to mean only self-sacrifice; or, at any rate, a mode of action which, while it brings some pleasure, has an accompaniment of self-surrender that is not pleasurable. But the sympathy which prompts denial of self to please others, is a sympathy which also receives pleasure from their pleasures when they are otherwise originated. The stronger the fellow-feeling which excites efforts to make others happy, the stronger is the fellow-feeling with their happiness however caused.

In its ultimate form, then, altruism will be the achievement of gratification through sympathy with those gratifications of others which are mainly produced by their activities of all kinds successfully carried on—sympathetic gratification which costs the receiver nothing, but is a gratis addition to his egoistic gratifications. This power of representing in idea the mental states of others, which, during the process of adaptation has had the function of mitigating suffering, must, as the suffering falls to a minimum, come to have almost wholly the function of mutually exalting men's enjoyments by giving everyone a vivid intuition of his neighbour's enjoyments. While pain prevails widely, it is undesirable that each should participate much in the consciousnesses of others; but with an increasing predominance of pleasure, participation in others' consciousnesses becomes a gain of pleasure to all.

And so there will disappear that apparently-permanent opposition between egoism and altruism, implied by the compromise reached in the last chapter. Subjectively looked at, the conciliation will be such that the individual will not have to balance between self-regarding impulses and other-regarding impulses; but, instead, those satisfactions of other-regarding impulses which involve self-sacrifice, becoming rare and much prized, will be so unhesitatingly preferred that the competition of self-regarding impulses with them will scarcely be felt. And the subjective conciliation will also be such that though altruistic pleasure will be attained, yet the motive of action will not consciously be the attainment of altruistic pleasure; but the idea present will be the securing of others' pleasures. Meanwhile, the conciliation objectively considered will be equally complete. Though each, no longer needing to maintain his egoistic claims, will tend rather when occasion offers to surrender them, yet others, similarly natured, will not permit him in any large measure to do this; and that fulfilment of personal desires required for completion of his life will thus be secured to him : though not now egoistic in the ordinary sense, yet the effects of due egoism will be achieved. Nor is this all. As, at an earlier stage, egoistic competition, first reaching a compromise such that each claims no more than his equitable share, afterwards rises to a conciliation such that each insists on the taking of equitable shares by others; so, at the latest stage, altruistic competition, first reaching a compromise under which each restrains himself from taking an undue share of altruistic satisfactions, eventually rises to a conciliation under which each takes care that others shall have their opportunities for altruistic satisfactions : the highest altruism being that which ministers not to the egoistic satisfactions of others only, but also to their altruistic satisfactions.

Far off as seems such a state, yet every one of the factors counted on to produce it may already be traced in operation among those of highest natures. What now in them is occasional and feeble, may be expected with further evolution to become habitual and strong; and what now characterizes the exceptionally high may be expected eventually to characterize all. For that which the best human nature is capable of, is within the reach of human nature at large.

§ 98. That these conclusions will meet with any considerable acceptance is improbable. Neither with current ideas nor with current sentiments are they sufficiently congruous.

Such a view will not be agreeable to those who lament the spreading disbelief in eternal damnation; nor to those who follow the apostle of brute force in thinking that because the rule of the strong hand was once good it is good for all time; nor to those whose reverence for one who told them to put up the sword, is shown by using the sword to spread his doctrine among heathens. The conception set forth would be received with contempt by that Fifeshire regiment of militia, of whom eight hundred, at the time of the Franco-German war, asked to be employed on foreign service, and left the Government to say on which side they should fight. From the ten thousand priests of the religion of love, who are silent when the nation is moved by the religion of hate, will come no sign of assent; nor from their bishops who, far from urging the extreme precept of the master they pretend to follow, to turn the other cheek when one is smitten, vote for acting on the principle— strike lest ye be struck. Nor will any approval be felt by legislators who, after praying to be forgiven their trespasses as they forgive the trespasses of others, forthwith decide to attack those who have not trespassed against them; and who, after a Queen's Speech has invoked "the blessing of Almighty God" on their councils, immediately provide means for committing political burglary.

But though men who profess Christianity and practise Paganism can feel no sympathy with such a view, there are some, classed as antagonists to the current creed, who may not think it absurd to believe that a rationalized version of its ethical principles will eventually be acted upon.

17

CHAPTER XV.

ABSOLUTE AND RELATIVE ETHICS.

§ 99. As applied to Ethics, the word "absolute" will by many be supposed to imply principles of right conduct that exist out of relation to life as conditioned on the Earth—out of relation to time and place, and independent of the Universe as now visible to us—"eternal" principles as they are called. Those, however, who recall the doctrine set forth in *First Principles*, will hesitate to put this interpretation on the word. Right, as we can think it, necessitates the thought of not-right, or wrong, for its correlative; and hence, to ascribe rightness to the acts of the Power manifested through phenomena, is to assume the possibility that wrong acts may be committed by this Power. But how come there to exist, apart from this Power, conditions of such kind that subordination of its acts to them makes them right and insubordination wrong. How can Unconditioned Being be subject to conditions beyond itself?

If, for example, any one should assert that the Cause of Things, conceived in respect of fundamental moral attributes as like ourselves, did right in producing a Universe which, in the course of immeasurable time, has given origin to beings capable of pleasure, and would have done wrong in abstaining from the production of such a Universe; then, the comment to be made is that, imposing the moral ideas generated in his finite consciousness, upon the Infinite Existence which transcends consciousness, he goes behind that Infinite Existence and prescribes for it principles of action.

As implied in foregoing chapters, right and wrong as conceived by us can exist only in relation to the actions of creatures capable of pleasures and pains; seeing that analysis carries us back to pleasures and pains as the elements out of which the conceptions are framed.

But if the word "absolute," as used above, does not refer to the Unconditioned Being—if the principles of action distinguished as absolute and relative concern the conduct of conditioned beings; in what way are the words to be understood? An explanation of their meanings will be best conveyed by a criticism on the current conceptions of right and wrong.

§ 100. Conversations about the affairs of life habitually imply the belief that every deed named may be placed under the one head or the other. In discussing a political question, both sides take it for granted that some line of action may be chosen which is right, while all other lines of action are wrong. So, too, is it with judgments on the doings of individuals: each of these is approved or disapproved on the assumption that it is definitely classable as good or bad. Even where qualifications are admitted, they are admitted with an implied idea that some such positive characterization is to be made.

Nor is it in popular thought and speech only that we see this. If not wholly and definitely yet partially and by implication, the belief is expressed by moralists. In his *Methods of Ethics* (1st Ed. p. 6.) Mr. Sidgwick says:—
" That there is in any given circumstances some one thing which ought to be done and that this can be known, is a fundamental assumption, made not by philosophers only, but by all men who perform any processes of moral reason-

ing."* In this sentence there is specifically asserted only the last of the above propositions; namely, that, in every case, what " ought to be done " " can be known." But though that "which ought to be done" is not distinctly identified with " the right," it may be inferred, in the absence of any indication to the contrary, that Mr. Sidgwick regards the two as identical; and doubtless, in so conceiving the postulates of moral science, he is at one with most, if not all, who have made it a subject of study. At first sight, indeed, nothing seems more obvious than that if actions are to be judged at all, these postulates must be accepted. Nevertheless they may both be called in question, and I think it may be shown that neither of them is tenable. Instead of admitting that there is in every case a right and a wrong, it may be contended that in multitudinous cases no right, properly so-called, can be alleged, but only a least wrong; and further it may be contended that in many of these cases where there can be alleged only a least wrong, it is not possible to ascertain with any precision which is the least wrong.

A great part of the perplexities in ethical speculation arise from neglect of this distinction between right and least wrong—between the absolutely right and the relatively right. And many further perplexities are due to the assumption that it can, in some way, be decided in every case which of two courses is morally obligatory.

§ 101. The law of absolute right can take no cognizance of pain, save the cognizance implied by negation. Pain is the correlative of some species of wrong—some kind of divergence from that course of action which perfectly fulfils all requirements. If, as was shown in an early chapter, the

---

* I do not find this 'passage in the second edition; but the omission of it appears to have arisen not from any change of view but because it did not naturally come into the re-cast form of the argument which the section contains.

conception of good conduct always proves, when analyzed, to be the conception of a conduct which produces a surplus of pleasure somewhere; while, conversely, the conduct conceived as bad proves always to be that which inflicts somewhere a surplus of either positive or negative pain; then the absolutely good, the absolutely right, in conduct, can be that only which produces pure pleasure—pleasure unalloyed with pain anywhere. By implication, conduct which has any concomitant of pain, or any painful consequence, is partially wrong; and the highest claim to be made for such conduct is, that it is the least wrong which, under the conditions, is possible—the relatively right.

The contents of preceding chapters imply throughout that, considered from the evolution point of view, the acts of men during the transition which has been, is still, and long will be, in progress, must, in most cases, be of the kind here classed as least wrong. In proportion to the incongruity between the natures men inherit from the pre-social state, and the requirements of social life, must be the amount of pain entailed by their actions, either on themselves or on others. In so far as pain is suffered, evil is inflicted; and conduct which inflicts any evil cannot be absolutely good.

To make clear the distinction here insisted upon between that perfect conduct which is the subject-matter of Absolute Ethics, and that imperfect conduct which is the subject-matter of Relative Ethics, some illustrations must be given.

§ 102. Among the best examples of absolutely right actions to be named are those arising where the nature and the requirements have been moulded to one another before social evolution began. Two will here suffice.

Consider the relation of a healthy mother to a healthy infant. Between the two there exists a mutual dependence which is a source of pleasure to both. In yielding its natural food to the child, the mother receives gratification; and to the child there comes the satisfaction of appetite—a satisfaction which accompanies furtherance of life, growth, and increasing enjoyment.   Let the relation be suspended, and on both sides there is suffering.   The mother experiences both bodily pain and mental pain; and the painful sensation borne by the child, brings as its results physical mischief and some damage to the emotional nature.   Thus the act is one that is to both exclusively pleasurable, while abstention entails pain on both; and it is consequently of the kind we here call absolutely right.   In the parental relations of the father we are furnished with a kindred example.   If he is well constituted in body and mind, his boy, eager for play, finds in him a sympathetic response; and their frolics giving mutual pleasure, not only further the child's physical welfare but strengthen that bond of good feeling between the two which makes subsequent guidance easier.   And then if, repudiating the stupidities of early education as at present conceived, and unhappily State-enacted, he has rational ideas of mental development, and sees that the second-hand knowledge gained through books should begin to supplement the first-hand knowledge gained by direct observation, only when a good stock of this has been acquired, he will, with active sympathy, aid in that exploration of the surrounding world which his boy pursues with delight; giving and receiving gratification from moment to moment while furthering ultimate welfare. Here, again, are actions of a kind purely pleasurable alike in their immediate and remote effects—actions absolutely right.

The intercourse of adults yields, for the reason assigned, relatively few cases that fall completely within the same category.   In their transactions from hour to hour more or less of deduction from pure gratification is caused on one or other side by imperfect fitness to the requirements.   The pleasures men gain by labouring in their vocations and receiving in one form or other returns for their services, usually have the drawback that the labours are in a considerable degree displeasurable. Cases, however, do occur where the energies are so abundant that inaction is irksome; and where the daily work, not too great in duration, is of a kind appropriate to the nature; and where, as a consequence, pleasure rather than pain is a concomitant. When services yielded by such a one are paid for by another similarly adapted to his occupation, the entire transaction is of the kind we are here considering: exchange under agreement between two so constituted, becomes a means of pleasure to both, with no set-off of pain. Bearing in mind the form of nature which social discipline is producing, as shown in the contrast between savage and civilized, the implication is that ultimately men's activities at large will assume this character. Remembering that in the course of organic evolution, the means to enjoyment themselves eventually become sources of enjoyment; and that there is no form of action which may not through the development of appropriate structures become pleasurable; the inference must be that industrial activities carried on through voluntary co-operation, will in time acquire the character of absolute rightness as here conceived. Already, indeed, something like such a state has been reached among certain of those who minister to our æsthetic gratifications. The artist of genius—poet, painter, or musician—is one who obtains the means of living by acts that are directly pleasurable to him, while they yield, immediately or remotely, pleasures to others. Once more, among absolutely right acts may be named certain of those which we class as benevolent. I say certain of them, because such benevolent acts as entail submission to pain, positive or negative, that others may receive pleasure, are, by the definition, excluded. But there are benevolent acts of a kind yielding pleasure solely. Some one who has slipped is saved from falling by a bystander: a hurt is prevented and satisfaction is felt by both. A pedestrian is choosing a dangerous route, or a fellow passenger is

about to alight at the wrong station, and, warned against
doing so, is saved from evil : each being, as a consequence,
gratified.   There is a misunderstanding between friends,
and one who sees how it has arisen, explains : the result
being agreeable to all.   Services to those around in the
small affairs of life, may be, and often are, of a kind which
there is equal pleasure in giving and receiving.   Indeed,
as was urged in the last chapter, the actions of developed
altruism must habitually have this character.   And so, in
countless ways suggested by these few, men may add to
one anothers happiness without anywhere producing unhappiness—ways which are therefore absolutely right.

In contrast with these consider the many actions which
from hour to hour are gone through now, with an accompaniment of some pain to the actor and now bringing results
that are partially painful to others, but which nevertheless
are imperative.   As implied by antithesis with cases above
referred to, the wearisomeness of productive labour as
ordinarily pursued, renders it in so far wrong; but then
far greater suffering would result, both to the labourer and
his family, and therefore far greater wrong would be done,
were this wearisomeness not borne.   Though the pains
which the care of many children entail on a mother, form
a considerable set-off from the pleasures secured by them
to her children and herself; yet the miseries, immediate and
remote, which neglect would entail so far exceed them, that
submission to such pains up to the limit of physical ability
to bear them becomes, morally imperative as being the least
wrong.   A servant who fails to fulfil an agreement in respect
of work, or who is perpetually breaking crockery, or who
pilfers, may have to suffer pain from being discharged ; but
since the evils to be borne by all concerned if incapacity or
misconduct is tolerated, not in one case only but habitually,
must be much greater, such infliction of pain is warranted
as a means to preventing greater pain.   Withdrawal of
custom from a tradesman whose charges are too high, or

whose commodities are inferior, or who gives short measure, or who is unpunctual, decreases his welfare, and perhaps injures his belongings; but as saving him from these evils would imply bearing the evils his conduct causes, and as such regard for his well-being would imply disregard of the well-being of some more worthy or more efficient tradesman to whom the custom would else go, and as, chiefly, general adoption of the implied course, having the effect that the inferior would not suffer from their inferiority nor the superior gain by their superiority, would produce universal misery, withdrawal is justified—the act is relatively right.

§ 103. I pass now to the second of the two propositions above enunciated. After recognizing the truth that a large part of human conduct is not absolutely right, but only relatively right, we have to recognize the further truth that in many cases where there is no absolutely right course, but only courses that are more or less wrong, it is not possible to say which is the least wrong. Recurrence to the instances just given will show this.

There is a point up to which it is relatively right for a parent to carry self-sacrifice for the benefit of offspring; and there is a point beyond which self-sacrifice cannot be pushed without bringing, not only on himself or herself but also on the family, evils greater than those to be prevented by the self-sacrifice. Who shall say where this point is? Depending on the constitutions and needs of those concerned, it is in no two cases the same, and cannot be by anyone more than guessed. The transgressions or short-comings of a servant vary from the trivial to the grave, and the evils which discharge may bring range through countless degrees from slight to serious. The penalty may be inflicted for a very small offence, and then there is wrong done; or after numerous grave offences it may not be inflicted, and again there is wrong done. How shall be determined the degree of transgression beyond which to discharge is less wrong than not to discharge? In like manner with the shopkeeper's misdemeanours. No one can sum up either the amount of positive and negative pain which tolerating them involves, nor the amount of positive and negative pain involved by not tolerating them; and in medium cases no one can say where the one exceeds the other.

In men's wider relations frequently occur circumstances under which a decision one or other way is imperative, and yet under which not even the most sensitive conscience helped by the clearest judgment, can decide which of the alternatives is relatively right. Two examples will suffice. Here is a merchant who loses by the failure of a man indebted to him. Unless he gets help he himself will fail; and if he fails he will bring disaster not only on his family but on all who have given him credit. Even if by borrowing he is enabled to meet immediate engagements, he is not safe; for the time is one of panic, and others of his debtors by going to the wall may put him in further difficulties. Shall he ask a friend for a loan? On the one hand, is it not wrong forthwith to bring on himself, his family, and those who have business relations with him, the evils of his failure? On the other hand, is it not wrong to hopothecate the property of his friend, and lead him too, with his belongings and dependents, into similar risks? The loan would probably tide him over his difficulty; in which case would it not be unjust to his creditors did he refrain from asking it? Contrariwise, the loan would very possibly fail to stave off his bankruptcy; in which case is not his action in trying to obtain it, practically fraudulent? Though in extreme cases it may be easy to say which course is the least wrong, how is it possible in all those medium cases where even by the keenest man of business the contingencies cannot be calculated? Take, again, the difficulties that not unfrequently arise from antagonism between family duties and social duties. Here is a tenant farmer whose political principles prompt him to vote in opposition to his landlord. If, being a Liberal, he votes for a Conservative, not only does he by his act say that he thinks what he does not think, but he may perhaps further what he regards as bad legislation : his vote may by chance turn the election, and on a Parliamentary division a single member may decide the fate of a measure. Even neglecting, as too improbable, such serious consequences, there is the manifest truth that if all who hold like views with himself, are similarly deterred from electoral expression of them, there must result a different balance of power and a different national policy : making it clear that only by adherence of all to their political principles can the policy he thinks right be maintained. But now, on the other hand, how can he absolve himself from responsibility for the evils which those depending on him may suffer if he fulfils what appears to be a peremptory public duty? Is not his duty to his children even more peremptory? Does not the family precede the State; and does not the welfare of the State depend on the welfare of the family? May he, then, take a course which, if the threats uttered are carried out, will eject him from his farm; and so cause inability, perhaps temporary perhaps prolonged, to feed his children. The contingent evils are infinitely varied in their ratios. In one case the imperativeness of the public duty is great and the risk of mischief to dependents small; in another case the political issue is of trivial moment and the possible injury which the family may suffer is great; and between these extremes there are all gradations. Further, the degrees of probability of each result, public and private, range from the nearly certain to the almost impossible. Admitting, then, that it is wrong to act in a way likely to injure the State; and admitting that it is wrong to act in a way likely to injure the family; we have to recognize the fact that in countless cases no one can decide by which of the alternative courses the least wrong is likely to be done.

These instances will sufficiently show that in conduct at large, including men's dealings with themselves, with their families, with their friends, with their debtors and creditors, and with the public, it usually happens that whatever course is taken in any case entails some pain somewhere; forming a deduction from the pleasure achieved, and making the course in so far not absolutely right. Further, they will show that throughout a considerable part of conduct, no guiding principle, no method of estimation, enables us to say whether a proposed course is even relatively right; as causing, proximately and remotely, specially and generally, the greatest surplus of good over evil.

§ 104. And. now we are prepared for dealing in a systematic way with the distinction between Absolute Ethics and Relative Ethics.

Scientific truths, of whatever order, are reached by eliminating perturbing or conflicting factors, and recognizing only fundamental factors. When, by dealing with fundamental factors in the abstract, not as presented in actual phenomena but as presented in ideal separation, general laws have been ascertained, it becomes possible to draw inferences in concrete cases by taking into account incidental factors. But it is only by first ignoring these and recognizing the essential elements alone, that we can discover the essential truths sought. Take, in illustration, the progress of mechanics from its empirical form to its rational form.

All have occasional experience of the fact that a person pushed on one side beyond a certain degree, loses his balance and falls. It is observed that a stone flung or an arrow shot, does not proceed in a straight line, but comes to the earth after pursuing a course which deviates more and more from its original course. When trying to break a stick across the knee, it is found that success is easier if the stick is seized at considerable distances from

the knee on each side than if seized close to the knee.
Daily use of a spear draws attention to the truth that by
thrusting its point under a stone and depressing the shaft,
the stone may be raised the more readily the further away
the hand is towards the end. Here, then, are sundry experiences, eventually grouped into empirical generalizations,
which serve to guide conduct in certain simple cases. How
does mechanical science evolve from these experiences?
To reach a formula expressing the powers of the lever, it
supposes a lever which does not, like the stick, admit of
being bent, but is absolutely rigid; and it supposes a fulcrum
not having a broad surface, like that of one ordinarily used,
but a fulcrum without breath; and it supposes that the
weight to be raised bears on a definite point, instead of
bearing over a considerable portion of the lever. Similarly
with the leaning body, which, passing a certain inclination,
overbalances. Before the truth respecting the relations of
centre of gravity and base can be formulated, it must be
assumed that the surface on which the body stands is unyielding; that the edge of the body itself is unyielding;
and that its mass, while made to lean more and more, does
not change its form—conditions not fulfilled in the cases
commonly observed. And so, too, is it with the projectile :
determination of its course by deduction from mechanical
laws, primarily ignores all deviations caused by its shape
and by the resistance of the air. The science of rational
mechanics is a science which consists of such ideal truths,
and can come into existence only by thus dealing with ideal
cases. It remains impossible so long as attention is restricted
to concrete cases presenting all the complications of friction,
plasticity, and so forth.   But now, after disentangling certain fundamental mechanical truths, it becomes
possible by their help to guide actions better; and it becomes
possible to guide them still better when, as presently happens,
the complicating elements from which they have been
disentangled are themselves taken into account. At an

advanced stage, the modifying effects of friction are allowed for, and the inferences are qualified to the requisite extent. The theory of the pulley is corrected in its application to actual cases by recognizing the rigidity of cordage; the effects of which are formulated. The stabilities of masses, determinable in the abstract by reference to the centres of gravity of the masses in relation to the bases, come to be determined in the concrete including also their characters in respect of cohesion. The courses of projectiles having been theoretically settled, as though they moved through a vacuum, are afterwards settled in more exact correspondence with fact by taking into account atmospheric resistance.   And thus we see illustrated the relation between certain absolute truths of mechanical science, and certain relative truths which involve them. We are shown that no scientific establishment of relative truths is possible, until the absolute truths have been formulated independently. We see that mechanical science fitted for dealing with the real, can arise only after ideal mechanical science has arisen.

All this holds of moral science. As by early and rude experiences there were empirically reached, vague but partially-true notions respecting the overbalancing of bodies, the motions of missiles, the actions of levers; so by early and rude experiences there were empirically reached, vague but partially-true notions respecting the effects of men's behaviour on themselves, on one another, and on society: to a certain extent serving in the last case, as in the first, for the guidance of conduct. Moreover, as this rudimentary mechanical knowledge, though still remaining empirical, becomes during early stages of civilization at once more definite and more extensive; so during early stages of civilization these ethical ideas, still retaining their empirical character, increase in precision and multiplicity. But just as we have seen that mechanical knowledge of the empirical sort can evolve into mechanical science, only by first omitting all qualifying circumstances, and generalizing in absolute ways the fundamental laws of forces ; so here we have to see that empirical ethics can evolve into rational ethics only by first neglecting all complicating incidents, and formulating the laws of right action apart from the obscuring effects of special conditions. And the final implication is that just as the system of mechanical truths, conceived in ideal separation as absolute, becomes applicable to real mechanical problems in such way that making allowance for all incidental circumstances there can be reached conclusions far nearer to the truth than could otherwise be reached; so, a system of ideal ethical truths, expressing the absolutely right, will be applicable to the questions of our transitional state in such ways that, allowing for the friction of an incomplete life and the imperfection of existing natures, we may ascertain with approximate correctness what is the relatively right.

§ 105. In a chapter entitled " Definition of Morality " in *Social Statics*, I have contended that the moral law, properly so-called, is the law of the perfect man—is the formula of ideal conduct—is the statement in all cases of that which should be, and cannot recognize in its propositions any elements implying existence of that which should not be. Instancing questions concerning the right course to be taken in cases where wrong has already been done, I have alleged that the answers to such questions cannot be given " on purely ethical principles." I have argued that—

"No conclusions can lay claim to absolute truth, but such as depend upon truths that are themselves absolute. Before there can be exactness in an inference, there must be exactness in the antecedent propositions. A geometrician requires that the straight lines with which he deals shall be veritably straight ; and that his circles, and ellipses, and parabolas shall agree with precise definitions—shall perfectly and invariably answer to specified equations. If you put to him a question in which these conditions are not complied with, he tells you that it cannot be answered. So likewise is it with the philosophical moralist. He treats solely of the *straight* man. He determines the properties of the straight man ; describes how the straight man comports himself ; shows in what relationship he stands to other straight men ; shows how a community of straight men is constituted. Any deviation from strict rectitude he is obliged wholly to ignore. It cannot be admitted into his premises without vitiating all his conclusions. A problem in which a *crooked* man forms one of the elements is insoluble by him."

Referring to this view, specifically in the first edition of the *Methods of Ethics* but more generally in the second edition, Mr. Sidgwick says :—

"Those who take this view adduce the analogy of Geometry to show that Ethics ought to deal with ideally perfect human relations, just as Geometry treats of ideally perfect lines and circles. But the most irregular line has definite spatial relations with which Geometry does not refuse to deal : though of course they are more complex than those of a straight line. So in Astronomy, it would be more convenient for purposes of study if the stars moved in circles, as was once believed : but the fact that they move not in circles but in ellipses, and even in imperfect and perturbed ellipses, does not take them out of the sphere of scientific investigation : by patience and industry we have learnt how to reduce to principles and calculate even these more complicated motions. It is, no doubt, a convenient artifice for purposes of instruction to assume that the planets move in perfect ellipses (or even—at an earlier stage of study—in circles) : we thus allow the individual's knowledge to pass through the same gradations in accuracy as that of the race has done. But what we want, as astronomers, to know is the actual motion of the ʜtars and its causes : and similarly as moralists we naturally inquire what ought to be done in the actual world in which we live." P. 19, Sec. Ed.

Beginning with the first of these two statements, which concerns Geometry, I must confess myself surprised to find my propositions called in question; and after full consideration I remain at a loss to understand Mr. Sidgwick's mode of viewing the matter. When, in a sentence preceding those quoted above, I remarked on the impossibility of solving " mathematically a series of problems respecting crooked lines and broken-backed curves," it never occurred to me that I should be met by the direct assertion that " Geometry does not refuse to deal " with " the most irregular line." Mr. Sidgwick states that an irregular line, say such as a child makes in scribbling, has " definite spatial relations." What meaning does he here give to the word " definite." If he means that its relations to space at large are definite in the sense that by an infinite intelligence they would be definable; the reply is that to an infinite intelligence all spatial relations would be definable: there could be no indefinite spatial relations— the word "definite" thus ceasing to mark any distinction. If, on the other hand, when saying that an irregular line has "definite spatial relations," he means relations knowable definitely by human intelligence; there still comes the question, how is the word "definite" to be understood? Surely anything distinguished as definite admits of being defined; but how can we define an irregular line? And if we cannot define the irregular line itself, how can we know its "spatial relations" definitely? And how, in the absence of definition, can Geometry deal with it? If Mr. Sidgwick means that it can be dealt with by the "method of limits," then the reply is that in such case, not the line itself is dealt with geometrically, but certain definite lines artificially put in quasi-definite relations to it: the indefinite becomes cognizable only through the medium of the hypothetically-definite.

Turning to the second illustration, the rejoinder to be made is that in so far as it concerns the relations between the ideal and the real, the analogy drawn does not shake but strengthens my argument. For whether considered under its geometrical or under its dynamical aspect, and whether considered in the necessary order of its development or in the order historically displayed, Astronomy shows us throughout, that truths respecting simple, theoretically-exact relations, must be ascertained before truths respecting the complex and practically-inexact relations that actually exist, can be ascertained. As applied to the interpretation of planetary movements, we see that the theory of cycles and epicycles was based on pre-existing knowledge of the circle: the properties of an ideal curve having been learnt, a power was acquired of giving some expression to the celestial motions. We see that the Copernican interpretation expressed the facts in terms of circular movements otherwise distributed and combined.

18

We see that Kepler's advance from the conception of circular movements to that of elliptic movements, was made possible by comparison of the facts as they are with the facts as they would be were the movements circular. We see that the subsequently-learnt deviations from elliptic movements, were to be learnt only through the pre-supposition that the movements are elliptical. And we see, lastly, that even now predictions concerning the exact positions of planets, after taking account of perturbations, imply constant references to ellipses that are regarded as their normal or average orbits for the time being. Thus, ascertainment of the actual truths has been made possible only by pre-ascertainment of certain ideal truths. To see that by no other course could the actual truths have been ascertained, it needs only to suppose any one saying that it did not concern him, as an astronomer, to know anything about the properties of circles and ellipses, but that he had to deal with the actual facts of the Solar System, to which end it was his business to observe and tabulate positions and directions and to be guided by the facts as he found them.   So, too, is it if we look at the development of dynamical astronomy. The first proposition in Newton's *Principia* deals with the movement of a single body round a single centre of force ; and the phenomena of central motion are first formulated in a case which is not simply ideal, but in which there is no specification of the force concerned : detachment from the real is the greatest possible. Again, postulating a principle of action conforming to an ideal law, the theory of gravitation deals with the several problems of the Solar System in fictitious detachment from the rest; and it makes certain fictitious assumptions, such as that the mass of each body concerned is concentrated in its centre of gravity. Only later, after establishing the leading truths by this artifice of disentangling the major factors from the minor factors, is the theory applied to the actual problems in their ascending degrees of complexity ; taking in more and more of the minor factors. And if we ask whether the dynamics of the Solar System could have been established in any other way, we see that here, too, simple truths holding under ideal conditions, have to be ascertained before real truths existing under complex conditions can be ascertained.

The alleged necessary precedence of Absolute Ethics over Relative Ethics is thus, I think, further elucidated. One who has followed the general argument thus far, will not deny that an ideal social being may be conceived as so constituted that his spontaneous activities are congruous with the conditions imposed by the social environment formed by other such beings. In many places, and in various ways, I have argued that conformably with the laws of evolution in general, and conformably with the laws of organization in particular, there has been, and is, in progress, an adaptation of humanity to the social state, changing it in the direction of such an ideal congruity. And the corollary before drawn and here repeated, is that the ultimate man is one in whom this process has gone so far as to produce a correspondence between all the promptings of his nature and all the requirements of his life as carried on in society. If so, it is a necessary implication that there exists an ideal code of conduct formulating the behaviour of the completely adapted man in the completely evolved society. Such a code is that here called Absolute Ethics as distinguished from Relative Ethics—a code the injunctions of which are alone to be considered as absolutely right in contrast with those that are relatively right or least wrong; and which, as a system of ideal conduct, is to serve as a standard for our guidance in solving, as well as we can, the problems of real conduct.

§ 105. A clear conception of this matter is so important that I must be excused for bringing in aid of it a further illustration, more obviously appropriate as being furnished by organic science instead of by inorganic science. The relation between morality proper and morality as commonly

18*

conceived, is analogous to the relation between physiology and pathology; and the course usually pursued by moralists is much like the course of one who studies pathology without previous study of physiology.

Physiology describes the various functions which, as combined, constitute and maintain life; and in treating of them it assumes that they are severally performed in right ways, in due amounts, and in proper order: it recognizes only healthy functions. If it explains digestion, it supposes that the heart is supplying blood and that the visceral nervous system is stimulating the organs immediately concerned. If it gives a theory of the circulation, it assumes that blood has been produced by the combined actions of the structures devoted to its production, and that it is properly aerated. If the relations between respiration and the vital processes at large are interpreted, it is on the pre-supposition that the heart goes on sending blood, not only to the lungs and to certain nervous centres, but to the diaphragm and intercostal muscles. Physiology ignores failures in the actions of these several organs. It takes no account of imperfections, it neglects derangements, it does not recognize pain, it knows nothing of vital wrong. It simply formulates that which goes on as a result of complete adaptation of all parts to all needs. That is to say, in relation to the inner actions constituting bodily life, physiological theory has a position like that which ethical theory, under its absolute form as above conceived, has to the outer actions constituting conduct. The moment cognizance is taken of excess of function, or arrest of function, or defect of function, with the resulting evil, physiology passes into pathology. We begin now to take account of wrong actions in the inner life analogous to the wrong actions in the outer life taken account of by ordinary theories of morals.

The antithesis thus drawn, however, is but preliminary. After observing the fact that there is a science of vital actions normally carried on, which ignores abnormal actions;

we have more especially to observe that the science of abnormal actions can reach such definiteness as is possible to it, only on condition that the science of normal actions has previously become definite; or rather, let us say that pathological science depends for its advances on previous advances made by physiological science. The very conception of disordered action implies a pre-conception of well-ordered action. Before it can be decided that the heart is beating faster or slower than it should, its healthy rate of beating must be learnt; before the pulse can be recognized as too weak or too strong, its proper strength must be known; and so throughout. Even the rudest and most empirical ideas of diseases, pre-suppose ideas of the healthy states from which they are deviations; and obviously the diagnosis of diseases can become scientific, only as fast as there arises scientific knowledge of organic actions that are undiseased.

Similarly, then, is it with the relation between absolute morality, or the law of perfect right in human conduct, and relative morality which, recognizing wrong in human conduct, has to decide in what way the wrong deviates from the right, and how the right is to be most nearly approached. When, formulating normal conduct in an ideal society, we have reached a science of absolute ethics, we have simultaneously reached a science which, when used to interpret the phenomena of real societies in their transitional states, full of the miseries due to non-adaptation (which we may call pathological states) enable us to form approximately true conclusions respecting the natures of the abnormalities, and the courses which tend most in the direction of the normal.

§ 106. And now let it be observed that the conception of ethics thus set forth, strange as many will think it, is one which really lies latent in the beliefs of moralists at large. Though not definitely acknowledged it is vaguely implied in many of their propositions.

From early times downwards we find in ethical specula-
tions, references to the ideal man, his acts, his feelings, his
judgments. Well-doing is conceived by Sokrates as the
doing of " the best man," who " as a husbandman, performs
well the duties of husbandry; as a surgeon, the duties of
the medical art; in political life, his duty towards the
commonwealth." Plato, in *Minos*, as a standard to which
State-law should conform, "postulates the decision of some
ideal wise man;" and in *Laches* the wise man's knowledge
of good and evil is supposed to furnish the standard:
disregarding "the maxims of the existing society" as un-
scientific, Plato regards as the proper guide, that " Idea of
the Good which only a philosopher can ascend to. Aristotle
(*Eth.* Bk. iii. ch. 4), making the decisions of the good man
the standard, says :—" For the good man judges everything
rightly, and in every case the truth appears so to him.
. . . . And perhaps the principal difference between the
good and the bad man is that the good man sees the truth
in every case, since he is, as it were, the rule and measure
of it." The Stoics, too, conceived of " complete rectitude of
action" as that " which none could achieve except the wise
man"—the ideal man. And Epicurus had an ideal standard.
He held the virtuous state to be " a tranquil, undisturbed,
innocuous, non-competitive fruition, which approached
most nearly to the perfect happiness of the Gods," who
" neither suffered vexation in themselves nor caused vexation to others."*

If in modern times, influenced by theological dogmas
concerning the fall and human sinfulness, and by a theory
of obligation derived from the current creed, moralists
have less frequently referred to an ideal, yet references
are traceable. We see one in the dictum of Kant—" Act
according to that maxim only, which you can wish, at the
same time, to become a universal law." For this implies

---

* Most of these quotations I make from Dr. Bain's *Mental and Moral
Science.*

the thought of a society in which the maxim is acted upon by all and universal benefit recognized as the effect : there is a conception of ideal conduct under ideal conditions. And though Mr. Sidgwick, in the quotation above made from him, implies that Ethics is concerned with man as he is, rather than with man as he should be; yet, in elsewhere speaking of Ethics as dealing with conduct as it should be, rather than with conduct as it is, he postulates ideal conduct and indirectly the ideal man. On his first page, speaking of Ethics along with Jurisprudence and Politics, he says that they are distinguished "by the characteristic that they attempt to determine not the actual but the ideal—what ought to exist, not what does exist."

It requires only that these various conceptions of an ideal conduct and of an ideal humanity, should be made consistent and definite, to bring them into agreement with the conception above set forth. At present such conceptions are habitually vague. The ideal man having been conceived in terms of the current morality, is thereupon erected into a moral standard by which the goodness of actions may be judged; and the reasoning becomes circular. To make the ideal man serve as a standard, he has to be defined in terms of the conditions which his nature fulfils—in terms of those objective requirements which must be met before conduct can be right; and the common defect of these conceptions of the ideal man, is that they suppose him out of relation to such conditions.

All the above references to him, direct or indirect, imply that the ideal man is supposed to live and act under existing social conditions. The tacit inquiry is, not what his actions would be under circumstances altogether changed, but what they would be under present circumstances. And this inquiry is futile for two reasons. The co-existence of a perfect man and an imperfect society is impossible; and could the two co-exist, the resulting conduct would not furnish the ethical standard sought.   In the first place, given the laws of life as they are, and a man of ideal nature cannot be produced in a society consisting of men having natures remote from the ideal. As well might we expect a child of English type to be born among Negroes, as expect that among the organically immoral, one who is organically moral will arise. Unless it be denied that character results from inherited structure, it must be admitted that since, in any society, each individual descends from a stock which, traced back a few generations, ramifies everywhere through the society, and participates in its average nature, there must, notwithstanding marked individual diversities, be preserved such community as prevents anyone from reaching an ideal form while the rest remain far below it.   In the second place, ideal conduct, such as ethical theory is concerned with, is not possible for the ideal man in the midst of men otherwise constituted. An absolutely just or perfectly sympathetic person, could not live and act according to his nature in a tribe of cannibals. Among people who are treacherous and utterly without scruple, entire truthfulness and openness must bring ruin. If all around recognize only the law of the strongest, one whose nature will not allow him to inflict pain on others, must go to the wall. There requires a certain congruity between the conduct of each member of a society and other's conduct. A mode of action entirely alien to the prevailing modes of action, cannot be successfully persisted in—must eventuate in death of self, or posterity, or both.

Hence it is manifest that we must consider the ideal man as existing in the ideal social state. On the evolution-hypothesis, the two pre-suppose one another; and only when they co-exist, can there exist that ideal conduct which Absolute Ethics has to formulate, and which Relative Ethics has to take as the standard by which to estimate divergencies from right, or degrees of wrong.

CHAPTER XVI.

THE SCOPE OF ETHICS.

§ 107. At the outset it was shown that as the conduct with which Ethics deals, is a part of the conduct at large, conduct at large must be understood before this part can be understood. After taking a general view of conduct, not human only but sub-human, and not only as existing but as evolving, we saw that Ethics has for its subject-matter the most highly-evolved conduct as displayed by the most highly-evolved being, Man—is a specification of those traits which his conduct assumes on reaching its limit of evolution. Conceived thus as comprehending the laws of right living at large, Ethics has a wider field than is commonly assigned to it. Beyond the conduct commonly approved or reprobated as right or wrong, it includes all conduct which furthers or hinders, in either direct or indirect ways, the welfare of self or others.

As foregoing chapters in various places imply, the entire field of Ethics includes the two great divisions, personal and social. There is a class of actions directed to personal ends, which are to be judged in their relations to personal well-being, considered apart from the well-being of others: though they secondarily affect fellow-men these primarily affect the agent himself, and must be classed as intrinsically right or wrong according to their beneficial or detrimental effects on him. There are actions of another class which affect fellow men immediately and remotely, and which, though their results to self are not to be ignored, must be judged as good or bad mainly by their results to others. Actions of this last class fall into two groups. Those of the one group achieve ends in ways that do or do not unduly interfere with the pursuit of ends by others—actions which, because of this difference, we call respectively unjust or just. Those of the other group are a kind which influence the states of others without directly interfering with the relations between their labours and the results; in one way or the other—actions which we speak of as beneficent or maleficent. And the conduct which we regard as beneficent is itself sub-divisible according as it shows us a self-repression to avoid giving pain, or an expenditure of effort to give pleasure—negative beneficence and positive beneficence.

Each of these divisions and sub-divisions has to be considered first as a part of Absolute Ethics and then as a part of Relative Ethics. Having seen what its injunctions must be for the ideal man under the implied ideal conditions, we shall be prepared to see how such injunctions are to be most nearly fulfilled by actual men under existing conditions.

§ 108. For reasons already pointed out, a code of perfect personal conduct can never be made definite. Many forms of life, diverging from one another in considerable degrees, may be so carried on in society as completely to fulfil the conditions to harmonious co-operation. And if various types of men adapted to various types of activities, may thus lead lives that are severally complete after their kinds, no specific statement of the activities universally required for personal well-being is possible.

But though the particular requirements to be fulfilled for perfect individual well-being, must vary along with variations in the material conditions of each society, certain general requirements have to be fulfilled by the individuals of all societies. An average balance between waste and nutrition has universally to be preserved. Normal vitality implies a relation between activity and rest falling within moderate limits of variation. Continuance of the society depends on satisfaction of those primarily personal needs which result in marriage and parenthood. Perfection of individual life hence implies certain modes of action which are approximately alike in all cases and which therefore become part of the subject-matter of Ethics.

That it is possible to reduce this division of Ethics to scientific definiteness, can scarcely be said. But ethical requirements may here be to such extent affiliated upon physical necessities, as to give them a partially-scientific authority. It is clear that between the expenditure of bodily substance in vital activities, and the taking in of materials from which this substance may be renewed, there is a direct relation. It is clear, too, that there is a direct relation between the wasting of tissue by effort, and the need for those cessations of effort during which repair may overtake waste. Nor is it less clear that between the rate of mortality and the rate of multiplication in any society, there is a relation such that the last must reach a certain level before it can balance the first, and prevent disappearance of the society. And it may be inferred that pursuits of other leading ends, are, in like manner, determined by certain natural necessities, and from these derive their ethical sanctions. That it will ever be practicable to lay down precise rules for private conduct in conformity with such requirements, may be doubted. But the function of Absolute Ethics in relation to private conduct will have been discharged, when it has produced the warrant for its requirements as generally expressed; when it has shown the imperativeness of obedience to them; and when it has thus taught the need for deliberately considering whether the conduct fulfils them as well as may be.

Under the ethics of personal conduct considered in

relation to existing conditions, have to come all questions
concerning the degree in which immediate personal welfare
has to be postponed, either to ultimate personal welfare or
to the welfare of others. As now carried on life, hourly
sets the claims of present self against the claims of future
self, and hourly brings individual interests face to face with
the interests of other individuals, taken singly or as associated. In many of such cases the decisions can be nothing
more than compromises; and ethical science, here
necessarily empirical, can do no more than aid in making
compromises that are the least objectionable. To arrive at
the best compromise in any case, implies correct conceptions
of the alternative results of this or that course. And,
consequently, in so far as the absolute ethics of individual
conduct can be made definite, it must help us to decide
between conflicting personal requirements and between
the needs for asserting self and the needs for subordinating
self.

§ 109. From that division of Ethics which deals with the
right regulation of private conduct, considered apart from
the effects directly produced on others, we pass now to
that division of Ethics which, considering exclusively the
effects of conduct on others, treats of the right regulation
of it with a view to such effects.

The first set of regulations coming under this head are
those concerning what we distinguish as justice. Individual
life is possible only on condition that each organ is paid for
its action by an equivalent of blood, while the organism as
a whole obtains from the environment assimilable matters
that compensate for its efforts; and the mutual dependence
of parts in the social organism, necessitates that, alike for
its total life and the lives of its units, there similarly shall
be maintained a due proportion between returns and
labours: the natural relation between work and welfare
shall be preserved intact. Justice, which formulates the

range of conduct and limitations to conduct hence arising, is at once the most important division of Ethics and the division which admits of the greatest definiteness. That principle of equivalence which meets us when we seek its roots in the laws of individual life, involves the idea of *measure;* and on passing to social life, the same principle introduces us to the conception of equity or *equalness,* in the relations of citizens to one another : the elements of the questions arising are *quantitative,* and hence the solutions assume a more scientific form. Though, having to recognize differences among individuals due to age, sex, or other cause, we cannot regard the members of a society as absolutely equal, and therefore cannot deal with problems growing out of their relations with that precision which absolute equality might make possible ; yet, considering them as approximately equal in virtue of their common human nature, and dealing with questions of equity on this supposition, we may reach conclusions of a sufficiently-definite kind.

This division of Ethics considered under its absolute form, has to define the equitable relations among perfect individuals who limit one another's spheres of action by co-existing, and who achieve their ends by co-operation. It has to do much more than this. Beyond justice between man and man, justice between each man and the aggregate of men has to be dealt with by it. The relations between the individual and the State, considered as representing all individuals, have to be deduced — an important and a relatively-difficult matter. What is the ethical warrant for governmental authority ? To what ends may it be legitimately exercised ? How far may it rightly be carried ? Up to what point is the citizen bound to recognize the collective decisions of other citizens, and beyond what point may he properly refuse to obey them.

These relations, private and public, considered as maintained under ideal conditions, having been formulated, there

come to be dealt with the analogous relations under real conditions—absolute justice being the standard, relative justice
has to be determined by considering how near an approach
may, under present circumstances, be made to it. As
already implied in various places, it is impossible during
stages of transition which necessitate ever-changing compromises, to fulfil the dictates of absolute equity; and
nothing beyond empirical judgments can be formed of the
extent to which they may be, at any given time, fulfilled.
While war continues and injustice is done between societies,
there cannot be anything like complete justice within each
society. Militant organization as well as militant action, is
irreconcilable with pure equity; and the inequity implied by
it inevitably ramifies throughout all social relations. But
there is at every stage in social evolution, a certain range of
variation within which it is possible to approach nearer to,
or diverge further from, the requirements of absolute equity.
Hence these requirements have ever to be kept in view that
relative equity may be ascertained.

§ 110. Of the two sub-divisions into which beneficence
falls, the negative and the positive, neither can be specialized.
Under ideal conditions the first of them has but a nominal
existence; and the second of them passes largely into a
transfigured form admitting of but general definition.

In the conduct of the ideal man among ideal men, that
self-regulation which has for its motive to avoid giving pain,
practically disappears. No one having feelings which
prompt acts that disagreeably affect others, there can exist
no code of restraints referring to this division of conduct.

But though negative beneficence is only a nominal part
of Absolute Ethics, it is an actual and considerable part of
Relative Ethics. For while men's natures remain imperfectly
adapted to social life, there must continue in them impulses
which, causing in some cases the actions we name unjust,
cause in other cases the actions we name unkind—unkind

now in deed and now in word; and in respect of these modes of behaviour which, though not aggressive, give pain, there arise numerous and complicated problems. Pain is sometimes given to others simply by maintaining an equitable claim; pain is at other times given by refusing a request; and again at other times by maintaining an opinion. In these and numerous cases suggested by them, there have to be answered the questions whether, to avoid inflicting pain, personal feelings should be sacrificed, and how far sacrificed. Again, in cases of another class, pain is given not by a passive course but by an active course. · How far shall a person who has misbehaved be grieved by showing aversion to him? Shall one whose action is to be reprobated, have the reprobation expressed to him òr shall nothing be said? Is it right to annoy by condemning a prejudice which another displays? These and kindred queries have to be answered after taking into account the immediate pain given, the possible benefit caused by giving it, and the possible evil caused by not giving it. In solving problems of this class, the only help Absolute Ethics gives, is by enforcing the consideration that inflicting more pain than is necessitated by proper self-regard, or by desire for another's benefit, or by the maintenance of a general principle, is unwarranted.

Of positive beneficence under its absolute form nothing more specific can be said than that it must become co-extensive with whatever sphere remains for it; aiding to complete the life of each as a recipient of services and to exalt the life of each as a renderer of services. As with a developed humanity the desire for it by every one will so increase, and the sphere for exercise of it so decrease, as to involve an altruistic competition, analogous to the existing egoistic competition, it may be that Absolute Ethics will eventually include what we before called a higher equity, prescribing the mutual limitations of altruistic activities.

Under its relative form, positive beneficence presents numerous problems, alike important and difficult, admitting only of empirical solutions. How far is self-sacrifice for another's benefit to be carried in each case?—a question which must be answered differently according to the character of the other, the needs of the other, and the various claims of self and belongings which have to be met. To what extent under given circumstances shall private welfare be subordinated to public welfare?—a question to be answered after considering the importance of the end and the seriousness of the sacrifice. What benefit and what detriment will result from gratuitous aid yielded to another?—a question in each case implying an estimate of probabilities Is there any unfair treatment of sundry others, involved by more than fair treatment of this one other? Up to what limit may help be given to the existing generation of the inferior, without entailing mischief on future generations of the superior? Evidently to these and many kindred questions included in this division of Relative Ethics, approximately true answers only can be given.

But though here Absolute Ethics, by the standard it supplies, does not greatly aid Relative Ethics, yet, as in other cases, it aids somewhat by keeping before consciousness an ideal conciliation of the various claims involved; and by suggesting the search for such compromise among them, as shall not disregard any, but shall satisfy all to the greatest extent practicable.

THE END.

For EU product safety concerns, contact us at Calle de José Abascal, 56–1°,
28003 Madrid, Spain or eugpsr@cambridge.org.

 www.ingramcontent.com/pod-product-compliance
Ingram Content Group UK Ltd.
Pitfield, Milton Keynes, MK11 3LW, UK
UKHW010348140625
459647UK00010B/907